BUILDING
SKILLS FOR
EFFECTIVE
PRIMARY
TEACHING

Sara Miller McCune founded SAGE Publishing in 1965 to support the dissemination of usable knowledge and educate a global community. SAGE publishes more than 1000 journals and over 800 new books each year, spanning a wide range of subject areas. Our growing selection of library products includes archives, data, case studies and video. SAGE remains majority owned by our founder and after her lifetime will become owned by a charitable trust that secures the company's continued independence.

Los Angeles | London | New Delhi | Singapore | Washington DC | Melbourne

2ND EDITION

BUILDING SKILLS FOR EFFECTIVE PRIMARY TEACHING

A GUIDE TO YOUR SCHOOL BASED TRAINING

RACHAEL PAIGE
SUE LAMBERT
REBECCA GEESON

Learning Matters
A SAGE Publishing Company
1 Oliver's Yard
55 City Road
London EC1Y 1SP

SAGE Publications Inc.
2455 Teller Road
Thousand Oaks, California 91320

SAGE Publications India Pvt Ltd
B 1/I 1 Mohan Cooperative Industrial Area
Mathura Road
New Delhi 110 044

SAGE Publications Asia-Pacific Pte Ltd
3 Church Street
#10-04 Samsung Hub
Singapore 049483

Editor: Amy Thornton
Senior project editor: Chris Marke
Project management: Deer Park Productions
Marketing manager: Lorna Patkai
Cover design: Wendy Scott
Illustrations: Becky Geeson
Typeset by: C&M Digitals (P) Ltd, Chennai, India
Printed in the UK

First edition published in 2017
Second edition published in 2020

Library of Congress Number: 2020933775

British Library Cataloguing in Publication Data

A catalogue record for this book is available from the British Library

ISBN 978-1-5264-9215-9
ISBN 978-1-5264-9214-2 (pbk)

At SAGE we take sustainability seriously. Most of our products are printed in the UK using responsibly sourced papers and boards. When we print overseas we ensure sustainable papers are used as measured by the PREPS grading system. We undertake an annual audit to monitor our sustainability.

Contents

Contents

The editors

Dr Rachael Paige is Head of Department for Primary Education at the University of Worcester. Previously she was the Head of Programmes: Primary and Early Years at Bishop Grosseteste University, Lincoln. She started her career as a primary school teacher, leading in areas such as special needs, English and music. Moving into a headship of a primary school, she completed her Master's in Leadership and Management, focusing upon improving behaviour systems through distributed leadership. Her work in initial teacher education has focused upon professional teaching skills, with a particular emphasis upon behaviour. Rachael's research interests are linked to social communication within the classroom and her doctorate is an exploration of the phenomenon of teacher presence.

Sue Lambert is Programme Leader for the PGCE Primary and Early Years' programmes at Bishop Grosseteste University, Lincoln. She taught for 19 years in primary schools, teaching all ages in the primary phase. She was a SENCo (Special Educational Needs Co-ordinator) for many years, an advisory teacher for history and a deputy head teacher. While in school, she mentored trainees, NQTs (Newly Qualified Teacher) and supported staff in developing their mentoring role. Her MA in Education focuses on the role of questioning and whole-school curriculum development. Sue is a Senior Fellow of the Higher Education Academy (SFHEA) has furthered her research in exploring trainees' reflective practice. Her work in initial teacher education has included all aspects of the professional role (particularly safeguarding), assessment, leading learning, the creative curriculum, behaviour and PE.

Rebecca Geeson is Programme Leader for the Undergraduate Primary ITT programmes at Bishop Grosseteste University, Lincoln. She taught for 12 years in primary schools, focusing in the main on Key Stage 2. She was a phase leader and an Advanced Skills Teacher (AST) in mathematics and art. Much of her AST outreach work was spent supporting NQTs and more experienced teachers in developing their classroom practice. Rebecca completed her MA in Education, focusing on the role of mentoring, and effective teaching approaches in teacher education. Her doctoral research considers the role of the teaching assistant, teaching assistants becoming teachers, reflection for professional development, and changes in professional identity during teacher training.

The contributors

Dr Emma Clarke taught in primary schools for 18 years, and has experience in nurture groups and pupil referral units. She completed her Master's degree in managing challenging behaviour and her Ph.D. focused on Teaching Assistants managing behaviour.

Dr Ashley Compton is a former primary school teacher and mathematics advisory teacher. Currently a Senior Lecturer in Primary Education at Bishop Grosseteste University, she has co-authored several education books on mathematics, music and creativity. She teaches on both undergraduate and postgraduate degree programmes, as well as supervising research students on Doctorate programmes. Ashley has also led teacher professional development for mathematics, including MaST (Mathematics Specialist Teachers). She has a range of research interests, including mathematics, assessment and creativity.

Andrew Dickenson is currently a Senior Lecturer in teacher development at Bishop Grosseteste University. He teaches on both undergraduate and postgraduate degree programmes. He also contributes to teacher professional development programmes throughout the Midlands, often teaching in settings to cement the application of his sessions. He also works for Lego Education (Denmark), writing materials for the Far East. Andrew's current research considers the relationship between media access and the cultural contexts in which horror imagery affects the emotional development of children.

Elizabeth Farrar is a former primary school teacher and headteacher with wide experience, particularly in small schools and mixed-year group teaching. Currently a Senior Lecturer at Bishop Grosseteste University and a Fellow of the HEA, she teaches on the PGCE Primary Education course. She also contributes to undergraduate programmes, and to the mentoring and coaching skills professional development course. Elizabeth's current doctoral research focuses on trainee teachers' perceptions of the impact of poverty on the educational outcomes of pupils and how this may inform programme development.

Dr Adam Hounslow-Eyre is a former primary school teacher and headteacher with a wide experience in small school and mixed-year group teaching. Currently Senior Lecturer in Education Studies in the School of Social Sciences at Bishop Grosseteste University, Adam teaches on both undergraduate and postgraduate degree programmes. Adam also contributes to teacher professional development programmes that develop mentoring and coaching in schools. His current research interests centre around complexity theory and the call for evidence-based teaching approaches.

Steve McNichol is currently a Senior Lecturer in Primary Education at Bishop Grosseteste University, where he leads the provision for developing the behaviour management skills of trainee teachers. Prior to this, Steve taught across the primary age range and held roles as a specialist behaviour teacher, Special Educational Needs Co-ordinator (SENCO) and deputy head teacher. Steve's current research interests centre around the role of midday supervisors in primary schools. He is also involved in research about the development of pre-service teachers' behaviour management skills during initial teacher training.

Ami Montgomery is a former primary school teacher with a wide experience of teaching in multicultural classrooms, where she held a variety of roles that included EAL provision and support. During this time, she developed a comprehensive understanding of the professional competence and theoretical implications of the practice of English Language Teaching, spending a substantial amount of time teaching English to newly arrived children. Ami is the Head of Programmes, Arts & Humanities at Bishop Grosseteste University and currently teaches across the undergraduate and postgraduate Teaching English to Speakers of Other Languages (TESOL) programmes. With an emphasis on the integration of theory and practice, she has acquired expertise in approaches and techniques to teaching English to non-native English learners and has developed a range of practical skills. Her current research project explores the linguistic and cultural resources of young plurilingual learners mobilised through language and communication in Lincolnshire primary schools.

Dr John Paramore taught in primary schools for 18 years before moving into initial teacher education in 2006. He recently retired from Bishop Grosseteste University where he taught on the PGCE Primary Education course. His writing and research interests focus on geography, assessment and critical pedagogy.

Shaun Thompson has worked as a teacher in a variety of mainstream and special education settings. He has also been a head teacher of a primary school prior to working in initial teacher education. His current research focuses upon pupils with autism, with a particular focus on the teaching and learning of mathematics.

Professor Richard Woolley is Professor of Education and Inclusion and Deputy Head of the School of Education at the University of Worcester. He is a Principal Fellow of the Higher Education Academy, and was awarded a National Teaching Fellowship in 2018. Richard has worked in primary, further and higher education. His teaching and research interests relate to diversity and equality, children's spirituality, special educational needs and disabilities, and Relationships and Sex Education, particularly in the primary phase of education. He has a longstanding interest in the controversial and sensitive issues often encountered by student teachers and those early in their careers.

Introduction

About this book

Who is this book for?

Trainee and mentor: this book is for both of you. We have designed the book so that the chapters help to develop skills for trainees and new teachers in key areas of professional practice, and also to support the mentor in reflecting upon their own practice, with prompts for mentoring and coaching discussion. This should support you both in gaining the most from the time you have in your mentor discussions, and also to create an opportunity for deeper understanding and reflection.

About the contributors

In each chapter you will gain a sense of enthusiasm and commitment to education from the authors. All the contributors work within the primary age phase and within teacher education, so you will sense the specialness we all feel for this important age phase. Each of the chapter authors are specialists within the topic presented in their chapter, and will offer practical ideas that are informed by research.

This book offers initial topics that will help you in beginning to build the skills to support you in becoming an excellent teacher. We have used the pictorial representation of jigsaw pieces to represent how different aspects of pedagogy and subject interlink. As you start to make the connections between the different pieces, the picture becomes clearer and has a greater sense of coherence. Take, for example, assessment and planning. While initially you may see assessment as one type of activity undertaken by the teacher (one piece of the jigsaw), and planning for a lesson as a separate activity (another piece of the jigsaw), as you become more proficient you will see how these two pieces of the jigsaw interlock and create a greater sense of the whole picture. You may already realise the important connection between planning and assessment, but other aspects of the professional role also interlink with each other: your pedagogic decisions about how you will engage the pupils in learning and behaviour management, and how you work with your Teaching Assistant, for example. All these things (and many more) interdepend and enhance each other. Trainee, at the moment it may feel like there are so many tasks, but as you develop your proficiency as a teacher you will see that aspects all contribute to the most important thing: supporting the learners in your class. Mentor, we encourage you to use the activities in this book as part of the trainee and mentor discussions to enable connections to be made and a deeper understanding of why teachers do what they do.

Key features of this book

Reflection and discussion activities

In each chapter, you will see reflection and discussion activities. These are an extremely important part of the book as they encapsulate our intention to support deeper reflection and quality dialogue between trainee and mentor. The intention is that you can use these suggestions in your meetings together and you can specifically select activities based upon your own personal targets. As an introduction, let us use the following to begin your journey of reflection and discussion together.

 Reflection and discussion activity

Reflection

Trainee and mentor, reflect upon what motivated you to decide to become a teacher. Identify two or three key influences upon that decision. Consider this aspect of motivation even further by considering how these influences relate to your own values. For example, an influence upon your decision could be, like Rachael, that education creates choices and possibilities which she has seen in her own family. This would link to the value of opportunity for all and a strong belief in inclusion. For Sue, it was about passion for learning, and this links to her value of all having opportunity to achieve and to be the best they can be. Rebecca was influenced by her parents and grandparents, all inspirational teachers who valued creativity in teaching and learning, and who really cared about the children whom they taught.

Discussion

Now, discuss your personal reflection with each other. Has anything changed in your understanding of the purpose of education and schooling in the time between when you decided to become a teacher and your stage of teaching now?

In the activity above, it is the intention to support you in thinking about what it is that motivates you to pursue a career in teaching. Certainly, your awareness of the political, social and economic situation will also impact your view of the work you do as a teacher and may change or influence your motivation at different times. As experienced educators, we encourage each of you to keep returning to your own values and motivations to support you in understanding the important work you do with pupils.

This reflection and discussion leads us to an important point that we trust is communicated throughout this book. You are part of an excellent profession that has the well-being of pupils always at the forefront of their practice. In education, the 'to do' list never appears to come to an end. A key skill is to prioritise and to think about the importance of the task. Sadly, sometimes opportunity to reflect and discuss with other professionals are seen as luxuries we do not have time to undertake, and sometimes the trainee and mentor meeting is full of operational tasks rather than a truly developmental discussion. However, we know that the impact of reflecting specifically and carefully is very powerful, and will enable you to become a much more effective teacher and mentor. Take time to read Rebecca Geeson's exploration of the impact of reflection in Chapter 1 and also Adam Hounslow-Eyre's discussion on mentoring and coaching in Chapter 16.

Find out more from [. . .] and Taking it Further [. . .]

Each author presents information about the chapter in a way that should enable you to easily contemplate key ideas. However, behind these ideas will be research and evidence-based approaches that have informed the author. If you want to find out more, then we have provided a feature that allows you to choose your level of engagement. Sometimes we have provided links to practical ideas or video clips to further illustrate or give you more information. Sometimes we have provided links to more academic writing, such as journal articles. This will require you to engage in a deeper way, considering the critical aspects of the topic.

Case studies

Another way we have enhanced the key points is to provide case studies, which place the topic of the chapter in to a real-life scenario. In some chapters, such as Rachael Paige's *Teacher Identity* (Chapter 2), you will follow the progress of a case through several short extracts about the same participants to support you in building up your own understanding of a topic. In other chapters, such as Learning and Teaching Approaches (Chapter 5), several case studies are presented to illustrate how different schools have implemented an approach. This feature should support you in understanding how aspects are translated to practice in the classroom. The examples from this chapter also supports you in understanding that there are a variety of ways that different schools approach the organisation and application of learning and teaching activity. For trainees, it is understanding that key principles motivate the decisions made about these approaches, and you need to develop as an evaluative and critical thinker, who is not just mimicking the practice they see, but has really thought about the reasons for a particular approach. These case studies should support you in doing just that.

Gratitude

It has been a team effort to create this book and, as the Editors, there are a few people to whom we owe gratitude and appreciation. First, to the chapter authors who have worked hard to communicate clear ideas that will support you in developing as practitioners. The photographs in Chapter 2 have been taken by Emily Bennett, and Julie Tinnion kindly agreed to be photographed to help illustrate the points in the chapter. This support and contribution is much appreciated. Rebecca Geeson has provided the cartoons at the beginning of each chapter, again enhancing the messages in the book. Helen Fairlie and Sarah Turpie have supported the editing and have advised us well along the way. Finally, to Amy Thornton and the team at Learning Matters: we appreciate the opportunity to share our ideas and contribute to the development of teachers.

We hope you will gain a great deal from the book. Remember, you can select the chapters that are most appropriate to you at particular times, and use the Reflection and discussion activity as part of your professional discussions together.

The Editors

1

Becoming a reflective learner and teacher

Rebecca Geeson

 This chapter will

- develop your understanding of reflection and reflexivity;
- consider how developing your ability to reflect will impact upon your practice;
- consider what to reflect upon, and what strategies you can use in order to reflect effectively;
- think about different approaches to reflection.

 Links to the Teachers' Standards

4 **Plan and teach well structured lessons,** specifically:
   - reflect systematically on the effectiveness of lessons and approaches to teaching.

8 **Fulfil wider professional responsibilities,** specifically:
   - develop effective professional relationships with colleagues, knowing how and when to draw on advice and specialist support;
   - take responsibility for improving teaching through appropriate professional development, responding to advice and feedback from colleagues.

Introduction

We have deliberately positioned the chapter on reflection at the start of this book, not because it is more important than aspects that are discussed in other chapters later on, but because the theme of reflection underpins everything in this book. Through the activities and discussions in each chapter, we encourage both trainees and mentors to engage in reflective practice, and consequently, develop your own effective practice as teachers and in your mentoring role.

Seminal authors

Donald Schön, one of the seminal writers on reflective practice, presents a very useful metaphor that helps us to think about what reflection is. In an ideal world, we would be able to position ourselves high on a hillside from which we could see a view before us of everything we need to know, and use this to create a map or plan of our professional lives. However, the reality is that we are down in the *swampy lowlands* (Schön, 1987) where we cannot see everything, and sometimes become stuck in the mud; we do not know everything, and we have to learn from the situations we encounter and the mistakes that we make as we go along. The way that Schön proposed that we develop a workable map of our professional worlds – one that we can use to navigate the unexpected road blocks or diversions that appear – is through reflection.

Schön's work (1983) centred on his distinction between *reflection-in-action* and *reflection-on-action*. Reflection-in-action is the process that you undertake with very little time and fairly immediately as and when you need to act in any situation. You will make use of your own previous knowledge and your understanding of theory as you decide how to act. Reflection-on-action is the reflective process that occurs after the event, usually once you have a little time and space to think through things.

Understanding these two ideas is central to the argument for developing reflective practice in teachers. Beaty (1997) guards us against becoming the teacher who has 20 years of experience, which is actually only one year of experience repeated 20 times over. If you simply respond to situations without engaging in reflection, you may apply the same action in a future situation. This may be the most appropriate action and will not necessarily be a negative response to a situation, but how will you know that the situation could not have been resolved in a different, and possibly better, way if you have not considered it in more depth? If you *reflect-on-action*, you will have the opportunity to consider alternatives, relate your actions to theory and, crucially, in doing so, develop a greater 'bank' of knowledge and theory upon which to draw next time you are *reflecting-in-action*.

It is important to point out here the mentor's key role in encouraging and developing reflective practice. Often, the mentor may be the one who initially points out aspects of practice that deserve further reflection, and can support and encourage the trainee in making links to theory and applying their learning to their future professional development (Argyris and Schön, 1974). Discussion with somebody else can be a beneficial part of reflection; trainees value the opportunity to talk about their experiences so that they can consider others' perspectives and appreciate having someone to encourage them to interpret and justify their ideas in order to make sense of them (Bain *et al.*, 1999).

Schön's work built on that of John Dewey, and this work can also help us to understand benefits of reflective practice. Dewey (1933, 1938) believed that the learner should be an active participant in learning, making their own sense of the world with encouragement from teachers who should foster an experimental approach to learning in their classrooms.

 Reflection and discussion activity

Reflection

Trainee: having considered Schön's ideas (1987) about reflection-in-action and reflection-on-action, think back to an event or situation that has occurred in the classroom recently. It could be how you responded to low-level disruption in the classroom, the resources you found to support a particular pupil during an English lesson or how you arranged groups in PE. It does not necessarily have to be something that you thought went badly. However, it should be a situation at which your mentor was present and also witnessed.

1. Briefly, letting your mentor know what you are planning to write about, note down what happened and what you did.

2. Write down what knowledge and theory you think you had about this beforehand. What do you think made you make your decisions?

Mentor: think about the situation or event that your trainee has identified to you.

1. Briefly note down your perception of the event. What happened? What did your trainee do?

2. Think about how you would have dealt with the situation. Write down other events that you have experienced that would have contributed to your own actions in the same situation.

Before you discuss this with your trainee, think back to Dewey's (1933, 1938) suggestion that the learner (or in this case, your trainee) should be encouraged by the teacher (or you, the mentor) to be experimental and to develop their own understanding of the world.

Discussion

Trainee and mentor, compare notes. First, consider whether you both saw things in the same way, and whether you relied upon the same prior knowledge and theory to inform your actions.

Now think back to Schön's (1987) *swampy lowlands*. You are *reflecting-inaction* to make your *reflection-on-action* more effective next time. How can you both use what you have learned to add to the trainee's 'map'?

Reflection, reflexivity and reflective practice

The terms 'reflection', 'reflexivity' and 'reflective practice' are sometimes erroneously used interchangeably. Effective *reflective practice* is made up of both *reflection* and *reflexivity*.

Reflection is the detailed consideration of events or situations, with careful thought about what happened, who was involved and the perception of the event. Considering why and how it happened and what theory can be applied can illuminate the situation further. There might be aspects that initially seemed inconsequential but, on further reflection, can be seen to have had a bigger impact on the situation than expected.

Reflexivity takes this in-depth consideration further and involves greater criticality. Argyris and Schön (1974) considered reflexivity to be the consideration of and possible tension between the values that a trainee or teacher claims to have (known as *espoused theory*) and what they actually do in practice (known as *theories-in-use*). To be *reflexive*, you should be asking questions about the event or situation relating to your own values and beliefs, your place within the school/classroom, your own background, etc.

Bolton suggests that the type of questions that might be asked by a *reflexive* practitioner might be as follows:

- *Why did this pass me by?*

- *What were my assumptions which made me not notice?*

- *What are the organisational etc. pressures or ideologies which obstructed my perception?*

- *How and in what way were my actions perceived by others?*

(Bolton, 2014, pp7–8)

The case study below is one that Matthews and Jessel (1998) used in their article, and the commentary that follows it illustrates ideas we have considered above.

—— 🧩 —— **Case study** ——————————————

Trainees' written reflection	Commentary
	The process of thinking and writing about this situation is reflection-on-action.
I just do not get on with my classes. They do not respect me and I cannot seem to establish my authority.	The trainee reflected-in-action during the lesson. Although we cannot tell, perhaps her own understanding of social interactions and what she expected in the pupils' responses to her based on her experience of working with other classes or seeing other teachers teach supported her reflection and informed this view.
The school-based tutor has suggested that I sit and work with a group of pupils during some lessons and talk to them to see how they are feeling . . .	The school-based mentor suggested an activity (Argyris and Schön, 1974) that might allow the trainee to construct her own understanding of the situation (Dewey, 1933, 1938).

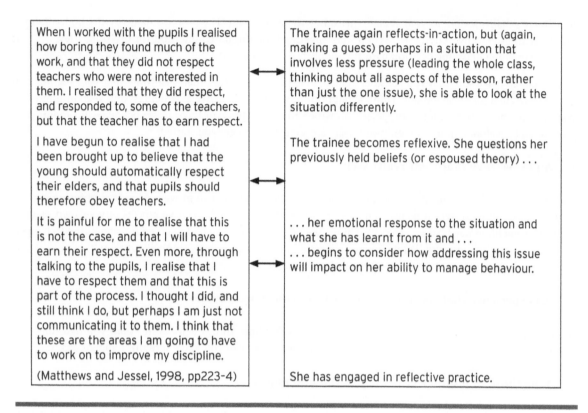

When I worked with the pupils I realised how boring they found much of the work, and that they did not respect teachers who were not interested in them. I realised that they did respect, and responded to, some of the teachers, but that the teacher has to earn respect.	The trainee again reflects-in-action, but (again, making a guess) perhaps in a situation that involves less pressure (leading the whole class, thinking about all aspects of the lesson, rather than just the one issue), she is able to look at the situation differently.
I have begun to realise that I had been brought up to believe that the young should automatically respect their elders, and that pupils should therefore obey teachers.	The trainee becomes reflexive. She questions her previously held beliefs (or espoused theory) ...
It is painful for me to realise that this is not the case, and that I will have to earn their respect. Even more, through talking to the pupils, I realise that I have to respect them and that this is part of the process. I thought I did, and still think I do, but perhaps I am just not communicating it to them. I think that these are the areas I am going to have to work on to improve my discipline.	... her emotional response to the situation and what she has learnt from it and ... ... begins to consider how addressing this issue will impact on her ability to manage behaviour.
(Matthews and Jessel, 1998, pp223-4)	She has engaged in reflective practice.

Discussion activity

Trainee and mentor: in thinking about the case study above, and questions that Bolton (2014) suggests, consider further questions that you could have also asked yourselves to develop reflexivity further.

We are not made aware in the excerpt above whether the school-based mentor knew that their suggested activity would provide the answers that the trainee needed. This is an important point to consider as both a teacher and as a mentor; experienced teachers and mentors are also wading through Schön's *swampy lowlands* (1987), albeit with hopefully a clearer map, and do not always have all the answers.

Choosing your focus for reflection

Before we consider *how* to reflect, we need to think about *what to reflect upon*.

It is important when you come to reflect that you choose a relevant focus for each reflection. It is better to analyse one or two experiences in depth, rather than attempt to consider everything. For example, do not use 'Today's maths lesson' as your theme; instead, perhaps focus on 'The progress made by the high-attaining pupils in the weighing activity' or 'When Max suggested an alternative method for division, I felt . . . '. It might be that you make the decision with the support of your mentor.

Over time, do make sure that you consider a range of experiences, rather than just those that your mentor suggested were areas for development. Think about both positive and negative experiences, and keep in mind that you need to choose something very specific on which to focus. Different types of experience will support your professional development in different ways. Here are some ideas to get you started:

- **An experience that went really well**

Trainee teachers often focus on the negative and ignore the things that went well. As well as pointing out the things that did not go well, it is just as important to be able to identify positive aspects of your own practice (and this sometimes needs some practice). Think about a time when you had planned for something to happen in a particular way and it did. While you are reflecting on this experience, think about why it went well and how you can use what you have learned in another context.

- **An experience that went much better than you expected it to**

At all stages in your career, you will surprise yourself; sometimes things work better than you had hoped or expected. These are particularly useful learning experiences. How can you make sure this happens again?

- **Something that didn't go as well as you had hoped**

You had perhaps planned something for a lesson, and thought it would work and it did not. These situations can be quite demoralising and knock your confidence. However, again, these experiences are very valuable. They often become targets for development, so it is particularly important that you confront them and decide how you can plan for a more positive outcome next time.

- **A situation where your mentor pointed out something (either a positive point or an area for development) that you had not noticed**

This often occurs when your mentor sees something going on in the classroom that you had not picked up on. As well as thinking about what they saw, also consider why you did not see it.

 Reflection and discussion activity

Reflection

Trainee: look back over a lesson and see if you can identify situations that would fit in each of the categories above.

Discussion

Trainee and mentor: thinking about too much at once will not enable in-depth reflective thinking. Of the four aspects you have chosen, discuss which will be the most valuable to reflect upon in more depth.

In the following chapters, you will be encouraged to reflect on a wide variety of areas relating to your teaching. As you do this always aim to consider:

- *Other perspectives*: What might different people's views be?

Think about those involved in the situation or experience – for example, you, your pupils, your mentor, other adults in the classroom.

Those others who know about the situation (other teachers in school, other trainees, parents, your university-based tutors).

Those in literature (who has written something about this?). Also consider why they may think in a particular way about the situation.

- *Causality*: What made this or that happen? Think about the people involved, timings, the context (would things have been different in a different lesson or with different groupings?).

How to reflect: using models of reflection

Many writers have proposed models to support reflection, and most are based on describing an experience, interpreting and analysing the experience, and then adapting one's approach in subsequent similar situations. Models for reflection are useful frameworks to support trainees in developing their reflective practice. Over time and with experience, you may find that you have adopted your own approach to reflection, but initially becoming familiar with, and making use of an approach, will support you.

Two particularly well-used cyclical models for reflection were presented by Kolb (1984) and Gibbs (1988).

Kolb's Learning Cycle

Kolb's Learning Cycle (1984) shows how you can learn from experiences through reflection and analysis in order to support you in future experiences.

Kolb (1984) suggested that any situation gives us opportunity to learn, but only if we have an opportunity to reflect upon it, interpret it and test out our interpretations.

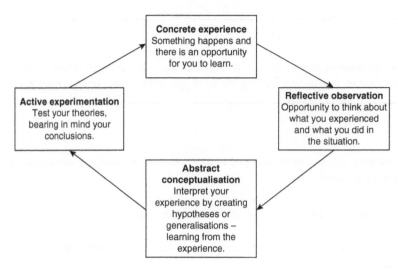

Figure 1.1 Kolb's Learning Cycle (adapted from Kolb, 1984)

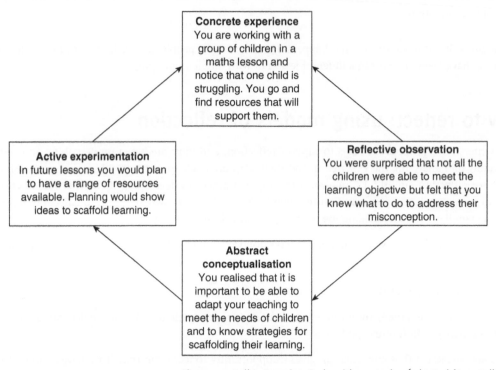

Figure 1.2 Kolb's Learning Cycle with examples (adapted from Kolb, 1984)

Gibbs' Reflective Cycle

Gibbs' (1988) Reflective Cycle includes six stages, and again encourages learning from an experience to enable greater understanding next time a similar situation occurs (see Figure 1.3).

It is important with each of these sections that you write a short account to allow you opportunity to think about each stage in the cycle, rather than briefly answering all.

- At the *Description* stage, you need to set the scene – some contextual information may be helpful here, but stick to what is relevant.

- When you come to think about *Feelings*, consider how your feelings may have differed at the time, immediately afterwards, and then a short while after the event.

- In your *Evaluation* of the situation, you should write about whether you think things went well or not.

- When you begin to engage in *Analysis*, it is useful to consider theory, thinking about different perspectives about the situation or similar situations.

- The *Conclusion* is a chance to think about whether you could have done anything differently. What have you learned from your experience?

- The *Action Plan* is the point where you consider what you will do differently next time a similar situation arises.

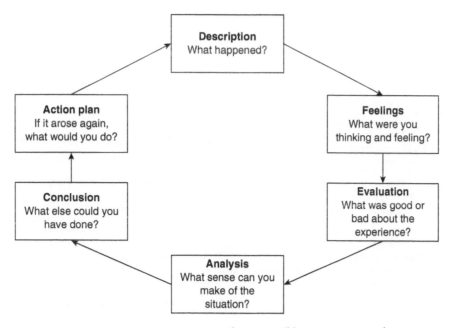

Figure 1.3 Gibbs' Learning Cycle (adapted from Gibbs, 1988)

While Kolb (1984) and Gibbs (1988) present their stages as cycles, in practice, it could be that you are reflecting on entirely different experiences in your next evaluation of your practice, so it may feel as if the 'cycle' ends after the action plan. However, as discussed above, this will support you so that next time a similar situation arises, you will have a greater body of knowledge upon which to draw when deciding your course of action; the cycle will continue, but there may be a hiatus between some stages.

Learning through reflection

It is useful to also consider Moon (1999) and Bain *et al.* (1999) who consider how learning occurs in their processes of reflection in more linear models.

Moon's levels of learning and learning journals

Moon (1999) suggests that it is only in the two final stages of the process that reflection on learning is likely to take place, and this was developed in her later work. She discussed the process of reflecting on specific critical incidents in learning journals, suggesting that deeper understanding is gained from drafting and redrafting a description of an incident, while asking more in-depth questions to develop deeper analysis (Moon, 2006).

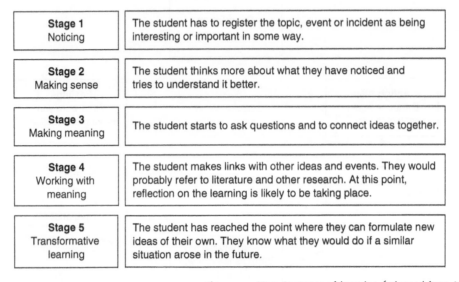

Stage 1 Noticing	The student has to register the topic, event or incident as being interesting or important in some way.
Stage 2 Making sense	The student thinks more about what they have noticed and tries to understand it better.
Stage 3 Making meaning	The student starts to ask questions and to connect ideas together.
Stage 4 Working with meaning	The student makes links with other ideas and events. They would probably refer to literature and other research. At this point, reflection on the learning is likely to be taking place.
Stage 5 Transformative learning	The student has reached the point where they can formulate new ideas of their own. They know what they would do if a similar situation arose in the future.

Figure 1.4 Moon's stages of learning (adapted from Moon, 1999)

Find out more from ... websites

Examples of the reflective writing process, with analysis of each draft, as well as more information about developing reflective writing are available from: **www.cetl.org.uk/UserFiles/File/reflective-writing-project/ThePark.pdf** (accessed 12 November 2019).

Bain's Framework (the 5Rs)

Bain *et al.* (1999) also proposed a similar five-stage model following research with Australian trainee teachers who were asked to reflect during their teaching placements.

Level 1 Reporting	The student describes, reports or retells with minimal transformation, no added observations or insights
Level 2 Responding	The student uses what they have reported in some way; they observe or make a judgement, ask a rhetorical question about the experience or share their emotional response to the situation.
Level 3 Relating	The student identifies aspects of the situation which have personal meaning, makes connections to current or prior experience, seeks a superficial understanding, identifies a strength/area for development and gives a superficial explanation for the reason something has happened, or identifies something they need to plan, do or change.
Level 4 Reasoning	The student integrates the experience with theoretical concepts, personal experiences and seeks a deeper understanding of why something has happened. They hypothesise, ask questions, look for answers, consider alternatives, and then attempt to explain their or others' behaviour with a greater depth of understanding.
Level 5 Reconstructing	The student engages in abstract thinking to generalise or apply their learning, drawing original conclusions from their reflections, generalising, formulating their own theory or position based on what they have learnt. They plan their own further learning based on their reflections.

Figure 1.5 Bain's Framework (adapted from Bain et al., 1999)

Reflection and discussion activity

Reflection

Trainee: think about the models for reflection discussed above. Bolton suggests that in order to reflect, we need to write (Bolton, 2014). Over a period of a few weeks, reflect on four different experiences using each of the models above.

Mentor: consider your own reflective practice too, and take time during this period to also reflect using the models discussed. Think about four different experiences that have occurred in your role as mentor. Also, consider Bain *et al.*'s (1999) findings - provide written feedback for your trainee on their reflection.

Discussion

Trainee and mentor: consider each reflective model, and decide which aspects you found most challenging, which model or models you found most useful for you. Would you adapt any of the models or take aspects of more than one to form a reflective model that is perfect for you? How does the mentor's written feedback help?

 Taking it further . . . research

There are many other models for reflection, some based on a linear or vertical model, such as those by Moon (1999) or Bain *et al.* (1999), and some that are iterative or cyclical, such as those developed by Kolb (1984) and Gibbs (1998). Others that are frequently cited and that were developed for nursing practitioners, but can also be applied to teacher training, are by Rolfe *et al.* (2001) and Johns (2009).

Rolfe *et al.*'s reflective model is based on three questions:

* What?
* So what?
* Now what?

Rolfe, G, Freshwater, D and Jasper, M (2001) *Critical Reflection in Nursing and the Helping Professions: A user's guide.* Basingstoke: Palgrave Macmillan.

Johns' model of reflection considers 'Looking out' as well as 'Looking in' and asks those who are reflecting to question the perspectives of others and the impact their actions have on others.

Johns, C (2009) *Becoming a Reflective Practitioner.* Chichester: Wiley-Blackwell.

Why reflect?

In order to 'buy into' the concept of reflection, it is important to briefly consider why we should all engage in reflective practice. Bolton (2014) summarises reasons that we should aspire to become reflective practitioners.

Reflective practice enables enquiry into:

- *what we know and wish or need to explore further;*

- *what we know but do not know we know;*

- *what we do not know and want to know;*

- *what we think, feel, believe, value, understand about our role and boundaries;*

- *how our actions match up with what we believe;*

- *how to value and take into account personal feelings.*

(Bolton, 2014, p2)

However, it is also important for you at this stage in your training to think about the short-term benefits of reflective practice. When speaking to recently qualified teachers, the reasons that they suggest they do not regularly engage in structured reflective practice are that they say they have not got time to reflect, they are not clear how this will improve what goes on in their classroom, or that they find the process embarrassing or upsetting.

In an ideal world (one with many more hours in the day), you would have the opportunity to reflect upon all aspects of your professional practice in great depth. However, a realistic approach is needed to ensure that reflective practice is valuable and meaningful, but also sustainable.

 Case study

Emma, who has been teaching for two years, does not write detailed reflections every day, but after developing and practising reflection during her training, she finds that she now routinely reflects on learners' progress, the success of the activities that she has planned and any problems that arose. She says: *It is important to reflect on each lesson, be it a quick ten-minute chat with teaching assistants or a more intense discussion with subject leads to support next steps. Reflecting ensures that I can deliver lessons that are engaging and specific to meet learners' needs. It also means that subsequent lessons can use a similar or alternative approach, dependent on the initial outcome. Reflecting with other members of staff is good for professional development as it can offer advice and support on structuring and teaching lessons or activities to include within it.*

Chapter summary

In this chapter, you have looked at different models that can support you in reflecting, but the model you use is up to you. Sometimes, you may want to use aspects of different approaches.

This chapter has presented the importance of ensuring that you reflect in some way to further improve your future practice.

 Taking it further ... research

The following research into the reflective practice was carried out recently in America and findings discuss the many positive outcomes of reflective practice for trainee teachers:

Slade, M, Burnham, T, Catalan, SM and Waters, T (2019) *The Impact of Reflective Practice on Teacher Candidates' Learning.*

Available at: **https://digitalcommons.georgiasouthern.edu/cgi/viewcontent.cgi?article=1821&context=ij-sotl** (accessed 12 November 2019).

References

Argyris, C and Schön, D (1974) *Theory in Practice: Increasing professional effectiveness.* San Fransisco, CA: Jossey-Bass.

Bain, J, Ballantyne, R, Packer, J and Mills, C (1999) Using journal writing to enhance student teachers' reflectivity during field experience placements. *Teachers and Teaching: Theory and Practice,* 5(1): 51–73.

Beaty, L (1997) *Developing Your Teaching Through Reflective Practice.* Birmingham: SEDA.

Bolton, G (2014) *Reflective Practice, Writing and Professional Development* (4th edn). London: SAGE.

Dewey, J (1933) *How We Think: A restatement of reflective thinking in the educative process.* Boston, MA: DC Heath & Co.

Dewey, J (1938) *Experience and Education.* New York: Kappa Delta Pi.

Gibbs, G (1988) *Learning by Doing: A guide to teaching and learning methods.* Oxford: Further Education Unit.

Kolb, DA (1984) *Experiential Learning: Experience as a source of learning and development.* Upper Saddle River, NJ: Prentice Hall.

Matthews, B and Jessel, J (1998) Reflective and reflexive practice in initial teacher education: A critical case study. *Teaching in Higher Education,* 3(2): 231–43.

Moon, J (1999) *Reflection in Learning and Professional Development: Theory and practice*. London: Kogan Page.

Moon, J (2006) *Learning Journals* (2nd edn). London: Routledge.

Schön, D (1983) *The Reflective Practitioner: How professionals think in action*. New York: Basic Books.

Schön, D (1987) *Educating the Reflective Practitioner*. San Fransisco, CA: Jossey-Bass.

Slade, M, Burnham, T, Catalan, SM and Waters, T (2019) The impact of reflective practice on teacher candidates' learning. *International Journal for the Scholarship of Teaching & Learning*, 13(2): 1–8.

2
Teacher identity

Rachael Paige

 This chapter will

- explore your developing identity as a teacher and what that means to you personally;
- introduce some ideas about how your teacher identity may develop over time;
- explore the importance of your own values and 'comfortableness' in your teacher identity.

 Link to Teachers' Standards

1   **Set high expectations which inspire, motivate and challenge pupils,** specifically:

- demonstrate consistently the positive attitudes, values and behaviour which are expected of pupils.

7   **Manage behaviour effectively to ensure a good and safe learning environment,** specifically:

- maintain good relationships with pupils, exercise appropriate authority, and act decisively when necessary.

8   **Fulfil wider professional responsibilities,** specifically:

- develop effective professional relationships with colleagues, knowing how and when to draw on advice and specialist support;
- take responsibility for improving teaching through appropriate professional development, responding to advice and feedback from colleagues.

Introduction: why is identity important?

Think for a moment about why you wanted to become a teacher. For some people, it was an aspiration from being quite young, potentially influenced by positive or negative experiences at school or perhaps being taught by a teacher who made a significant difference to them. For other people, it could be an opportunity for a change of career, moving towards a role that is perceived to be more fulfilling and in a professional context where they feel they can make a difference. It would be unusual to hear that people chose to become a teacher because they just need a job – any job – or that they were motivated by financial reward solely. Being a teacher and what that means in terms of professional and personal identity is probably something that you have not considered in depth before. However, your identity as a teacher is played out in your behaviours and is influenced by your values and perception of self. In this chapter we will explore your developing teacher identity and also look at how you can develop your own 'comfortableness' in your own identity.

Who do you think you are?

Our professional identity is important because it shapes how we behave in the classroom and influences our interactions with a range of people in our professional role. You may hear some people say that teaching is an act, and I explore this approach in the next chapter (Chapter 3) when I discuss teacher presence. O'Connor (2011) shares the views of three teachers about identity in her study and these teachers explain that there is an aspect of acting in that you share a professional self in the classroom, and while this can still be an expression of who you are, as an individual, there are some aspects that are chosen to be exaggerated or even repressed. When we think about teacher identity, there is a sense of bringing something of yourself (Meijer *et al.*, 2009) and who you believe you are and what you believe you can bring to this important role. I recall when I first began my role as a headteacher in a primary school several years ago now: I could not imagine that I was the headteacher, that I was actually leading this school. I did not wear my badge which said 'Headteacher' for the first week because it had not become part of who I thought I was. By wearing the badge, I would have to accept the role and the responsibility. Part of the challenge for me was that being the leader in the school was not part of my professional identity, yet. I ask the trainee teachers with whom I work at different points throughout their initial teacher education and training programme: 'Do you feel like a teacher?' At the beginning of the programme the reaction is usually nervous laughter and I retort that to the children in the class you are a teacher, however much that is part of what you think about yourself or not. It may not be quite part of your identity, yet, so you play the role of the teacher initially. The intention is that this chapter helps you think about how your work with the pupils in your class can further become meaningful and how your identity as a teacher can influence and support the commitment, dedication and enthusiasm you give to your teacher role.

Our professional identity is also influenced by our personal identity, which is multi-layered with our affinity to personal and social groups with which we align – for example, religion, ethnicity, gender, social background, etc. In terms of our identity, these aspects may be more or less prominent for different people, and this will be influenced by personal experiences and whether we identify with a group that has been under-represented or oppressed in the past. Already, we can see that our identity can be multi-layered and influenced by external and internal factors.

When we think about professional identity there are many aspects that cumulatively impact on our identity and self-perception: our values and ideals, our experiences and our developing professional skills. In this chapter, I want to present some key ideas to you that may initially appear paradoxical: that we need to understand our professional identity and know ourselves well so that we can bring authenticity to the classroom (Rodgers and Raider-Roth, 2006) and something of ourselves to the role. However, our professional identity is not fixed and can change over time as we gain more experience or learn more from research and evidence (Day *et al.*, 2006). Identity has been understood in different ways over time and an early view was that our identity was fixed (Day *et al.*, 2006), that it was a natural state and life events, or even deliberate decisions, did not impact that identity. So, I wonder who you would say you are at this moment in time? Take some time to reflect on this idea in the reflection and discussion activity below.

 Reflection and discussion activity

Trainee and mentor: we are going to think about different aspects of identity and this first reflection activity gives you opportunity to consider your own identity and the aspects that contribute to that construction.

First, which aspects would you attribute to yourself as important to your identity and who you are? For example, your cultural heritage, gender affiliation, or religion may be key to your own perception of self and identity.

Next, think about the values and attributes that you think are important and that you would recognise as part of your identity - for example, kindness, ambition, empathy.

Finally, consider your motivations in your professional context. We could call this your professional philosophy. What is it that drives you and enthuses you to be the best teacher you can be? As an example, when I first became a teacher I was motivated by the philosophy that education gives choices and I was committed, as I still am, to opportunities for social mobility and personal development, and fulfilment for all.

In the activity above you will have started to consider how your teacher identity is multi-layered and that there are many influences upon our identity. This activity has started from your own perception of self and a reflection from your own perspective. Be alert to feedback you gain from other professionals as this will support you in considering how your teacher identity can develop and also how you can use aspects of your identity to support your delivery in the classroom through effective communication and interactions.

What do we mean by identity?

Several writers have explored what we mean by identity – for example, O'Connor (2008); Day *et al.*, (2006). In simple terms, identity relates to the type of person who is presented in specific situations and contexts (Gee, 2000). O'Connor (2008) holds a similar perspective to the one I present in this chapter, in that personal beliefs, values and philosophies are lived out in actions and behaviours within your teacher role, and this presents your identity in practice. This representation of your identity in the social spheres, and in terms of your teacher identity that is in your school context, can be thought of as your professional identity. However, your personal and professional identity are interlinked (Day *et al.*, 2006) and it is the representation of these aspects of your interlinked identity that you will negotiate within the professional context. In time, that representation will become embedded in your actions and behaviours in the classroom and the comfortableness that you see in many established teachers will be something you will experience, too. There is also a strong aspect of reflection where individuals can understand their feelings, motivations and responses, as well as use social interactions and communication with others to develop and evolve your professional identities. This idea of developing your professional identity leads on to another key idea I would like you to consider.

Earlier in the chapter, I introduced an initial idea of identity in that it was viewed as a fixed, natural state that was little influenced by external or internal factors (Day *et al.*, 2006). This idea has evolved in research and you will already sense from this chapter that this is a view that I am challenging. If our identity is fixed, and when we talk about being genuine and authentic we mean reverting to what we believe is our fixed nature, then this is problematic if we want to adopt a range of approaches and strategies to support us in communicating and leading the learning in our classrooms effectively. You may have heard of the term 'looking-glass self' (originally Cooley, 1902). This concept of identity is drawn upon even in contemporary ideas to understand self and identity through not only self-reflection, but also through feedback from others. This relates to the definition I shared earlier where self-reflection and communication with others are key to supporting the development of your professional identity. This idea of how our professional teacher identity develops suggests that we build and construct our identity as we reflect upon situations, take feedback from others, and consider how the way we behave outwardly aligns with those key things that we feel are important in our identity: our personal attributes alongside our beliefs, values and philosophies.

 Taking it further . . . research

I have already referred to Kate O'Connor's (2008) research and here I recommend her work for follow-up reading. The ideas from O'Connor's work is influential in my own thinking both for the topic of this chapter and because it also links well with the ideas in the next chapter about teacher presence. O'Connor has written a paper that reports qualitatively about the experiences of three teachers in a secondary school context and what influences their professional decision making. A key conclusion from the study was that a deliberate choice to care about students was part of identity, and that there is a sense of the public and professional identity where the right amount of care and concern for pupils has to be maintained.

You can read the paper by accessing the journal *Teaching and Teacher Education*, 24(1). The full reference is listed at the end of the chapter.

Following on from these initial ideas about teacher identity, here is a key idea aspect for you to think about that draws upon post-modern construction of identity: that identity is not fixed. Identity can be understood to be situational and adaptable (Akkerman and Meijer, 2011; Day *et al.*, 2006). This means that we draw on different aspects of our identity when in different situations, rather than relying on our single way of being, interacting and communicating. Therefore, it is argued from a post-modern perspective, that identity is not stable (Day *et al.*, 2006); it is changing and evolving all the time. The next reflection and discussion activity supports deeper thinking about this idea.

Reflection and discussion activity

Akkerman and Meijer (2011) argue that identity can be *multiple yet unitary, discontinuous and continuous, social and individual* (p309).

Take a moment to think about what this quote means and what these authors are suggesting. I interpret this quote to mean our identity is not fixed and yet is fixed (and Day *et al.*, 2006, present this idea as well). Do you agree that our identity can be described in this way and, if so, what does that mean for you as a new teacher or a teacher with more experience and mentoring a colleague new to the profession?

Think about the attributes and values you listed in the first reflection and discussion activity. How fixed are these in your identity?

Talk to your mentor about how their teacher identity has developed over their career so far. Are the same things important in terms of their underpinning philosophy and values, and are these then lived out in their behaviours and interactions in the classroom? Are there any conflicts or disconnects between identity and the teacher role, perhaps linked to changing policy, for example?

The quotation in the reflection and discussion box by Akkerman and Meijer (2011) appears to be a paradox, but it describes a phenomenon of stability and instability (Day *et al.*, 2006) that I would like to suggest to you can co-exist. This supports an idea of situational identities where a core identity will ever be present but there is an adaptation to the context – there is something that is continuous but elements that need to change to aid engagement with others or success in your school context. Akkerman and Meijer (2011) describe this in the context of still being your authentic and genuine self, but that an adaptation is necessary for engagement with others and also as you progress in your career holding different things as important. I refer back to my own personal example of moving into a senior leadership role. Different aspects of my identity became important to that situation and context – for example, thinking in a strategic way and what I call 'raising your head' – that is, looking beyond your own and immediate situation to understand other perspectives and impact. Over my career, I have also understood that aspects of my continuous identity, such as being compassionate, kind and caring, can be applied in differing contexts and that I can choose to use these aspects of my identity in a deliberate way. That is why I like O'Connor's (2008) idea of *choosing* to care: with an awareness of self and commitment to developing your professional identity you can make choices about how your sense of self, values and attributes are lived out. The challenge for teachers is to remain within the parameters of individual identity: to avoid the fake and superficial pretence that can hinder communication. I argue that it is in this place of lived-out identity that we find our comfortableness in the classroom, and we develop confidence in who we are as teachers and the actions we take in the learning environment.

 Case study

In my own doctoral research, I worked with four Key Stage 2 teachers exploring their perception of teacher presence. In these case studies some of the teachers talked about identity, how this can change in context and the impact of not feeling sure about your identity. Below, I share with you two of these case studies.

(Continued)

(Continued)

Paul has been teaching for about five years in a primary school located in an area that has experienced difficulty in recruiting teachers mainly due to the rural location in which the school is located. When Paul joined the school as a Newly Qualified Teacher (NQT), it had been graded as requiring improvement by Ofsted. Paul had a military career prior to becoming a teacher. When he changed career, he was undertaking an instructor role in the military and could see how skills he had learnt could be transferable to education. His motivation and desire to teach had also arisen from the satisfaction he had felt in his instructor role. However, in the shared conversation (unstructured interview) I had with him, he expressed the challenges he had during his NQT year when he took what he thought was a professional approach to the teacher role in which he was more detached and authoritarian (his word), not really bringing the aspects of his personality that could have supported connection with the pupils in his class. Paul identifies how reflection has been a key approach to developing but also verbalises how he had to 'take off' his previous identity: 'And I was literally having to take off a helmet and put on a mortar board . . . where I had a definite identity, a role, institutionalisation etc. basically having to get rid of the baggage.'

Duncan has been a Year 5 and 6 teacher for five years as well. Duncan also changed career to come in to teaching, like Paul. His background was in hospitality prior to teaching. In the dialogue with Duncan, he spoke about sharing selected aspects of who you are with the children so that trust and relationships were secured. This was seen in the classroom as well, where I was able to observe Duncan with his class. Duncan had established a classroom environment in which he appeared confident, relaxed and comfortable, and was able to deploy some of his humour, playfulness and even make a mistake in front of a visitor (me). In the first extract he is talking about what distinguishes him in terms of being the teacher and he refers to the formal attire he wears in the classroom: 'I am the kind of person who would also be confident with regard to what I'm wearing but I think it is about creating impression, almost. And, just that little barrier almost of professional identity. So, the children look at you in a slightly different way.'

However, Duncan goes on to say that it is important that the pupils do see who you are and that this can be a in a *showperson* way, or an *overinflated version* of yourself.

After reading the case studies above, take a moment to think about these real-life situations and how these teachers have taken previous life experiences and who they thought they were in terms of identity and adapted. O'Connor (2008) states that we take aspects of our identity and either exaggerate or repress, according to the situation. Paul and Duncan have been able to provide some examples of this in their reflections.

 Find out more from . . . TED talk

Timmy Sullivan explores the difference between a teacher and an educator from the viewpoint of a pupil. In this talk, Timmy shares how an educator, in his view, is different from fulfilling a teacher role: they bring something of themselves as people and take time to connect with their students, with care and concern for the pupils obvious in actions and priorities.

Available at: **www.youtube.com/watch?v=POMxyIYPOyI** (accessed 23 March 2020)

Chapter summary

In this chapter, you have been introduced to some modern and post-modern ideas about teacher identity. You have been challenged to think about the idea of having some continuous or fixed aspects to your identity that will be applied in different situations, but also to consider how you can use self-reflection and feedback to support development of your teacher identity. Developing confidence in your own teacher identity leads to a comfortableness in your teacher role in the classroom, supporting good communication and a connection to the pupils in your class.

References

Akkerman, S and Meijer, P (2011) A dialogic approach to conceptualizing teacher identity. *Teaching and Teacher Education*, 27(2): 308–19.

Cooley, C (1902) *Human Nature and the Social Order*. New York: Scribner.

Day, C, Kington, A, Stobart, G and Sammons, P (2006) The personal and professional selves of teachers: stable and unstable identities. *British Educational Research Journal*, 32(4): 601–16.

Gee, J (2000) Identity as an analytic lens for research in education. *Review of Research in Education*, 25: 99–125.

Meijer, P, Korthagen, F and Vasalos, A (2009) Supporting presence in teacher education: the connection between the personal and professional aspects of teaching. *Teaching and Teacher Education*, 25(2): 297–308.

O'Connor, K (2008) 'You choose to care': teachers, emotions and professional identity. *Teaching and Teacher Education*, 25(2): 297–308.

Rodgers, C and Raider-Roth, M (2006) Presence in teaching. *Teachers and Teaching: Theory and Practice*, 24: 177–26.

Clips from the internet:

TED talk by Timmy Sullivan: **www.youtube.com/watch?v=P0MxylYP0yI** (accessed 23 March 2020)

3
Teacher presence
Rachael Paige

 This chapter will

- introduce you to some strategies to help you have a 'presence' in the classroom;
- discuss what it means to have presence, both techniques and developing your own confidence in the classroom;
- support you in reflecting upon which characteristics create presence and how you can develop your skills.

 Link to Teachers' Standards

1   **Set high expectations which inspire, motivate and challenge pupils,** specifically:

- establish a safe and stimulating environment for pupils, rooted in mutual respect;
- demonstrate consistently the positive attitudes, values and behaviour which are expected of pupils.

7   **Manage behaviour effectively to ensure a good and safe learning environment,** specifically:

- have clear rules and routines for behaviour in classrooms, and take responsibility for promoting good and courteous behaviour both in classrooms and around the school, in accordance with the school's behaviour policy;
- manage classes effectively, using approaches which are appropriate to pupils' needs in order to involve and motivate them;
- maintain good relationships with pupils, exercise appropriate authority, and act decisively when necessary.

Introduction: is presence the 'X factor' of teaching?

Think about someone you know who you would identify as having presence. What is it about them? The clothes they wear or the way they use their body language? Is it the way they speak or how they interact with other people? It is quite difficult to say exactly what it is that gives some people that special something, that 'X factor', which makes them stand out from the crowd or encourages other people to stop and listen to them.

To have presence can be very useful (and sometimes essential), not only in the classroom but also in meetings and situations where you want to have an influence. In fact, this phenomenon is written about in a range of fields: leadership and management (Senge *et al.*, 2004), business (Carney *et al.*, 2010) and also within the context of behaviour management (Jones, 2007). It appears to be something important in our interactions with both pupils and other adults, but is quite difficult to completely define. In Chapter 9 (written by Emma Clarke and Steve McNichol), you will also read of Canter's assertive discipline approach which has an emphasis upon the direction (assertion) of the teacher towards the pupils, which can be interpreted as having a presence in the classroom. Within this chapter, I will argue that effective presence is more subtle than Canter describes, but the importance of the teacher role – which Canter and Canter (1992) identify – remains a theme.

In education, teacher presence is not often written about explicitly (and is certainly not framed as an approach to communication, as I will present in this chapter), but it is talked about often. In fact, the lack of presence can be a significant barrier to trainee teachers (and qualified teachers) in having that positive influence in the classroom that inspires children to engage in the learning. In this chapter, we will look more closely at 'what is teacher presence?' and introduce you to some techniques that can help you develop this aspect of your teacher role. For mentors, this chapter should challenge you to think about the feedback you give to trainees and ensure that vague terms, such as 'presence', are unpicked to support professional development.

 Reflection and discussion activity

Reflection

Before reading the next part of the chapter, consider the following.

Trainee: list the qualities or characteristics that you think create presence in the classroom. You perhaps know someone who has presence, so try to describe them and what it is that makes you identify them as someone with presence.

Mentor: think about when you might have used the term 'presence' in your mentoring role and unpick some of the features you are expecting to see from the trainee. Be as specific as possible.

Discussion

Trainee and mentor: now compare your lists. Start to discuss similarities and differences in the lists. Is presence something some people have, or can we learn some of these strategies?

What is presence and can it be learned?

In the first trainee and mentor reflection activity, you may have thought of someone who you would identify as having presence. It is likely that some of the characteristics are related to non-verbal communication: use of gesture, smile, position in the classroom and an enthusiastic approach, for example. You may also have listed some ways in which they use their voice: intonation, change in pitch and volume. People who are identified as having a presence often also present as confident, whether that is genuine confidence or presenting in that way (see Figure 3.2 and Amy Cuddy's work later in this chapter). These are all ideas that we will explore together in detail throughout this chapter. As we start to unpick the concept of teacher presence, hopefully you are beginning to realise that we can learn some techniques to help us in the classroom (and other professional situations requiring influence and effective communication). It is true to say that some people do seem to have that instinctive way of asserting their presence and having an influence in different situations. Some of this is related to confidence (genuine or presented) or a willingness to overcome any inhibitions when engaging the pupils in their learning. While identifying techniques is reasonably easy, developing your persona so that you present as confident and use an engaging style with the pupils takes more self-reflection and rehearsal. It is far more complex to truly believe in your own competence as a teacher and then present that confidence in the classroom. That is why it is so important to develop as a reflective practitioner, and the mentor role is significant in coaching trainees to become more reflective, willing to attempt new things (and sometimes fail) and develop a confidence in your own professional practice.

When considering this phenomenon – and whether techniques can be learnt or developed to increase presence – it is helpful to make a few initial assertions. First, presence is viewed by this author as a communication tool and is related to engaging others and having influence. As we look at some research and case studies throughout the chapter, you will see how this perspective is supported by others (such as Babad *et al.*, 2004; Rodgers and Raider-Roth, 2006; Korthagen and Vasalos, 2009; Salter, 2016). This perspective is important as communication is a key aspect in a positive classroom environment to enable all pupils to participate in learning. Second, within literature there is a very interesting distinction between *having presence* and *being present*. *Having presence* relates to the techniques the teacher uses and reflects a somewhat behaviourist approach to communication (see Chapter 9). Behaviourism, in its broadest sense, suggests that a certain stimulus can encourage a particular response. The use of stickers, or rewards, to reinforce positive behaviour is an example. In this context of communicating through teacher presence, it could be that a positive and enthusiastic persona presented by the teacher may encourage pupils to engage and participate. Alternatively, *being present* (a concept promoted by Rodgers and Raider-Roth, 2006), has a different emphasis. While the outward communication by the teacher remains important, these authors identify that a genuine and authentic relationship with the pupils, built upon mutual respect and trust, is more important than acting or learning techniques. It is this genuine *being present* (p271) and *in the moment* (p279), when nothing else matters but the learning, the students and the subject matter, that culminates in true teacher presence according to these authors.

These two ways of viewing presence will help to shape the discussion in this chapter.

Case study

David is a trainee primary teacher following a School Direct route into teaching. He is in his first term with a school he knows quite well from volunteering with them prior to starting the course. David says that he is happy at the school and has a good relationship with his mentor, Tim. David has been leading groups consistently and well during the first part of his placement. He has also led a sequence of English lessons with Tim in the classroom and worked with small groups. David has felt confident leading the English lessons because English is a specialism for him and he has observed Tim leading English previously.

This week David taught a science lesson and Tim observed him. After the lesson, Tim asked David to reflect specifically upon the progress children made and their engagement in the lesson. David realised that many of the children had not been focused on the lesson, and instead were off-task during practical activities. David was able to explain how he used the behaviour systems in place and he felt that the children needed to be more committed to the lesson and listen to the instructions. The following day, Tim provided David with some formal written feedback. In the areas for development Tim suggested: 'Have more presence.'

Reflection and discussion activity

Mentor: although we may feel that we have discussed a situation with our trainee and that they understand the targets set, sometimes we make assumptions. Reflect on what assumptions may have been made by Tim. What do you think Tim actually meant by 'have more presence'? When providing follow-up written support to trainees, think about how you communicate those more complex concepts, such as presence or persona.

Trainee: presently, in this case study we only really know what David thought and the written feedback that Tim provided. We will return to the case study later to explore what Tim said in the verbal feedback. Take time to think about the target: 'Have more presence.' What do you think this might mean? What do you think may have influenced the perceived lack of presence in this lesson?

Trainee and mentor: begin to draft a more specific target that would help David progress. Perhaps your target will be linked to being confident in the science subject matter so that David can be fully 'in the moment' of learning. Or perhaps you will concentrate on his non-verbal behaviours or use of voice.

Having presence: developing techniques

You may have heard of the 'Dr Fox Effect'. This term refers to a study in the 1970s by Naftulin *et al.* (1973) in which student evaluation ratings were given to 'Dr Myron L. Fox' for his lecture entitled 'Mathematical games theory as applied to physician education'. During the lecture, Dr Fox used techniques to engage the audience, which included humour and giving an enthusiastic presentation. However, what the learners failed to notice (and the learners were a group of experienced educators themselves, such as social worker educators) was that Dr Fox was giving something of a nonsense lecture, with contradictions throughout, neologisms and conclusions that did not support the previous statement. You may have realised: Dr Fox was an actor. His rapport and enthusiasm had, according to Naftulin *et al.*, 'seduced' the group.

Find out more from . . . internet clips and research

The Dr Fox lecture is available on YouTube: **www.youtube.com/watch?v=RcxW6nrWwtc** (accessed 12 November 2019).

You may wish to read the academic journal article – see the References list at the end of the chapter.

While there have been some more recent studies that have criticised this idea of 'seduction' (this term is used by Naftulin *et al.* (1973) to mean that learners are seduced into thinking they have learned something by a charismatic teacher), the way you present yourself as the teacher is important. You need to show enthusiasm and interest in the subject yourself before you can expect your learners to engage. I am sure you can think of examples from sessions you have attended when the delivery of the content has been so 'dry' and 'boring' that it is very hard to concentrate however committed you are as the learner. This may seem like an obvious statement, but for trainee teachers sometimes there is so much to think about: the subject content, the pedagogical approaches you are using, ensuring positive learning behaviours and perhaps your mentor is observing. It is easy to become overwhelmed with so many priorities and consequently not communicate the love of learning and enjoyment of the subject as you would wish. Peel and Babad (2014) replicated Naftulin *et al.*'s study, and while they found that learners were not as naive as originally presented by the original research team in thinking they learned significantly new things just because the teacher was charismatic, this recent study does support that learners value the enthusiasm and energy shown in the delivery by the teacher. Neill and Caswell (1993) call it *nonverbal pzazz*; White and Gardner (2012) call it the *classroom X-Factor*, but a key message for you is to be enthusiastic: enjoy (and show that you enjoy) leading the learning in your class.

Building upon the point that having enthusiasm and building rapport with your learners is a positive starting point, we will start to unpick the different ways we communicate and establish a presence, including some exercises for you to try. Another familiar (mis)quoted researcher leads us to think about non-verbal communication. Mehrabian is well known for his work in the area of non-verbal communication and it is from his 1972 work that the '7–38–55' distinction has emerged relating to when communicating attitudes or feelings: according to Mehrabian, 7 per cent of the communication of attitudes and feelings are in the words we say, 38 per cent in the way we say them and 55 per cent in facial expression. Research in this area has moved forward from this simplistic formula, and there are authors who argue fervently that words are just as important as the way we say them and the non-verbal behaviours we exhibit. However, the delivery of your words and your use of non-verbal behaviours can have a significant impact upon the presence we have in the classroom. In fact, the message you are communicating is at its strongest when your actual words, the way you say them (intonation) and your non-verbal communication are all in synchronisation.

Which non-verbal behaviours help create presence in the classroom?

Some interesting research studies have looked at teachers' non-verbal behaviours and students' perceptions of those teachers. Some examples of this research can be found in Ambady and Rosenthal (1993) and Babad *et al.* (2003, 2004). These researchers were particularly interested in how participants who did not know the teacher rated them when they only watched short clips of non-verbal behaviours with no sound content (they call these 'thin slices'). These initial ratings were compared to the overall evaluations of the actual class at the end of the teaching semester. Those initial 'thin slices' predicted the end ratings that actual classes of students gave to the teacher. It appears that we communicate a great deal through our body language and non-verbal behaviours, and those initial impressions seem to remain when teaching over a longer period of time. It is important to acknowledge that these researchers did focus mainly upon high school and college students in USA and Israel, but Babad, with other researchers (Babad *et al.*, 1991; Babad and Taylor, 1992), also extended their work to look at those in fourth grade, which would equate to Year 5 in the UK.

This body of research identifies three important aspects of communication in the classroom:

a)   self-presentation;

b)   social perception;

c)   social interaction.

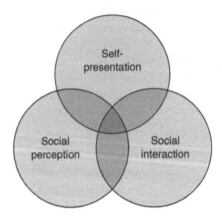

Figure 3.1 Presence as an integrated social experience (adapted from Babad et al., 2004)

Figure 3.1 provides a helpful way to view teacher presence, which includes the things that you do and the way you present as a teacher (self-presentation), the way that your pupils perceive you (social perception) and the relationships you have with your pupils (social interaction).

Later in the chapter, when we look at what it means to 'be present' and the importance of the relationships within the classroom, social perception and social interaction will be addressed. So, let's think about you as the teacher and how you can use techniques to help present yourself in a confident and influential way.

Self-presentation

One of the most important things to reflect upon is how you demonstrate a confident and calm manner in the classroom. Carney *et al.* (2010) explore how our body language can not only give the impression of confidence to the audience, but their research also suggests that when we adopt a strong and confident stance, it actually impacts the genuine confidence we have in ourselves.

Find out more from ... TED Talks

In her 2012 TED Talk, Amy Cuddy addresses how our body language can help us in presenting as confident in high-stress situations, such as a job interview. Her research (with Carney *et al.*, 2010) asked participants to practise 'high-power' poses. Have a look at Amy's talk here: **www.ted.com/talks/amy_cuddy_your_body_language_shapes_who_you_are?language=en** (accessed 12 November 2019).

Try some of these high-power poses when preparing yourself for your day of teaching.

Also, notice your own body language and when you may exhibit body language that does not exude confidence. Cuddy (2012), as you will see in the talk, uses the phrase 'fake it 'til you make it'. Consider how your non-verbal behaviours, as well as your verbal behaviours, exhibit the teacher you want to be.

Which body language should we use to show confidence and presence in the classroom?

Along with Amy Cuddy, other researchers in this field – for example, Rodenburg, 2009 – agree that there are some key ways in which we can use our body language. A key tip is to think carefully about open and closed body language. When we fold our arms or cross our legs, this can be interpreted as closed body language and those who observe us may feel we are not approachable or that we are very nervous. Alternatively, display open, positive body language such as some of the suggestions below.

Posture: Ensure that your posture is good by straightening your back and keeping your shoulders extended rather than hunched.

Figure 3.2 Straight back, shoulders extended

Use of gesture: Open palms are a positive way to communicate willingness to listen to others, openness to ideas and warmth towards your pupils.

Figure 3.3 Open palms

Assertive gesture: The use of 'palms down' is an assertive gesture. It can help you communicate your point strongly or show that the discussion has ended.

Figure 3.4 Palms down

Facial expression: Ensure that you have a positive expression. A smile is extremely powerful in building rapport and creating a positive climate for learning. However, recipients can tell the difference between real and fake smiles. Real smiles are also seen in the eyes as well as the mouth. Use eye contact well to show interest in what the learners are saying or doing (or to show that you have seen what the learners are doing).

Figure 3.5 Smile!

Babad *et al.* (2004) also identified some other characteristics of good teacher behaviours when they are teaching.

- A relaxed persona with positive body language.

- Stands rather than sits when addressing the whole group.

- Expressive in hand, body, face and voice.

- Moves around the space (but not excessively).

- Has a strong orientation towards the learners. This means that you are not just talking to an audience but that you are really engaging and noticing your pupils, and allowing yourself to explore ideas deeper with your pupils (rather than distracted by the next point on the lesson plan).

Grounded: When you are in the classroom, use a 'grounded' stance (Churches and Terry, 2007) to show that you are confident and comfortable in front of an audience. This involves ensuring that you are standing with your legs side by side with your weight equally distributed (not leaning to one side), good posture (shoulders extended not hunched) and arms by your side (not hidden in pockets, folded or behind your back). Ensure that you are looking at the class and showing that you are acknowledging your learners.

Figure 3.6 Grounded stance

Taking it further . . . research

In my own research, I conducted a study with some trainee teachers at the end of their programme. In two separate focus groups, the trainee teachers were asked to watch four clips of teachers teaching for 30 seconds. Unlike the studies by Ambady and Rosenthal (1993) and Babad *et al.* (2003), the participants were able to listen to the words being spoken as well as the non-verbal actions. They were then asked to discuss 'Which characteristics create presence?' Using thematic analysis (drawing out key themes from what was said) of the participants' responses, a key message that emerged from both focus groups was that confidence, or at least appearing confident, is important. From reading this chapter so far, you will see that this links very closely to the work of Carney *et al.* (2010). That confidence, according to these trainee teachers, is evident in the positive body language exhibited by the teacher, the eye contact (including 'the teacher look'), and the intonation and careful use of voice to communicate and maintain interest. Also, the position of the teacher in the classroom and the way in which the space in the classroom is used was important.

The four categories identified in this small-scale research are helpful in starting to unpick some of the techniques that can be used in the classroom. However, while these participants were able to verbalise those techniques used to create a presence, or exhibit confidence, in the classroom, the importance of relationships and knowing the individuals in the class was a very strong theme. This particular group of trainee teachers felt that you could not have technique without genuine connectedness to your pupils. Salter (2016) suggests that connectedness is a key component of presence, and the outcomes of my own doctoral work in this area has concluded that connection to your pupils, comfortableness in your delivery and confidence in your ability are all key to presence in the classroom. Kornelsen (2006, p79) identifies a *shift from a way of doing to a way of being*, which teachers described as they progressed within their career. While the participants in my study did not describe this idea of a journey that Kornelsen found when talking to new teachers, there is definitely an acknowledgement that technique cannot stand alone when working with real children in your classroom.

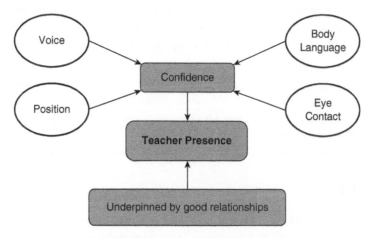

Figure 3.7 A representation of the themes emerging from the focus groups

Case study

Let's return to the conversation between David (the trainee in the case study) and Tim (the mentor).

David had received written feedback from Tim which said: 'Have more presence.' David asked Tim to explain more of what he meant, and here is an excerpt from their conversation.

Tim: When we discussed the lesson, you acknowledged that the children were not on task and they were not really taking notice of you when you gave them instructions. Your voice was very quiet and you were addressing them from the corner table, where you were working with your group. I could tell that you were getting worried about the lack of focus during the lesson because you stopped looking around the room; you just focused on your group and some of the others were not achieving very much.

David: I did realise that some of the children were not on task, but I had told everyone what to do before I went to my group. The children should have got on with the task.

 Reflection and discussion activity

Trainee and mentor: look at the targets you drafted earlier. Which one would you suggest now? What advice would you give to David to support his own self-reflection and support him in accepting constructive feedback?

In the case study, David is obviously exhibiting some behaviours that are demonstrating his lack of confidence in that particular session. He has not moved himself from the place where he is sitting to address the entire class (positionality) or used eye contact and positive body language to reassert himself in the classroom. In fact, from Tim's observation, it appears that David was either avoiding looking at the pupils (due to the fact that he was not confident in tackling any lack of engagement) or he was so engrossed in working with his group that he had lost that global view of the classroom that is so important. Tim also mentioned the use of voice. Using intonation, pitch and volume well is important for communication. You need to look after your voice, too, in teaching, and developing good habits and practice will support you in using your voice flexibly and effectively.

 Find out more from ... websites

The National Education Union (NEU) has some advice for voice care: **https://neu.org.uk/advice/voice-care-teachers** (accessed 12 November 2019).

Being present

Throughout this chapter, you will have realised that it is not enough to simply learn some techniques to create a presence in the classroom. You need to take time to build relationships with your learners and get to know them and how they respond to you. Rodgers and Raider-Roth define presence in teaching as:

a state of alert awareness, receptivity, and connectedness to the mental, emotional, and physical workings of both the individual and the group in the context of their learning environments, and the ability to respond with a considered and compassionate best next step.

(2006, p266)

Discussion activity

Read the definition from Rodgers and Raider-Roth (2006). What do you think this means in terms of:

- your view of yourself as the teacher in the classroom;

- the way you interact with the pupils in your class;

- the way you structure your learning activities;

- the way you manage the classroom;

- the way you set up the learning environment?

Think about your own practice. Reflect upon how you can change any habits or practices that hinder that opportunity to be 'connected' to all aspects of the pupil's learning development.

This definition has many implications for practitioners, especially in a primary classroom. This quotation challenges us to ensure that we know our pupils as individuals and the dynamics of those individuals as a class: to be sensitive and aware of any changes that may affect pupils in our care and respond to that appropriately. Schön (1983) calls this *reflection in action*: being able to think about what is happening in the here and now, and what would be the most effective action. You will also notice in the quotation that these authors use words such as 'compassionate'. The importance of our engagement with pupils on a human level, rather than being so preoccupied with getting from the beginning to the end of our plan, can set us apart as teachers who are really able to respond to our pupils and ensure they are progressing in all aspects. As Rodgers and Raider-Roth term it, to *be* present.

These authors do state explicitly that they do not agree that teaching can be reduced to a series of behaviours or techniques (p266), but that their concept of presence (as defined above) makes the difference in the classroom. They identify four dimensions of presence:

- self-awareness or connection to the self;

- connection to students;

- connection to subject matter and pedagogical knowledge;

- the context or current situation.

Implications of the four dimensions

If we take these four dimensions as essential aspects of our professional practice, then there are skills that we need to develop beyond those that often appear in lists of professional competencies. The dimensions appear to be essential for developing that classroom presence where pupils take notice, not because you are using techniques and dramatic actions to gain attention, but because the pupils have developed respect for you and want to listen to what you have to say. This is something that takes time and has to be part of the professional identity that you develop. To build that trust and respect, pupils need to see that you are able to manage your own emotions and present a safe environment. Daniel Goleman (2006) in his book *Emotional Intelligence* identifies the importance of managing our own emotions and knowing ourselves well so that we are able to respond and behave in a measured and calm way, while still being true to ourselves. This is where there is a difference between *having presence* and *being present*. Having presence is about presenting yourself in a particular way, but it is very difficult to maintain that persona if your genuine thoughts, feelings and emotions are not in line with your outward expression. For example, you may be feeling very anxious and worried about a situation (perhaps it is an observation by your mentor). You can use techniques such as those suggested in previous sections of this chapter, and we know from the research that these are helpful techniques to influence and communicate with our class, but maintaining that character or persona can drain our energy and make us feel detached from what is really happening. This is especially true if we have to maintain this false persona over a long period of time. Pupils in our primary classes are with us for significant periods of time and will see the inconsistencies. Korthagen and Vasalos (2009), who perpetuate this definition of presence being explored in this section in their work, say that true presence is part of a 'u' model: it starts with self-reflection and self-knowledge – they call this *open mind, open heart, open will* (p9) – this leads to presence (as defined by Rodgers and Raider-Roth (2006)) and this enables the individual to be open in responding to situations and problems.

In summary, these authors believe that rather than learning dramatic poses and adjusting non-verbal communication, genuine behaviours and actions will flow from a reflective practitioner who brings their genuine self to the classroom, who has developed openness and an understanding of how they can just *be*. The following extract from Meijer *et al.* (2009) demonstrates how a trainee teacher has this realisation during a mentoring conversation. Paulien has been struggling with establishing presence in the classroom and has been using a reflection model, supported by coaching conversations with Angelo, to support her development. Here she has a significant breakthrough in her understanding of teacher presence in the classroom:

> *Paulien (trainee teacher): I do believe that I am much more, that more and more I learn to **genuinely be**. It gives such a happy feeling [laughs]. It specifically comes to me in sudden realizations. Then there is this sudden insight and then BANG, **I am**. Something like that. Then I'm very aware of, well, yes, of me.*

> *Angelo (mentor): And what does this mean to you, when you teach from this sense of being, or, being a teacher who's able to teach from her inner sense of being? Imagine you would always be able to teach from your sense of being, your inner self? What would this mean?*

> *Paulien: Well, it would save so much of your energy. If you're really yourself – I know it's strange, but it's really hard to be yourself – but if you finally succeed in being yourself, everything just comes naturally. But I find it very difficult, when I lose touch with myself, to reconnect with myself.*

Meijer *et al.* (2009, p306)

Reflection and discussion activity

Read the extract above between Paulien and Angelo. There are some interesting ideas here that you can start to think about and discuss with your mentor.

- What does it mean as a teacher to 'genuinely be', as Paulien describes? Angelo begins to unpick this description by saying that it is 'teach(ing) from your sense of being'. What does this concept mean to you?

- Paulien says that when she loses touch with herself it is very difficult to reconnect. This can be interpreted as those moments in teaching when we no longer feel relaxed, or that we are able to be ourselves in the classroom because of the different pressures and distractions. Think about a situation you have had in the classroom where you have felt similar to Paulien. What were the barriers or distractions? In those situations, how can you reconnect?

 Chapter summary

Within this chapter, we have thought about techniques you can use to engage learners by having an enthusiastic persona, using positive non-verbal body language and portraying an open approach to your classroom management. We have looked at some research in the first part of the chapter which suggests some effective non-verbal behaviours to support your delivery, such as open hand gestures and a good posture. We have thought about the significance of confidence, or presenting as confident, until you are able to genuinely interact with your class from a place of personal security in your own competence ('fake it 'til you make it'). Finally, we have been challenged to think about teacher presence from a different perspective, away from techniques: the important place of genuine interactions (rather than a performance) and developing relationships where influence is based upon mutual respect. This type of presence takes time to build and develop, which is why I have presented in this chapter these two perspectives. Techniques can help us make initial impressions with our class (which are so important) and can help us communicate in an interesting and engaging way. However, this type of performance can quickly fade, so it is paramount that teacher presence in the long term is built upon relationships, genuine compassion for your learners and a flexibility to respond to the circumstance and in the moment.

References

Ambady, N and Rosenthal, R (1993) Half a minute: predicting teacher evaluations from thin slices of non-verbal behavior and physical attractiveness. *Journal of Personality and Social Psychology*, 64(3): 431–41.

Babad, E and Taylor, P (1992) Transparency of teacher expectancies across language, cultural boundaries. *Journal of Education Research*, 86: 211–34.

Babad, E, Avni-Babad, D and Rosental, R (2003) Teachers' brief nonverbal behaviors in defined instructional situations can predict students' evaluations. *Journal of Educational Psychology*, 95(3): 553–62.

Babad, E, Avni-Babad, D and Rosental, R (2004) Prediction of students' evaluations from brief instances of professors' nonverbal behavior in defined instructional situations. *Social Psychology of Education*, 7(1): 3–33.

Babad, E, Bernieri, F and Rosenthal, R (1991) Students as judges of teachers' verbal and nonverbal behavior. *American Educational Research Journal*, 28: 211–34.

Canter, L and Canter, M (1992) *Assertive Discipline: Positive behavior management for today's class room* (2nd edn). Santa Monica, CA: Lee Canter & Associates.

Carney, D, Cuddy, A and Yap, A (2010) Power posing. *Psychological Science*, 21(10): 1363–8.

Churches, R and Terry, R (2007) *NLP for Teachers: How to become a highly effective teacher*. Wales: Crown House Publishing.

Jones, F (2007) *Tools for Teaching: Discipline, instruction, motivation*. Santa Cruz, CA: Fredric H Jones & Associates.

Goleman, D (2006) *Emotional Intelligence*. New York: Bantam Books.

Kornelsen, L (2006) Teaching with presence. *New Directions for Adults and Continuing Education*, 111: 73–82.

Korthagen, F and Vasalos, A (2009) From reflection to presence and mindfulness: 30 years of developments concerning the concept of reflection in teacher education. EARLI Conference, The Netherlands.

Mehrabian, A (1972) *Nonverbal Communication*. New Brunswick, NJ: Aldine Transaction.

Meijer, P, Korthagen, F and Vasalos, A (2009) Supporting presence in teacher education: the connection between the personal and professional aspects of teaching. *Teaching and Teacher Education*, 25(2): 297–308.

Naftulin, D, Ware, J and Donnelly, F (1973) The Doctor Fox lecture: a paradigm of educational seduction. *Journal of Medical Education*, 48: 630–5.

Neill, S and Caswell, C (1993) *Body Language for Competent Teachers*. London: Routledge.

Peel, E and Babad, A (2014) The Doctor Fox research (1973) re-revisited: 'educational seduction' ruled out. *Journal of Educational Psychology*, 106(1): 36–45.

Rodenburg, P. (2009) Presence: How to use positive energy for success. London: Penguin Books.

Rodgers, C and Raider-Roth, M (2006) Presence in teaching. *Teachers and Teaching: Theory and Practice*, 12(3): 265–87.

Salter, R. (2016) *Classroom Presence*. Hampshire: Teachers' Pocketbooks.

Schön, DA (1983) *The Reflective Practitioner: How professionals think in action*. New York: Basic Books.

Senge, P, Scharmer, C, Jaworski, J and Flowers, B (2004) *Presence: Exploring profound change in people, organizations and society*. London: Nicholas Brearley.

White, J and Gardner, J (2012) *The Classroom X-Factor*. London: Routledge.

4

Principles of teaching for learning

Sue Lambert

This chapter will

- provide opportunities to think about what we mean when we say 'learning';
- see how different theories and approaches have influenced teaching for learning in the classroom;
- reflect on these theories and approaches, recognising when and why particular approaches may be more or less useful in the classroom.

Links to the Teachers' Standards

2 **Promote good progress and outcomes by pupils,** specifically:
- be aware of pupils' capabilities and their prior knowledge, and plan teaching to build on these;
- demonstrate knowledge and understanding of how pupils learn and how this impacts on teaching.

4 **Plan and teach well structured lessons,** specifically:
- plan and teach well-structured lessons;
- impart knowledge and develop understanding through effective use of lesson time;
- promote a love of learning and children's intellectual curiosity;
- reflect systematically on the effectiveness of lessons and approaches to teaching;
- contribute to the design and provision of an engaging curriculum within the relevant subject area(s).

(Continued)

(Continued)

5 **Adapt teaching to respond to the strengths and needs of all pupils,** specifically:

- know when and how to differentiate appropriately, using approaches which enable pupils to be taught effectively;

- have a secure understanding of how a range of factors can inhibit pupils' ability to learn, and how best to overcome these;

- demonstrate an awareness of the physical, social and intellectual development of children, and know how to adapt teaching to support pupils' education at different stages of development;

- have a clear understanding of the needs of all pupils, including those with special educational needs; those of high ability; those with English as an additional language; those with disabilities; and be able to use and evaluate distinctive teaching approaches to engage and support them.

Introduction

As teachers, it is important to remember that learning can be interpreted and defined in many different ways and that it can look different depending on what you are trying to learn.

 Reflection and discussion activity

Reflection

Trainee: how do you learn best?

- When things are presented in blocks of information?

- When things are presented in a cross-curricular or creative way?

- When you have a say in the direction of learning?

- When you use new or unfamiliar materials?

- When you are given the 'big picture' and see the purpose of the learning?

- When you work with someone else to discuss things or ask and answer questions?

- When you teach someone else?

- Does it vary? Why?

Mentor: think about how you vary your approach to teaching and learning, and why. Can you think of some examples to share with the trainee? For example, when you teach in blocks, in a more cross-curricular way or when pupils have taken the lead in the direction of the learning?

Discussion

Trainee and mentor: discuss why the approach to teaching and learning might vary. Discuss whether you think this is important.

As a teacher, you need to understand the theories and research that have influenced what you teach and how you teach it. Nothing is more important than knowing the pupils that you teach and what will 'hook' them into the learning and why. You need to feel confident that this is giving pupils the best opportunities to learn. You need to be able to reflect on the approaches that will be most successful for supporting pupils to make progress in their learning and to evaluate how successful these have been.

As Hattie explains:

> *There is no fixed recipe for ensuring that teaching has the maximum possible effect on student learning and no set of principles that apply to all learning for all students. But there are practices that we know are effective and many practices that we know are not.*

(2012, p4)

There are many theories about how pupils learn, based on research and practice from Ancient Greek times through to the most recent theories, focusing on the importance of children having a range of skills to enable them to learn in the rapidly changing world of new technologies (connectivism) (Siemens, 2005). It is not possible to look at every approach in one chapter, but I will present some examples and links to other materials, as well as give you opportunities to reflect. Through these activities, you will be able to learn more about different principles of teaching for learning. This will help you to think about what this might look like in the classroom, deepening your understanding of how you might teach and why. As MacBlain (2014) notes, it is important to understand historical and cultural influences that shape practice, but also to recognise that new approaches or developments about learning will continue to be influential. There are many different ways to teach and theories about learning, and some of these will be explored more fully in later chapters such as Learning and teaching approaches (Chapter 5) and Questioning to stimulate dialogue (Chapter 8).

 Reflection and discussion activity

Reflection

Trainee: think about something that you have had to learn. Was there a teacher you had that really helped you? What was it about their teaching that helped you to learn?

(Continued)

(Continued)

Discussion

Mentor: share some examples of helpful ways you have found to 'hook' pupils into the learning, particularly any reluctant learners. Unpick why you approached the learning in a particular way.

Trainee and mentor: discuss what you think are things that can help or hinder pupils being able to engage in learning and what you need to consider to successfully 'hook' pupils into learning.

Theories that influence classroom practice

This section will briefly discuss some theories and principles of teaching for learning and give examples of what this might look like in the classroom. If you want to look at some of the things discussed in more detail, the Find out more from . . . sections have some references to further reading and websites.

Behaviourist theories

Behaviourist theories focus on learned behaviours, usually in response to stimuli. Exponents state that behaviours become more automatic with repeated practice or reinforcement. You may be familiar with Pavlov's dog. Ivan Pavlov conditioned a dog to respond to a bell when food was present. He did this repeatedly to the point where he could ring the bell and the dog would salivate even if there was no food, because the dog was conditioned to associate the bell with food. This is known as classical conditioning. The other area is operant or behavioural conditioning. Thorndike (cited in Shunk, 2012) and Skinner (1974) are well-known authors in this area. Thorndike found that not all positives motivated learners and negatives did not always lessen unwanted behaviours. He argued that you need to know exactly what it is you want to teach and how you want to teach it. If you know what responses you should get, you can reinforce these behaviours. Trial and error are important ways of learning. Skinner (1974) agreed with much of Thorndike's work and felt that reinforcing a behaviour using rewards to promote positive behaviours or sanctions to prevent inappropriate or negative behaviour enabled children to be active learners. Repetition reinforces the behaviour that is desired through consequences for the actions. Most behaviourists emphasise the importance of positive reinforcement.

 Reflection and discussion activity

Scenario

Alyena is making noises on the carpet when you are teaching the whole class about multiplying and dividing by two. This happens quite often and when you ask her for an answer to a question she gets the answer right but you do not praise her. The rest of the pupils do not seem to be distracted by her behaviour so you ignore it. You praise the other pupils for their correct answers and listening to each other. After several sessions, the noises stop and when asked for an answer, you praise her for the answer. If pupils get the answers wrong, there is no praise.

Reflection

Trainee: think about the impact of this approach on Alyena's learning and that of the other pupils. If it helps, think about how you responded to praise or not having efforts recognised.

Mentor: think about how you use praise for correct responses and how you address things if pupils give an incorrect answer. Think about when this approach may be useful or less useful for the pupils so that you can discuss it with the trainee.

Discussion

Mentor and trainee: think about what the strengths and limitations of this approach might be. Here are a few things to start you off. Stimulus and response do not necessarily mean understanding. Pupils become used to the rewards so they lose their impact. It can be useful for rote learning and where rewards can be given for correct response.

 Find out more from ... websites and books

A short film that looks at the behaviourist theorists, Pavlov, Skinner and Watson: **www.youtube.com/watch?v=xvVaTy8mQrg** (accessed 6 November 2019).

Skinner, BF (1978) *Reflections on Behaviorism and Society.* Englewood Cliffs, NJ: Prentice-Hall.

Cognitivist theories

This is an approach to learning which recognises that, for pupils to be successful learners, they need to be aware of their own learning and how they learn. This helps them to know how to improve their learning. Teachers often help pupils to do this by modelling and explaining the learning process and expectations. Giving pupils a clear focus for the learning and outlining how they will know they have been successful in their learning are important. This approach encourages dialogue: the teacher supports pupils to articulate their learning, such as how they solved a worded problem in mathematics, while errors or misconceptions are used to unpick the learning. A well-known theorist in this area is Howard Gardner (1999) and you may have heard of his research suggesting that we have multiple intelligences. He believed that there is not one global intelligence but that we have a range of intelligences, so our learning in one area may be stronger than in another (Muijs and Reynolds, 2007).

Table 4.1 Intelligences identified by Gardner

Intelligence	Characteristics
Bodily kinaesthetic intelligence	• Can use their body to express emotion • Can play games effectively • Can invent a game • Can choreograph dance and sequences of movement
Interpersonal intelligence	• Notices differences in people – i.e. contrasts in their moods, temperaments, motivations and intentions • Is empathetic • Can effectively lead, organise and manage
Linguistic intelligence	• Can order meanings and rhythm of words • Can decode rules of grammar • Can invent new language • Enjoys playing with words
Musical intelligence	• Is sensitive to rhythm, pitch and timbre • Appreciates timing and tone • Enjoys creating and listening to music • Can recognise melodies accurately
Visual/special intelligence	• Can make representations of the visual world • Can create mental images • Can use visual and special awareness in unfamiliar circumstances
Logical/ mathematical intelligence	• Can work logically • Can make deductions • Can use reasoning to find answers and solutions • Is a problem solver • Can categorise, calculate and hypothesise • Likes to experiment • Can develop arguments
Naturalistic intelligence (added 1999)	• Can identify and group particular plant or animal species • Can identify different weather formations and climates • Can classify natural things such as rocks, types of mountains and geographical landscapes • Can apply knowledge of nature for such as farming, landscaping, or animal training
Existential intelligence (added 1999)	• Prefers activities that allow them to choose • Looks for connections in things across the curriculum and more widely • Can develop questions to investigate because they can think reflectively • Appreciates and values the world around them • Can see things from a range of perspectives

Source: Table based on the multiple intelligences outlined in Gardner (1983, 1999).

Gardner (1999) also cautions that labelling things as learning styles is not helpful and can make the focus of teaching and learning too narrow (see Table 4.1). For pupils who have different intelligences, accessing, for example, learning that is language heavy or mathematical learning may be challenging, so as a teacher you need to consider this. As Pritchard notes:

> *individual learners have preferred ways of working, thinking and learning. If an individual's preferred approach to a learning task is ignored in the ways that a teacher expects them to work, there is a distinct possibility that their learning will not progress as efficiently and effectively as it might.*

(2009, p56)

There is a lot of debate about intelligence: whether it is fixed or changeable, and what it actually is, but there is some evidence to suggest that intelligence can be developed and enhanced. It may not be helpful to see pupils as having higher or lower intelligence (Lazear, 2004; Hymer and Michel, 2002), or even if there are multiple intelligences (Kincheloe, 2004). This links with the discussion of the mastery approach in Chapter 5 in terms of having a growth mindset for all pupils.

 Reflection and discussion activity

Reflection

Trainee: why might it hinder your teaching if you assume that pupils have fixed intelligence or if pupils think they have fixed intelligence?

Mentor: can you think of ways that you have avoided labelling pupils in terms of intelligence? Can you think of pupils who have surprised you by what they could do because you approached the learning in a way that enabled them to 'shine'?

Discussion

Mentor and trainee: discuss the previous points and how your approach to planning and learning might take this into account.

Long- and short-term memory (which includes working memory) also need some consideration when thinking about planning teaching for learning (Sousa, 2011). There are some useful publications and links in the Find out more from . . . section. For many years, there was a focus on getting information into long-term memory so that it was a permanent part of learning. Working memory is temporary and can only store, deal with or retrieve things for a limited amount of time, and this varies with how old you are. Those younger than 5 years have less capacity than between 5 years and adolescence (Sousa, 2011). This has implications for the amount of information we expect pupils to store and use: *Less is more!* (Sousa, 2011, p52).

As Sousa notes, working memory needs to connect with the learner's past experiences and, depending on the answer to the two questions below, it is either saved or rejected.

'Does this make sense?' This question refers to whether the learner can understand the item based on past experience. Does it 'fit' into what the learner knows about how the world works? When a student says 'I don't understand,' it means the student is having a problem making sense of the learning.

'Does it have meaning?' This question refers to whether the item is relevant to the learner. For what purpose should the learner remember it? Meaning, of course, is a very personal thing and is greatly influenced by that person's experiences. The same item can have great meaning for one student and none for another. Questions like 'Why do I have to know this?' or 'When will I ever use this?' indicate that the student has not, for whatever reason, perceived this learning as relevant.

(2011, p52)

Sousa's questions also link with learning the constructivist approach, discussed later in the chapter.

 Reflection and discussion activity

Scenario

You are doing a lesson about instruction writing in English. You share with the pupils that you are writing instructions for planting seeds, which will be part of your science lesson later. The pupils already know about the key features such as using the imperative verb, time connectives and writing in the second person present tense. You begin by reminding the pupils about what they already know and show them a list of key features which you pin up on the wall as a reminder. You explain that they will be planting the seeds in their science lesson and that they need instructions to be able to do this correctly. You then use an example of an instruction writing frame on the interactive board to model writing instructions and talk through the process with the pupils as you model it, asking them for responses to questions to reinforce the key points that you want them to remember. Some pupils seem to be struggling to focus and engage once you start to model writing the instructions.

Reflection

Trainee: think back to the early reflection about how you learn 'best' and the discussion above about different intelligences and memory. Why might some of the pupils be less engaged during the modelling part of the lesson?

Mentor: think about how you have ensured pupils who learn in different ways have been able to access the learning. If it is helpful, link it to the scenario example, and in the discussion share with the trainee how you keep all the pupils engaged.

Discussion

Mentor and trainee: discuss some of the ways you involve the pupils in learning and how you might have approached the case study differently. How might this affect how you plan your teaching?

Find out more from ... internet clips

Howard Gardner discusses and reflects on multiple intelligences: **www.youtube.com/watch?v=I2QtSbP4FRg** (accessed 6 November 2019).

Bridging behaviourist and cognitivist theories

Albert Bandura (1977) felt that behaviourist theories provided an incomplete picture because you do not only learn from your own experiences but also from things that you observe, can imitate or see modelled. Learners also learn *where there is no immediate or apparent reward* (Pound, 2014, p57). They can use all of this to develop their ability to problem solve and consider consequences. Bandura believed that people can control their behaviour to some degree and learn. This is known as social learning theory. He believed that helping learners achieve success meant that they would be better able to achieve further success and take on challenges. Observing others complete something successfully and having this reinforced motivates others to do the same. You need to role model positive behaviours, ways to solve conflicts and things such as reading yourself in class when pupils read so they see that you think this is important (Pound, 2014).

Reflection and discussion activity

Scenario

You are doing a maths lesson about solving worded problems. You model an example as a class about how to solve a worded problem by looking for key words that identify what the calculation is and how to answer the question. You ask a pupil who is confident to come out and do the calculation, talking through the process with the pupil and asking them to explain what they are doing. You praise the pupil for the correct answer and showing the other pupils how they worked it out. You praise all the pupils and say that you know they will be able to do a calculation of their own now that they have seen someone else show them how to do it. The pupils are then asked to have a go independently at a different worded problem using the same calculation method. The pupils still have your example on the board and most have a go, although a few still struggle to complete it correctly on their own.

Reflection

Trainee: think about why this might be a helpful approach for pupils and what the issues might be for those who still struggle.

Mentor: think of examples of when this approach has been helpful in your teaching and when it has not been as helpful.

Discussion

Trainee and mentor: discuss what you have both decided are possible strengths and limitations of this approach.

Find out more from ... internet clips

Watch this introduction to social learning theory: **www.youtube.com/watch?v=ZqDMjOd9T2o** (accessed 6 November 2019).

Cognitive constructivist and social constructivist theories

Constructivists think that you learn best when you build on your existing knowledge, skills and understanding, and when you construct your own learning and build new knowledge. Learning is an active process and prior learning is a key feature of this approach. Muijs and Reynolds (2007) note that this means that what each child might learn from a lesson may be slightly different.

Piaget (in Piaget and Inhelder, 2000) is probably the best-known name associated with the cognitive constructivist approach to learning. He developed an approach to learning based on stages of development, broadly associated with different age bands (see Table 4.2). This is an example of Piaget's stages of development and I have added the column to show what this might look like in practice.

Table 4.2 Piaget's stages of development

Stage of development	What happens at this stage	What it might look like
Sensori-motor stage	Knowledge and understanding come from physical actions and senses. Children are self-centred.	Children learn by looking, listening, tasting, touching and smelling. They learn to move and experience the environment by doing things physically. They are playing with things – e.g. toys in the bath.
Pre-operational stage	Children learn to use and control their environment more. They start to use words and language for objects and this helps support ideas for play. They do not have complete knowledge, so may have misconceptions that may not be logical.	Children may use language incorrectly as they learn – e.g. 'I goed to the shops' instead of 'I went to the shops' – and they may also have misconceptions about things such as all big things sink and all small things float.
Concrete operational stage	Children develop more logical thinking. This is usually only with things they can see or are concrete.	Looking at the example above, at this stage (when looking at things that float or sink), they will begin to see that size is not necessarily a factor. They can recognise that many ships are very big and heavy but still float and begin to think about other reasons for things to float and sink.

Stage of development	What happens at this stage	What it might look like
Formal operational stage	Thinking becomes more ordered and logical. This means that they can work with abstract ideas, predict and hypothesise and see the implications of their thinking and that of others.	At this stage, children and young adults can offer reasoned explanations for things. For example, they might say that two things that weigh the same but are shaped differently will either float or sink based on what they know already about water resistance, boats, seeds transported by water, etc.

Source: Adapted from How Children Learn *(Pound, 2014).*

Piaget also emphasised the importance of thinking and giving children thinking time (Fisher, 2005, p13). Piaget suggested that we build links between things we know (schema) and these are added to so that new schema are created all the time. The links within and across schema enable us to learn and make progress. If each developmental stage is not completed, then it can cause problems for further learning. Context can impact on learning too, so a pupil might be able to do something within the classroom but may not see how to use this learning in a different context or environment, which may limit their learning. More successful learning occurs when pupils can link it to 'real-life' situations and see the purpose of the learning.

As Pritchard (2009) notes, *Effective learning is learning which is lasting and capable of being put to use in new and different situations* (px). However, Gray and MacBlain (2015) note that in Piaget's work there is little emphasis on the role of the teacher.

 Reflection and discussion activity

Reflection

Trainee: think about Piaget's stages of development and the importance he attaches to completing each stage. What do you think could be issues for pupils and teachers if any stages are not fully developed?

Mentor: think of any pupils who have a delay in their development. What do you do to support these children in your planning and teaching?

Discussion

Trainee and mentor: share a discussion about what the issues for pupils may be and the ways that your planning and teaching needs to take this into account to support them in their learning.

Within constructivist theory there is *social constructivism*. Probably the best-known theorists in this area of learning are Vygotsky (2012, in Vygotsky *et al.*) and Bruner (1977) who recognised both the role of the teacher and the impact of cultural background as key to learning. They proposed that social interaction was important for learning to be able to take place, and prior and current knowledge enabled new learning to develop from the interactions. This could be with peers, teachers, parents and carers, sometimes but not always, a *more knowledgeable other* (MKO) to enable further learning to take place. Learning can take place anywhere. Usually in a school setting the teacher is in the role of the MKO. You may be familiar with the term 'scaffolding learning'. The teacher breaks down the learning into manageable steps for pupils to enable them to build new learning onto what they already know. Vygotsky called this the *Zone of Proximal Development* (ZPD) – i.e. a level just above the level of knowledge, skills and understanding that the pupils already have and where they need help to make progress. Teachers scaffold in different ways – for example, through discussion, use of resources, encouraging group discussion and targeted questioning. Repetition helps to embed the learning.

John Dewey ([1916] 1961) is influential in terms of his views that children learn by doing and enquiring, and that the teacher is the facilitator of learning. He argued that learning did need to be structured and although you cannot change past experiences you can influence the present and future learning of children (Gray and McBlain, 2015). Trial and error are seen as a positive part of the learning process. This links with enquiry and investigative approaches to learning. This is explored in more detail in Chapter 5.

 Find out more from . . . websites

Easy-to-read information about Vygotsky and Piaget with a short video about the differences between their theories of learning: **www.simplypsychology.org/vygotsky.html#piaget** (accessed 6 November 2019).

Bronfenbrenner (1917–2005) further explored the influence of ecological systems theory to explain how everything in a child and the child's environment affects how a child grows and develops. His theory explored different systems that impact on child development what are called nested systems, moving from those nearest to the child to those furthest away. The early model included four systems and was criticised for not including the child in an active role in their own development, so a fifth system was added. Below are links to find out more about Brofenbrenner and his ecological systems theory.

 Find out more from . . . the internet

An introduction to Brofenbrenner's theory with a diagram showing the systems and how they are organised: **www.psychologynoteshq.com/bronfenbrenner-ecological-theory** (accessed 7 November 2019).

Taking it further . . . research article

Christensen, J (2016) A critical reflection of Brofenbrenner's Development Ecology Model. *Problems of Education in the 21st Century*, 69: 22-8: **http://oaji.net/articles/2016/457-1460961906.pdf** (accessed 7 November 2019).

This article reflects on Brofenbrenner's approach, considering possible limitations and strengths. It also provides useful background information about the nested systems that Brofenbrenner identifies and possible missing elements - e.g. consideration of resilience.

Other approaches to teaching for learning

Emotional intelligence

Several authors have considered the influence that emotional intelligence (EI) (otherwise known as emotional quotient (EQ)) has on how well pupils progress (Alexander, 2010; Goleman, 2006). How a person 'feels' about a learning situation determines the attention it gets, so you need to use emotion intelligently (Sousa, 2011). As a teacher, you need to be aware of the impact that emotion can have. Basically, if you can be self-aware in terms of your own emotions and manage these emotions and those of others, you are better able to learn.

Goleman (2006) identified five 'domains' of EI; three are to do with knowing and managing your emotions and motivation, and the other two concern recognising and understanding the emotions of others and managing relationships. If emotions are not managed, learning can be inhibited. There is more about this in Chapters 3 and 15.

Reflection and discussion activity

Reflection

Trainee: think about times when pupils have not seemed able to learn because of something that happened, perhaps at a breaktime. What did you or the teacher do to help the pupil manage their emotions?

Mentor: think about examples of successful approaches that you have used when pupils were struggling with their emotions or in relating to other pupils.

Discussion

Mentor and trainee: think about what useful approaches you could develop to help pupils develop emotional intelligence. There are some ideas for this in Chapter 15 too.

Find out more from ... YouTube

Daniel Goleman introduces Emotional Intelligence: **www.youtube.com/watch?v=Y7m9eNoB3NU** (accessed 6 November 2019).

Thinking skills and problem-solving approaches

Skills-based approaches to learning and building learning around thinking skills are also ideas you may encounter in schools. These approaches provide a framework for developing thinking skills and solving problems. Learning is about understanding, so advocates of skills-based approaches and developing thinking skills promote the idea that developing the skills gives context to the knowledge. There are elements of a number of the learning theories discussed in these approaches. In the Find out more about . . . section below, there is a link to Belle Wallace's (2001) Thinking Actively in a Social Context (TASC) approach and Edward de Bono's (2000) *Six Thinking Hats*. The focus becomes more about developing skills for learning rather than acquiring knowledge because the skills will enable pupils to find out things they need to know. De Bono developed a toolkit for ways of thinking. Each hat encourages different approaches.

Find out more from ... internet clips, websites

An example of de Bono's six hats in the primary classroom: www.youtube.com/watch?v=yUliluJrWKg (accessed 7 November 2019).

A link to more information about the six hats: **www.debonogroup.com/six_thinking_hats.php** (accessed 7 November 2019).

Information about the TASC approach including pdfs and PowerPoints: **http://teachertools.londongt.org/?page=classroomThinkingSkills** (accessed 7 November 2019).

Lorin *et al.* (2001) provided a revised version of Bloom's taxonomy to show how thinking develops to higher levels. Bloom used his taxonomy to support his argument that learning needs to be broken down into levels – and as you develop you have higher level thinking and learning. Some schools use this to help them develop higher order questions, and this is further explored in Chapter 8 which looks at questioning and dialogue. In the Find out more . . . section, there are links to examples of Bloom's taxonomy and a simple example of what skills might be demonstrated at each level.

Reflection and discussion activity

Reflection

Trainee: think back to the beginning of the chapter when you were asked to think about how you learn best, reflecting on the different principles and approaches. Are there approaches that you think are more helpful to support learning?

Discussion

Trainee and mentor: discuss why it is important to know about the principles for learning and teaching, and how this may help you as you develop your own teaching for learning.

 Find out more from . . . websites and books

Examples of the levels of thinking in Bloom's taxonomy including the revised taxonomy:

http://thepeakperformancecenter.com/educational-learning/thinking/blooms-taxonomy/blooms-taxonomy-revised/ (accessed 6 November 2019).

Gershon, M (2015) *How to Use Bloom's Taxonomy in the Classroom: The complete guide.* Charlestown, SC: CreateSpace.

 Chapter summary

This chapter has given you a brief overview of some key learning theories and approaches.

You can see that many of the principles for learning and teaching are used within lessons to help pupils learn. The approach used depends on what pupils are learning and how you plan your teaching to make sure their learning is effective. As Hattie notes:

> It matters what teachers do but what matters most is having an appropriate mind frame relating to the impact of what they do . . . having a mind frame in which they see it as their role to evaluate their effect on learning.

> (2012, p15)

It is not really about the principles for teaching and learning per se, but about knowing why you teach what you teach in particular ways. This teaching needs to be grounded in an understanding of how pupils learn, having the ability to reflect and having confidence in why you do what you do.

▬▬▬▬▬ References ▬▬▬▬▬

Alexander, R (ed.) (2010) *Children, Their World, Their Education: Final report and recommendations of the Cambridge Primary Review*. Abingdon: Routledge.

Bandura, A (1977) *Social Learning Theory*. New York: General Learning Press.

Bruner, JS ([1960] 1977) *The Process of Education* (2nd edn). Cambridge, MA: Harvard University Press.

De Bono, E (2000) *Six Thinking Hats*. London: Penguin.

Dewey, J ([1916] 1961) *Democracy and Education*. New York: Macmillan.

Fisher, R (2005) *Teaching Children to Think* (2nd edn). Cheltenham: Nelson Thornes.

Gardner, H (1983) *Frames of Mind: The theory of multiple intelligences*. London: HarperCollins.

Gardner, H (1999) *Intelligence Reframed: Multiple intelligences for the 21st century*. New York: Basic Books.

Goleman, D (2006) *Emotional Intelligence: Why it can matter more than IQ* (2nd edn). London: Bloomsbury.

Gray, C and MacBlain, S (2015) *Learning Theories in Childhood* (2nd edn). London: SAGE.

Hattie, J (2012) *Visible Learning for Teachers: Maximising impact on learning*. Abingdon: Routledge.

Hymer, B and Michel, D (2002) *Gifted and Talented Learners: Creating a policy for inclusion*. London: David Fulton.

Kincheloe, J. (2004) *Multiple Intelligences Reconsidered*. New York: Peter Lang.

Lazear, D (2004) *Multiple Intelligences Approach to Assessment*. Carmarthen: Crown House.

Lorin W, Anderson, LW, Krathwohl, DR and Bloom, BS (2001) *A Taxonomy for Learning, Teaching, and Assessing: A revision of Bloom's taxonomy of educational objectives*. New York: Longman.

MacBlain, S (2014) *How Children Learn*. London: SAGE.

Muijs, D and Reynolds, D (2007) *Effective Teaching: Evidence and practice* (3rd edn). London: SAGE.

Piaget, J and Inhelder, B (2000) *The Psychology of the Child*. New York: Basic Books.

Pound, L (2009) *Contemporary Thinking and Theorists: An overview of contemporary educational and psychological theorists*. London: Practical Pre-School Books.

Pound, L (2014) *How Children Learn: Educational theories and approaches – from Comenius the father of modern education to giants such as Piaget, Vygotsky and Malaguzzi*. London: Practical Pre-School Books.

Pritchard, A (2009) *Ways of Learning: Learning theories and learning styles in the classroom*. Abingdon: Routledge.

Shunk, D (2012) *Learning Theories: An educational perspective* (6th edn). Boston, MA: Pearson Education. Available at: **http://server2.docfoc.com/uploads/Z2015/12/26/1koY3p4pMU/5a9f4b6679bd468fb0e9a9d541487e09.pdf**

Siemens, G (2005) Connectivism: a learning theory for the digital age. *International Journal of Instructional Technology and Distance Learning*, 2(1): 3–10.

Skinner, BF (1974) *About Behaviorism*. New York: Vintage Books.

Sousa, D (2011) *How the Brain Learns* (4th edn). London: SAGE.

Vygotsky, LS, Hanfmann, E, Vakar, G and Kozulin, A (2012) *Thought and Language*. Cambridge, MA: MIT Press.

Wallace, B (ed.) (2001) *Teaching Thinking Skills Across the Primary Curriculum: A practical approach for all abilities*. Abingdon: David Fulton.

5
Learning and teaching approaches

Ashley Compton, Andy Dickenson and Sue Lambert

 This chapter will

- introduce you to some definitions and approaches that you may consider using to engage pupils, with practical ideas for your class, including a mastery approach;
- consider ideas for variation (differentiation) and intervention;
- discuss approaches for developing opportunities for engagement and ensuring that all pupils have the opportunity to achieve;
- support you in considering approaches you may wish to incorporate into your own practice and practices that you may see in school;
- reflect upon the characteristics of approaches.

Links to the Teachers' Standards

4   **Plan and teach well structured lessons,** specifically:

- impart knowledge and develop understanding through effective use of lesson time;
- promote a love of learning and children's intellectual curiosity;
- contribute to the design and provision of an engaging curriculum within the relevant subject area(s).

Introduction

What approaches can be used to support the learning of pupils?

Ideas change over time and teachers implement approaches to learning in different ways for their pupils. Sometimes certain approaches (such as a mastery or topic-based approach) are seen in schools, or a specific theme is used that takes its lead from National Curriculum subjects (such as Space, or the Victorian Era). There are many differing approaches, such as a cross-curricular approach, immersive learning, enquiry-based learning or the Forest Schools approach. In schools, you may see other methods such as the International Primary Curriculum (topic), Mantle of the Expert (pupils in role working on a commission for a client), Take One Picture and Montessori philosophy (play based), to name a few. Not all of these can be covered in this chapter, but below are links to finding out more about some approaches not discussed.

These concepts are also linked to the ITT Core Content Framework Classroom Practice (EEF, 2019) and Standard 4 – 'Plan and teach well-structured lessons'. There are key ideas in this chapter which shall be explored:

1. Effective teaching can transform pupils' knowledge, capabilities and beliefs about learning.

2. Explicitly teaching pupils metacognitive strategies linked to subject knowledge, including how to plan, monitor and evaluate, supports independence and academic success.

3. Questioning is an essential tool for teachers; questions can be used for many purposes, including to check pupils' prior knowledge, assess understanding and break down problems.

🔆 — Find out more from . . . the internet

- This website provides teachers' notes about using artwork as the stimulus for learning across the curriculum: **www.nationalgallery.org.uk/learning/teachers-and-schools/teachers-notes** (accessed 7 November 2019).

- This website provides an introduction to the mantle of the expert approach and links to planning ideas to use in the classroom: **www.mantleoftheexpert.com** (accessed 7 November 2019).

- Teacher TV clip about the Montessori approach: **https://uk.video.search.yahoo.com/yhs/search?fr=yhs-itm-001&hsimp=yhs-001&hspart=itm&p=montesori+approach#id=3&vid=47bba9e1a6f2c9510bf25530 5b00437b&action=view** (accessed 7 November 2019).

- This website provides an introduction to the International Primary Curriculum: **https://fieldworkeducation. com/curriculums/primary-years/about-the-ipc?e=371** (accessed 7 November 2019).

A mastery approach

Although mastery as a teaching approach has existed for many years, a renewed emphasis has been placed upon this approach to learning. This approach links with the intended application of the National Curriculum that all should have the opportunity to master skills and knowledge to ensure depth of understanding, and that learning is embedded rather than rushing on to the next objective. This has serious implications for ideas about attainment and differentiation/variation. The influence of Singapore maths and Mathematics mastery is particularly evident in primary schools.

What is mastery?

Mastery is not a new concept. Around 50 years ago, Bloom (1968) was promoting the concept of mastery learning and researching the different conditions in which this would work. This approach spread in the United States and beyond during the following decades, although it was not tightly defined. In the 1970s, Bloom tried to synthesise the various definitions:

> There are many versions of mastery learning in existence at present. All begin with the notion that most students can attain a high level of learning capability if instruction is approached sensitively and systematically, if students are helped when and where they have learning difficulties, if they are given sufficient time to achieve mastery, and if there is some clear criterion of what constitutes mastery.

(1976, p4)

Bloom (1968, 1976) noted that mastery learning required a change in thinking for both teachers and students: you need to believe that the vast majority of pupils can achieve mastery rather than thinking that only some of the pupils will achieve, and that some pupils will never achieve. He felt that aptitude for a subject was not about whether a student could learn something, but about how long it would take them. Thus, students with a high aptitude for a subject would learn quickly – students who are now referred to sometimes as 'fast graspers'. Bloom (1976) compared the process of mastery learning to working with a personal tutor who would respond to your individual needs, adapting the teaching as necessary and allowing you the time you need to learn. Unfortunately, this is hard to do in a school situation where one teacher has to cater for the individual needs of 30 pupils in the class during the lesson time allocated. In order to respond to the individual needs of the pupils and achieve mastery, Bloom (1968, 1976) said that you need to:

WALT   success criteria.

- have focused objectives with clearly defined outcomes;

- be aware of the prerequisite knowledge and skills for the new learning;

- have frequent formative assessments to check progress in learning;

- be prepared to adapt teaching in response to the formative assessments:

  o by providing alternative explanations;

  o more concrete illustrations;

- o additional examples;

- o varying the degree of independent versus highly structured learning;

- o altering the type and quantity of positive reinforcement; *links to behaviour?*

- o finding more motivating contexts.

When formative assessments show that the pupils are ready, you then undertake a summative assessment as a final check. These are usually written tests (for subjects like mathematics and history), but could also be physical tasks (for subjects like PE and art). Bloom (1968) suggested that the formative and summative results should be described as mastery or non-mastery rather than being given grades such as A or C. Those who had not achieved mastery would get feedback that provided specific advice on what aspects still needed to be addressed and how to achieve these, while those who had already achieved mastery would be given enrichment activities. It is perhaps significant that Bloom talked about mastery learning rather than mastery teaching. In addition to the teaching strategies outlined above, Bloom emphasised the importance of the pupil's willingness to learn and respond to feedback and perseverance in overcoming difficulties.

England has seen a renewed interest in mastery teaching following international comparisons with areas like Singapore and Shanghai, which ranked highly in mathematics and science in the 2009 PISA tests. NCSL (2013) organised a research trip for UK teachers to Shanghai and Ningbo, China, to study how they taught mathematics and science. Some aspects they discovered were about conditions for teachers: less curriculum content; subject specialist teachers were used for mathematics and science; all teachers took part in Teaching Research Groups and observed other teachers to learn from each other; and teachers spent only about 25 to 30 per cent of their time with the class, allowing them ample time for planning, assessing and providing individual support. About 20 per cent of the pupils received individual support, which took place at lunchtime, after school or during planned intervention time. During the lessons there was a mastery approach with teacher explanations, class and group discussions, and individual practice, where all pupils did the same activities using national textbooks. Although there was evidence of over-learning through repetition of the same concept, the delegates did not see the rote approach they had expected. Instead, they found an emphasis on pupils explaining their thinking rather than just giving answers.

The National Centre for Excellence in the Teaching of Mathematics (NCETM) has produced a collection of materials to support teaching for mastery. Their explanation for mastery fits with Bloom's mastery learning and the expectations of the National Curriculum. It is split into four aspects:

Mastery approach – belief that all pupils can learn mathematics;

Mastery curriculum – that all pupils should access the same curriculum;

Teaching for mastery – keeping the class together while simultaneously addressing individual needs;

Achieving mastery – having a deep conceptual understanding that allows the pupil to apply the concept in new contexts.

(Askew *et al.*, 2015, pp5–6)

Although the NCETM definition for a mastery approach refers to learning mathematics, this could apply to any area of the curriculum, but it depends on teachers having a growth mindset (Dweck, 2012) towards their pupils. This challenges some existing models of differentiation where pupils are put into different attainment groups (Marks, 2013).

Some schools in England trialled a programme called Mathematics Mastery in Year 1 and Year 7, based on mastery teaching from Singapore. The programme involved keeping the class together until mastery was achieved, using objects and pictures to represent mathematical concepts, emphasis on problem-solving skills, relational understanding (Skemp, 1976), high expectations and a growth mindset (see Chapter 7). Keeping the class together was a big change for many of the schools that were used to having different objectives for different attainment groups. In order to keep the class together, all pupils had the same objectives. Those who struggled with them were given same-day interventions, with extra teaching and practice, so that they did not fall behind the class. Those who understood the objectives quickly were not moved on to the next topic but given problems to deepen their understanding of the objective, through considering it in different contexts. The evaluation after one year of implementation found that there was a small increase in progress compared to the control group (Vignoles et al., 2015). The evaluators noted that the study was limited because it looked at only one year of implementation, immediately after it was finished, so could not say what the impact would be in the long term after pupils had followed the programme throughout Years 1 to 9.

What does differentiation/variation look like in mastery?

George (2014, p65) talks about the importance of *equity rather than equality*, with teaching more tailored to individual needs but with an expectation that all can succeed. In the Shanghai example, this was done through individual support by teachers who had considerable non-contact time, although the NCSL report (2013) pointed out that around 80 per cent of the pupils were also getting private tutoring outside school. These levels of staffing and parental support are unlikely to be found in most UK schools, so other options must be considered, especially for same-day interventions.

If we go back to Bloom (1968, 1976), several of his suggestions can be planned into the lesson by preparing alternative explanations, additional examples, motivating contexts and concrete illustrations. These are things that would help those struggling with the concept, while providing reinforcement for those who have already grasped it. Remember that those who have grasped the concept quickly might not yet understand it deeply. Another suggestion was varying the degree of independent versus structured learning. You could undertake a quick assessment of understanding after some individual practice and then follow up with an open-ended problem for those who understood, allowing you to work more closely on a structured task with those who were struggling. The key to avoiding the problems related to ability grouping and low expectations is to base your support on assessments of that concept on that day and not on more generalised beliefs of the pupil's abilities.

 Case study

Southwood School has introduced mastery teaching in mathematics, which has involved changes to the school timetable. In Neha's Year 2 class, the mathematics lesson is from 9:30 to 10:05am. This involves direct

(Continued)

(Continued)

teaching, with the pupils completing a small number of examples independently. There are marking stations where the pupils can check whether they have the correct answers. The pupils also self-assess to indicate how confident they are about the work. From 10:05 to 10:20 the teaching assistant leads some practice activities, focusing on counting, number bonds or times tables while the teacher checks the pupils' work from the lesson. At 10:20 the pupils go out to play while the teacher plans the next steps for the pupils she has identified as needing further intervention, either because they were making mistakes or because they lacked confidence. After playtime, the pupils have another 20 minutes of mathematics, either as part of the intervention group or the deepening group. The deepening group apply the key idea from the lesson in a new context or in a problem-solving activity that was planned by Neha before the lesson.

St Hugh's school is applying mastery to English and mathematics lessons, and has taken a different approach to timetabling. Ian spends the first ten minutes of the lesson with a small group of pupils he has identified from previous lessons as being likely to struggle with the day's objectives. During these ten minutes, Ian goes over aspects from previous lessons that are necessary for today's learning and explains key vocabulary. The rest of the pupils have a silent reading time. On Tuesdays and Thursdays, Ian plans longer interventions based on the assessments from Monday and Wednesday's lessons. The pupils who do not need the intervention will apply the concept in varied contexts. On Fridays, all the pupils work on deepening their understanding by applying the concept in varied and less predictable contexts.

Forster school has embraced the idea of mastery across the curriculum. In the core subjects (English, mathematics and science), they have lessons that are 75 minutes long. The usual structure is to teach the whole class 'ping-pong' fashion for the first half hour – a series of inputs in which the teacher gives a short explanation or demonstration with the pupils trying an example following each input, and this is then discussed. This is followed by 15 minutes of intervention for some pupils, based on a quick assessment of the pupils' understanding, while the rest of the class do further exercises. The last half hour is spent with the whole class on deepening by working on a single large problem or by applying the concept in varied contexts. The approach is less tightly structured with the rest of the curriculum. There is an emphasis on teachers observing and assessing while the pupils work so that they can intervene quickly during the lesson with individuals, small groups or the whole class depending on the needs identified.

 Reflection and discussion activity

Reflection

Trainee: you might find that planning is a complex and time-consuming process. Most mastery intervention models require a quick planning response to the misconceptions that the pupils present during the lesson. What preparation could you do before the lesson to help you make this quick response to your assessment of the pupils during the lesson?

Mentor: what organisation do you think would work best for interventions for you and your school? Do you feel a mastery approach with quick interventions to prevent pupils falling behind is appropriate for all subjects?

Discussion

Trainee and mentor: work together to plan a lesson that includes or is followed by a quick intervention. Think about the roles of each adult, how the pupils will be assessed and what the pupils who do not need the intervention will be doing.

Mastery hinges on a belief that all pupils can and should succeed in learning if given enough time, individualised support, frequent formative assessment, quick interventions and an appropriate curriculum with common, clearly defined objectives. This differs from an ability grouping approach with differentiation/variation in objectives, and may require a change in mindset from both teachers and pupils. Although there is some evidence in the UK and abroad demonstrating good progress through a mastery approach, implementing it in the UK comes with many challenges, such as how to deliver quick interventions without substantial non-contact time.

Cross-curricular, topic and theme-based approaches to learning, including enquiry-based approaches

Adopting a topic- or theme-based curriculum is very much about finding concrete links between discrete subjects. It can seem a bit overwhelming if you are starting from the very beginning of planning and resourcing lessons for a topic, as this can take a lot of work. However, these approaches are also extremely rewarding and provide opportunities for you to be creative and child-centred.

Within a cross-curricular approach, pupils gain a range of experiences through enrichment. For example, in a topic about the Romans, pupils could construct their own pupil-scale Roman army shields in DT and art lessons. These are then used outside the classroom to re-enact the battle formation of the tortoise.

If you give pupils the tools and opportunities to develop investigative skills, they can become more competent in beginning their own investigations. A positive way to develop independence in investigation is to use technology to enable pupils to follow a specific line of enquiry, or for them to construct their own response to a question. Allowing pupils to discuss what they have experienced throughout a lesson and generate their own questions will often lead to discovery of the most relevant lines of enquiry being asked independently by the pupils. A way to capture these questions is to use a 'Post-it' wall, where they add questions and answers, as they discover new knowledge. This develops an excellent peer-support approach and continues to build curiosity. For example, if a pupil asks if a nut is a seed, others should be given the opportunity to respond and prove that their answer is correct.

Enquiry-based learning is an approach where pupils analyse evidence in order to form and test hypotheses, which may use a teacher-guided enquiry method. When using enquiry-based learning, a teacher may choose a theme or aspect of a subject that is pertinent to the lesson they are teaching, or link to a previous session so that the pupils are actively building on their prior learning. For this approach, the lesson can begin with an investigation, a starting point activity or demonstration that can provide inspiration and inspire curiosity, so that the pupils want to learn more. This could also provoke questions from the pupils. As a class, or within small groups, the pupils (possibly along with the teacher) create a question to investigate and start designing a method to answer that question. In most instances, the initial ideas are created with teacher guidance, before narrowing down the areas to one specific focus. There is a distinct difference between investigation and enquiry. With investigation, the teacher's questions, or the learning objective for the lesson, directs pupils from a starting point towards acquiring the knowledge necessary to find a result; the teacher leads the pupils along a pathway and uses a series of specific prompts to facilitate the 'correct' answer. Within an enquiry-based learning environment, the pupils create their own questions, such as 'How did the Romans arrive in Britain?' or 'Where does soil come from?'. They will use a series of personal observations or conjectures to formulate a response. In such cases the pupils become, what Vygotsky would call, *the more knowledgeable other (MKO)*, sharing what they have already gathered as evidence with others. In Vygotsky's theory the MKO denotes someone who has superior understanding, ability or skills than a learner, linked to a task, concept or process (Ismail *et al.*, 2015). The students need to be engaged in the enquiry, so they will have to be provided with a range of information that enables them to form an initial hypothesis. They should be able to select from a range of resources, documents and other sources that offer different viewpoints and evidence; these will then support the investigation of the enquiry question.

After the pupils have been presented with evidence to sift through, they can be given opportunities to analyse evidence, and time needs to be allocated to allow enquiries to be revised. Pupils should be encouraged to share all their thoughts, so that these can be filtered into a single question or something they can enquire about. By eliciting pupils' initial ideas as a class, they will begin to formulate plans to help them answer the question and to consider what resources they may need to do this.

Table 5.1 Example of the teacher's role in enquiry-based approaches

Teachers	Pupils
• Establish the task • Facilitate the process	• Pursue their own line of enquiry • Draw on existing knowledge • Highlight learning needs • Find/collect, analyse and present relevant evidence

 Reflection and discussion activity

Scenario

As part of a topic about flight, you have a discussion with the pupils about what sorts of things they know that can fly. You ask them to think about toys they have or have seen, living things and anything else that they can think of that can fly. The pupils are encouraged to come up with a list with a partner, and these are then shared in a class discussion. You guide the pupils to look at key features of things that can fly and use questioning to make sure that they are looking at materials, shapes and key features. You then explain that they are going to make something that they think can fly and you are going to take the finished things outside to see which can fly the furthest across the playground. The pupils are given a range of materials and pictures of things that fly, including natural things such as butterflies and seeds as well as kites, planes etc. The pupils work in friendship groups of three or four. You give them some time to explore the materials and to create a design. While they are doing this, you work with each group guiding them with key questions such as 'Why have you decided to use this material?' or 'What has made you decide that this is a good shape for something that is going to fly?' Depending on their responses, you guide them to think about why choices may or may not work so they can revise and adapt what they are doing.

Reflection

Trainee: think about the importance of the teacher's role in this example. What might be the issues for the teacher in planning this approach to learning? Do you think this is a good approach to support learning? Why?

Mentor, think about how you group pupils and ways that you help them by scaffolding the learning with different resources, use of questions and amount of support.

Discussion

Trainee and mentor: discuss different ways of scaffolding learning and what you need to consider when thinking about how the pupils can access the learning.

Benefits of using enquiry-based learning include beginning with the pupils (sometimes with support) reflecting on and taking responsibility for their own learning. In many cases the use of an enquiry model helps to build resilience and persistence; where the ability to formulate and ask their own questions to clarify and confirm the accuracy of their understandings helps to deepen the level of understanding. Pupils also begin to use higher order thinking skills to solve problems and make judgements about their own work and that of others; they learn about alternative models or points of view, as well as begin to understand the importance of unbiased evidence when building reasoned arguments and viewpoints.

Immersive learning

Immersive learning is an approach where schools adopt its methods fully or utilise experience for a significant period of time. Most schools that became fully immersive settings have since returned to using a more traditional style of teaching but still make use of experiences.

There are several definitions explaining what immersive learning is. According to Gartner (2012), immersive learning environments can be *learning situations that are constructed using a variety of techniques and software tools, including game-based learning, simulation-based learning and virtual 3D worlds* (2012, p1).

— 🧩 — **Case study** ═══════════════════════

Within a dedicated classroom, at a school located in Lincolnshire, pupils use one such multimedia environment to allow them to visit rainforests, travel around our solar system and engage with a storyteller to look at the story of Jack and the Beanstalk from the giant's perspective. This school links the immersion to projects based on the world outside the classroom, as they consider this purposeful learning and make links to continuing learning at home.

The other main definition for immersive learning stems from the less technologically based use of the classroom. Here the walls and floor space are decorated and utilised to create an environment where the pupils become immersed in the theme in a much more theatrical way, almost becoming actors on the stage of their own learning. Within the context of this style of learning, the pupils choose their own learning space and work to produce the objectives of the lesson in a variety of ways, whether on tablets, on paper, in books or as a collaborative piece.

When considering the use of an immersive approach, there are several aspects that need to be thought through. First, adopting this approach fully will usually be a whole-school decision, especially as it is heavily reliant upon resources. As a space, your classroom should be set out so that the pupils can find areas to contemplate and work. The spaces for learning also need to have a firm link to the topic or theme. This may sound similar to the topic-based approach, but with immersive learning the entire room is transformed (not just areas for role play) to re-create as realistic an experience as possible.

The learning spaces are specifically designed so that the pupils become part of the experience, and in some cases the teacher assumes a role that encompasses the theme. Successful immersive spaces allow pupils to engage fully in the topic they are learning. Where success has been evident, environments have been created so that classrooms have become pirate ships, oceans and factories where props are available to add to the overall reality. These spaces help establish a realm of cross-curricular learning opportunities and support the progress of pupils across the curriculum.

— 💡 — **Find out more from . . . websites** ═══════════

Marsh, J (2015) What is immersive learning, and how can it benefit your school? (26 January): **www.innovatemyschool.com/ideas/what-is-immersive-learning-and-how-can-it-benefit-your-school** (accessed 7 November 2019).

It may be beneficial to use elements of immersive learning alongside an enquiry approach – for example, by utilising a police incident room, placing 'Post-it' notes on a board where hypotheses can be shared and then discussed later. Creating an element of detection can instil a greater focus for the pupils. If they act as 'reflective detectives' (this is where discussion of progress between peers takes place, feedback is given and pupils are given an opportunity to act on this) the pupils should be able to ask for the opinions of others, and assess the strengths and areas to develop in their own work, and provide feedback that supports their peers.

The Forest School approach

It may seem odd to have uncaged fires, use outdoor toilets, openly encourage pupils to experiment with tools and hold lessons outside in all weathers. As one head teacher told their staff, 'There is no such thing as the wrong weather, just the wrong clothes'. The ethos of the Forest School approach has spread across the UK over the last few years: maintaining a focus on using all the senses, embracing the outdoors, and a philosophy of child-led learning and discovery. It may seem to the untrained eye, with pupils examining insects through magnifying glasses or sitting in treehouses or tents to read and complete work, that this is nothing more than disorganised play. However, Vygotsky (1978) put the child at the centre of his own experiences and learning. Here the importance was that when pupils experience the world around them, with appropriate levels of support, they explore without preconceptions and directions; the teacher's input is a starting point, but the learning develops as the pupils discover through the use of the world around them and through the use of the natural environment.

The Forest School philosophy states that pupils should be encouraged to take more risks, be more active and have more independence learning. Pupils are encouraged to use imagination and develop hypotheses through discovery. It also focuses on the emotional, social and developmental benefits of education. Using nature encourages the pupils to better understand the world around them and have a greener approach to life. To fully embrace the Forest School approach, teachers minimise the use of technology so the natural world drives the learning and pupils look through their own eyes. A key phrase is 'positive outdoor experiences', where pupils are free to learn within a 'safe' outdoor classroom. Even if the setting seems to flow in a very natural manner, the areas for learning are prepared so that injuries can be minimised (remember: for all outdoor learning environments, to be safe for the pupils, a risk assessment should be completed as an important part of planning the lesson). Staff leading Forest School sessions are also trained.

Research shows that there is a direct link between the Forest School approach and creativity. Fjørtoft (2005) found that the natural surroundings of Forest Schools are pivotal in increasing the cognitive development of pupils who participate in creative and inventive play. The link between Early Years' learning and Forest Schools is incredibly strong, linking with fine and gross motor skills. The links are also seen in independent and group play, as well as social interaction; all elements of the developmental stages that can be enhanced by learning in an outdoor environment. As later Key Stages see the benefits of the physical nature of the Forest School approach, they also see the enhanced opportunities of outdoor classrooms, providing overt links to the world outside the familiar four walls.

The biggest challenge with the Forest School approach is the lack of natural space available to some schools or where an urban environment lacks flora and fauna, which impacts on the ability to utilise these to assist in learning opportunities. Here, many schools create a 'nature zone', usually linked to a pond, or they make use of local parks, so that pupils can experience the natural world and its learning possibilities. Spaces in urban environments can be created using large raised beds that contain trees, dustbins, buckets and recycled lorries/tractors.

Taking it further ... research articles and books

Bell, S (2010) Project-based learning for the 21st century: skills for the future. *The Clearing House: A Journal of Educational Strategies, Issues and Ideas*, 83(2): 39–43.

Clark, RCC and Mayer, RE (2011) *E-learning and the Science of Instruction: Proven guidelines for consumers and designers of multimedia learning* (3rd edn). San Francisco, CA: John Wiley & Sons.

Mayer, RE (2001) *Multimedia Learning*. New York: Cambridge University Press.

Chapter summary

This chapter will have provided you with an insight into different approaches to learning that schools may use to deliver the curriculum. It has demonstrated that there is no right or wrong way to support pupils to learn and that the importance of planning and use of the whole learning environment is key for you as a teacher. It has hopefully shown you than getting pupils involved as active learners who can see the purpose of the learning is the most important thing to 'hook' them into wanting to learn and that a growth mindset is key to an inclusive approach.

References

Askew, M, Bishop, S, Christie, C, Eaton, S, Griffin, P, Morgan, D and Wilne, R (2015) *Teaching for Mastery: Questions, tasks and activities to support assessment*. Oxford: Oxford University Press.

Bloom, B (1968) Learning for mastery. *Evaluation Comment*, 1(2): 1–12.

Bloom, B (1976) *Human Characteristics and School Learning*. New York: McGraw-Hill.

Department for Education (2019) *Initial Teacher Training (ITT): Core Content Framework*. Available at: **www.gov.uk/government/publications/initial-teacher-training-itt-core-content-framework** (accessed 7 November 2019).

Dweck, CS (2012) *Mindset*. London: Robinson.

Fjørtoft, I (2005) Landscape as playspace: the effects of natural environments on children's play and motor development. *Children, Youth and Environments*, 14(2).

Gartner (2012, July 31). Immersive learning environments (ILEs) – Gartner IT glossary. Available at: **www.gartner.com/en/information-technology/glossary** (accessed 7 November 2019).

George, P (2014) Made for mathematics? Implications for teaching and learning. In Leslie, D and Mendick, H (eds) *Debates in Mathematics Education*. Abingdon: Routledge, pp7–16.

Hart, R (2016) Lab coats paint a thousand words. Elementary (3–5). Available at: **www.plt.org/educator-tips/lab-coats-paint-a-thousand-words** (accessed 1 December 2016).

Ismail, N, Ismail, K and Aun, N (2015) *The Role of Scaffolding in Problem Solving Skills Among Children*. Ipedr.com. Available at: **www.ipedr.com/vol85/019-PB00004.pdf** (accessed 7 November 2019).

Kirschner, PA, Sweller, J and Clark, RE (2006) Why minimal guidance during instruction does not work: An analysis of the failure of Constructivist, discovery, problem-based, experiential, and inquiry-based teaching. *Educational Psychologist*, 41(2): 75–86.

Marks, R (2013) 'The Blue Table Means You Don't Have a Clue': The persistence of fixed-ability thinking and practices in primary mathematics in English schools. *Forum: for Promoting 3–19 Comprehensive Education*, 55(1): 31–44.

NCSL (2013) *Report on Research into Maths and Science Teaching in the Shanghai Region*. Available at: www.gov.uk/government/uploads/system/uploads/attachment_data/file/340021/report-on-research-into-maths-and-science-teaching-in-the-shanghai-region.pdf (accessed 7 November 2019).

Skemp, RR (1976) Relational understanding and instrumental understanding. *Mathematics Teaching in the Middle School*, 12(2): 88–95. Originally published in *Mathematics Teaching*.

Vignoles, A, Jerrim, J and Cowan, R (2015) *Mathematics Mastery Primary Evaluation Report*. London: Education Endowment Foundation.

6

Planning for learning

Rebecca Geeson

This chapter will

- consider the reasons for lesson planning;
- become more familiar with the key aspects included in lesson plans;
- consider the reasons for including different elements in your lesson plan;
- develop your ability to plan efficiently.

Links to the Teachers' Standards

4 **Plan and teach well structured lessons:**
- impart knowledge and develop understanding through effective use of lesson time;
- promote a love of learning and children's intellectual curiosity;
- set homework and plan other out-of-class activities to consolidate and extend the knowledge and understanding pupils have acquired;
- reflect systematically on the effectiveness of lessons and approaches to teaching;
- contribute to the design and provision of an engaging curriculum within the relevant subject area(s).

8 **Fulfil wider professional responsibilities**, specifically:
- deploy support staff effectively.

Introduction

Even if you are at the very early stages of your teaching career, it is likely that you are already aware of lesson planning. You may have been introduced to your school's or training provider's planning format, have been given lesson plans to look at or to work from, and even had a go at planning lessons already. It is also likely that when you looked at your first lesson plan, it appeared to be a confusing grid which included lots of information, and your initial thoughts were, 'Do I really have to do one of those for *every* lesson I teach?'. This chapter initially aims to develop your understanding of why teachers plan so that you are able to see that the task of lesson planning is purposeful. Consideration of the elements that make up a successful plan will follow. Once you understand what you are doing, why you are doing what you are doing and what strategies you can use to help you through the process, your lesson planning will become more efficient and effective.

Why do we plan?

It is important initially to clarify the difference between *writing lesson plans* and *planning*. Quite simply, the process of planning does not require any paperwork at all; we all constantly undertake planning, or make decisions about the future. However, the writing of lesson plans, or lesson planning, involves recording the thoughts that a teacher has during the process of deciding how to ensure that pupils make progress in their learning. This chapter will consider both: why teachers plan lessons and why teachers write lesson plans.

Why plan lessons?

Standing in front of a class of pupils, probably with other experienced adults around you and teaching can seem a little daunting in your early training. However, standing in front of that audience with no idea what you are going to say or do is even more frightening. At the early stages of your training, it is likely that you will not be 'let loose' to teach a class of pupils unless you have presented a plan beforehand, so you will not yet have experienced the feeling of attempting to teach a class without having prepared. Later on in your career, you will inevitably have occasions when you will find yourself suddenly having to take over a class; it will be at times like these that you will remember how important it is to be prepared.

Many approaches to teaching suggest that pupils need to take ownership of and lead their own learning. However, these valuable approaches rely on the teacher having the knowledge and ability to skilfully lead and encourage pupils to learn new knowledge or a particular concept or to develop a skill through their chosen interest. Without this direction and encouragement from the teacher, there would be no way to ensure that pupils make progress.

The crucial thing to remember is that planning and preparing can happen in many ways (Hattie, 2012). Schools usually require lessons to be prepared *in one form or another* before the start of the lesson, and while the way that these plans are presented will differ immensely from school to school, there certainly is no 'best' way to present planning. The underlying purpose of the process of planning remains the same, though: in order to ensure that pupils' learning progresses, decisions have to be made.

Learning is central to the planning process. Pupils' learning and progress is at the heart of education, and school leaders are responsible for and held accountable for this progress. One of the ways that some schools monitor learning and progress in their schools is through the planning process. While it is unlikely that most school leaders sit and analyse individual lesson plans on a weekly basis, having a lesson-planning process in place serves a number of purposes, all linked to pupils' learning and progress. Lesson planning:

- ensures that pupils' prior learning is developed and built upon from lesson to lesson, between subjects, across year groups;

- allows for the learning and progress of individuals and groups to be considered;

- provides a plan for how teachers are going to assess the progress of their learners and provide a starting point for the next sequence of learning.

Ramos has been teaching for two years, and sees pupil progress as the heart of lesson planning:

Planning has been an important tool for structuring lessons. It has helped me to organise the content of my sessions and ensures I deliver the content in the most effective way to suit the needs of the learners. Across a strand, planning enables me to see a clear progression of learning: focusing on knowledge, skills and understanding. I plan individual lessons that consider the needs of pupils with all abilities – ensuring pupils have access to learning. Subsequent lessons build on formative assessment to ensure progression occurs.

Figure 6.1 The plan, do, assess cycle

This can be seen as a cyclical process. Observations will form an ongoing part of your teaching career: people such as mentors in school, training providers and school leaders will come and observe your teaching. Again, the ultimate reason for this is to ensure that the pupils in your class are learning and making progress.

School inspectors generally do not ask to see lesson plans. In fact, Ofsted explicitly state that they do not require schools to provide lesson plans, nor do they specify how planning should be set out or the amount of detail it should include (Ofsted, 2016). Whether planning is effective will be evidenced elsewhere – for example, through what the pupils say, how they behave and respond to questions and the work that they produce in a lesson and over time. However, particularly during training, the lesson planning document may still be a valuable tool for supporting observers' understanding of how you plan to ensure progress in the lesson. Your analysis of the lesson plan, of a lesson in which pupils did not make expected progress, after the event can be very useful to help you work out why and plan for improvements next time. Just as importantly, you can use the lesson plan to also help you to identify your strengths.

 Reflection and discussion activity

Choose a time when the trainee can observe the mentor teaching the class.

Reflection

Mentor: ensure that your lesson plan is presented with the level of detail you would expect from your trainee. Point out to them how you are planning to check progress during the lesson.

Trainee: carry out a focused lesson observation, looking particularly at how your mentor is ensuring the pupils make progress in the lesson. Are they asking questions? What type of questions? Are they working with individuals/groups? Do they observe pupils' discussions? Are they sticking to the lesson plan that they have given you? If not, why do you think they have adapted their plans and does this relate to progress? Do they stop groups or the whole class at unplanned points to explain or clarify?

Discussion

Trainee and mentor: after the lesson, discuss how the pupils' progress was assessed in the lesson. Also, look at the learning in pupils' books together and use this to add to your understanding of progression in the lesson.

Following the above activity, you may have seen misconceptions occur. Early on in our teaching careers, hearing pupils give the 'wrong' answer can be a worry and cause self-doubt: 'Is this because I did not explain properly? I clearly did not plan this well enough!' but this level of reflection is actually very valuable. More experienced teachers expect misconceptions, and value them. One pupil's incorrect response is likely to be the tip of the iceberg; others may also have not understood, and by finding out more, a good teacher can immediately respond ensuring the pupil's learning is back on track for that lesson, but also help identify where the learning will move on to in subsequent lessons.

Developing your understanding of planning

In Table 6.1 below, there are some broad phases for planning as a trainee teacher.

Reflection and discussion activity

Reflection

Trainee: where are you now? Just as you will be encouraging the pupils in your class to reflect on their own prior learning, think about your understanding of planning lessons at this point. Look at the phases described in Table 6.1 - where are you now?

Mentor: what does your trainee need now? As teachers, we know that different learners need different levels of support at different times. Before you begin to set expectations of your trainee concerning what you require from them in their planning, there is a need to consider their current level of understanding and provide them with activities that build on what they already know. Think about where you feel the trainee is now based on Table 6.1, and be prepared to provide examples/evidence to support your views.

Discussion

Discuss where both of you feel the trainee's current level of understanding is and think about what support the trainee will need in order to progress.

Here are some broad phases of planning as a trainee teacher. The mentor/trainee relationship is something that requires commitment and work from both sides to ensure an effective working partnership. For you as a trainee, it is important to consider that the purpose for planning lessons is to ensure that learners make good progress. It could be that you sometimes forget that your mentor has to consider your learning and progress, too.

Table 6.1 The development of planning skills

Stage	How does the trainee plan at this stage?	What can the mentor do to support the trainee's planning at this stage?	What does the trainee need to develop their planning skills further?
Pre-introductory phase *Mentor plans.*	Trainee uses mentor's plans to teach lessons.	Mentor's own shorthand will need explaining. Mentor will need to discuss the planning with trainee, explaining reasons for their planning choices. Mentor will need to explain pupils' prior learning in depth.	Trainee should focus on gaining an understanding of the pupils' prior knowledge. Observe mentor's teaching and annotate their plan during the lesson, raising questions to discuss after the lesson.

(Continued)

Table 6.1 (Continued)

Stage	How does the trainee plan at this stage?	What can the mentor do to support the trainee's planning at this stage?	What does the trainee need to develop their planning skills further?
Introductory planning phase *Mentor and trainee work together to plan.*	Trainee uses mentor's ideas and mentor's understanding of pupils' prior learning and uses mentor's planning as a model and begins to plan aspects of subsequent lessons (parts of the lesson, group activities etc.).	Mentor can support through modelling the planning of small aspects of the lesson. Mentor may need to step in during the lesson to explain/support – sometimes what has been explained by mentor has been misinterpreted by trainee. If planning is done as a team, invite trainee to attend.	Trainee should explain and show where the planning has come from (NC, long-/medium-term plans, published schemes, etc.). Trainee should attempt to assess and evaluate prior learning before moving on to planning more independently.
Developing planning phase *Trainee working more independently after initial input and before feedback.*	Through this phase, trainee moves from simply adapting mentor's plans to planning larger parts of the lesson with less need for support. Initially, trainee relies heavily upon the plans or schemes used by the school. Further through this stage, trainee adapts these to meet the needs of the class with more confidence and includes more of their own ideas and adaptations.	Trainee seeks advice from mentor before planning the lesson to ensure that their understanding of prior learning is correct. Mentor should suggest initial ideas and then trainee attempts to write the plan independently. Trainee seeks advice after the plan is written for confirmation. Mentor encourages trainee to 'submit' their plans to mentor well in advance of the lesson so that mentor has opportunity to offer feedback and there is time for this process to happen more than once. Mentor should remain aware that trainee's developing confidence may be misplaced, so support will still be needed during planning.	Trainee should be starting to build up own 'bank' of ideas, resources, approaches, strategies that can be used or adapted in lessons. Trainee should be gaining confidence with their assessments of the pupils' learning.

Stage	How does the trainee plan at this stage?	What can the mentor do to support the trainee's planning at this stage?	What does the trainee need to develop their planning skills further?
Extending planning phase *Trainee works independently, with mentor checking at particular stages.*	Trainee suggests and discusses their planning verbally with mentor before attempting plans independently. Trainee starts writing individual lesson plans without a huge amount of input from mentor and is generally able to gauge prior learning accurately and independently.	Mentor supports with the ideas stage, but expects trainee to explain prior learning and expected progress of pupils.	If appropriate, trainee should work with planning team in school to consider and contribute ideas to medium-term planning.
	Trainee plans individual lesson plans independently, drawing from their own assessment of prior learning.	Trainee presents mentor with a plan which they feel is 'just about there' and may only need a few amendments. Less feedback time should be needed in advance of the lesson.	Trainee should engage with the longer term planning process within school.
	Trainee plans individual lessons with complete autonomy, making use of longer term planning in schools (where appropriate) and engaging in the creation of longer term plans.	Mentor only needs to consider plans after some lessons in order to reflect on effectiveness of teaching.	Trainee should aim to increase efficiency in the planning process.

 Case study

The following account is from a new mentor.

I worked with my first trainee last year - I'll call her Sophie - and her planning was not great. It wasn't so much that what she put in the plan wasn't right; she usually had appropriate learning objectives that built on prior learning (although her success criteria weren't great), and activities she had planned were generally appropriate. The main problem was that she didn't let me see it until just before the lesson, despite me gently (and then more forcibly) reminding her that I needed to see it at least a day beforehand.

(Continued)

(Continued)

There had been some lessons I watched that frankly were unsatisfactory; hardly any progress was made by the majority of the pupils, and when I looked at her plans I could see why. There were usually different reasons for the weaknesses in the lesson. On one occasion she entirely missed out explaining some key vocabulary; on another she had tried to build on prior learning, but as she was asking the pupils to apply it in an entirely different context, she hadn't realised that she needed to make the link more explicit. I was annoyed that she hadn't shared her plans with me in advance. I know the class and would have been able to give her ideas to avoid so many of the problems she was encountering in the lesson.

As I was new to mentoring, and not long out of training myself, I was quite worried about discussing this with Sophie, but I knew I had to. I was going to be held accountable for the pupils' progress during the year, and if the pupils did not make progress in the six weeks she was teaching my class, I would have problems. I also wanted to make sure that Sophie's time in the school was of value. When I talked to her, it turned out that she was working in a part-time job some evenings, so getting planning done, let alone sending it to me, was a challenge. This explained things. I can remember how long lesson plans used to take me when I was training. Sophie also admitted that she had not even thought about things from my perspective; she knew that the pupils' progress was the most important thing, but did not see how lesson planning supported it until we discussed it. Once she could see how to track progress through her planning and realised how it would impact on pupils' learning, things got better. It was not a fun conversation, but once things were out in the open, our relationship seemed to improve too, and, thankfully, so did Sophie's teaching and the pupils' progress.

As you can see from this mentor's story, Sophie had not allowed time for her mentor to give her feedback and support the trainee in her learning. The lesson plan itself is merely a record of your preparation, but particularly in the early stages of your career, the advice gained from more experienced teachers is invaluable *before* you teach each lesson.

Who is the plan for?

Lesson plans can be present in many different formats, but the key point to remember is that ultimately the lesson plan is not for anyone other than you, as a trainee. It is a reminder for you of your thought processes during the planning stage, so that when you are in front of the class, you will have the confidence to say that the learners are making progress.

It is very rare (and best avoided) that teachers read from their lesson plan as they are teaching. However, having an *aide-mémoire* can be helpful to remind you of organisational details during the lesson. For this reason, 'wordy' plans tend to be less effective – the information that needs to be found quickly is hidden within less relevant text; try succinct bullet points instead.

However, at all stages of your career, it is important to remember that while the lesson plan is mainly for you, others may also need to be able to decipher it. Along with your mentor, and perhaps the senior leadership team, teaching assistants who work in the class will need to be able to understand your plans for the lesson to ensure pupil progress. A balance, therefore, is needed between what you need to support your teaching of the lesson and what others may need to be able to understand from the plan.

The Early Years Foundation Stage Framework and the National Curriculum

In many schools, the National Curriculum (2013) forms the basis for long-term plans as *maintained schools are legally required to follow the statutory national curriculum* (DfE, 2013, p5). Learning outcomes are presented in the National Curriculum, and then schools use these to form the basis of their long-term plans. Different approaches are needed depending on the subject being considered; the learning outcomes for the 'core' subjects of mathematics, English and science are presented in year-by-year detail in the National Curriculum, whereas the learning outcomes for whole Key Stages are provided for other (or 'foundation') subjects, so there is an opportunity to organise aspects more flexibly.

It is important to note that the National Curriculum is designed to provide *an outline of the core knowledge* that pupils need and is *just one element in the education of every child* (DfE, 2013, p6). It is designed to allow time for schools to develop a wider curriculum that extends pupils' knowledge, skills and understanding beyond the National Curriculum specifications. This enables schools to have some freedom beyond the statutory requirements. However, along with other schools that are able to choose not to use the National Curriculum, a long-term planning stage supports schools in mapping out what will be taught, when to ensure progress, when to avoid repetition, and, in the case of maintained schools, how to show evidence that legal requirements are met.

The Statutory Framework for Early Years Foundation Stage (EYFS) seeks to provide quality and consistency in all settings and a secure foundation for pupils' learning and development (DfE, 2017). This means that schools will generally start their planning process with the Statutory Framework for EYFS, and the National Curriculum for pupils in Key Stages 1 and 2. Whether or not schools label the subsequent stages as in the table below, they will all go through a process of gradually fine-tuning broad learning outcomes until a focused, specific, measurable learning objective can be created for an individual session.

As above, maths, a core subject for which detailed year-by-year outcomes are provided, may be approached differently from art, a foundation subject.

Different schools organise the different stages of planning in different ways. Sometimes, a long-term plan may include only very brief learning outcomes and the medium-term plan will include further details. This may then be followed up with a short-term, or daily plan, and at the training stage, a daily session plan is advisable, whether or not your school does expect this of their experienced members of staff. In other cases, a long-term plan will have a great deal of depth and detail, which may make the medium-term stage less necessary. The important thing to note is that while all schools will plan in EYFS from the EYFS Framework, some schools will be basing their KS1 and KS2 curricula on the National Curriculum, while others will not. However, to ensure that progress is made, a mapping process will have taken place before you come to plan your lesson.

Table 6.2 Learning outcomes to learning objectives

Maths	Planning stage	Art
In year 3 *Pupils should be taught to measure, compare, add and subtract: lengths (m/ cm/mm); mass (kg, g); volume/capacity (l/ml) (DfE, 2013, p117).*	**National Curriculum**	At the end of KS1 *Pupils should be taught to use drawing, painting and sculpture to develop and share their ideas, experiences and imagination and to use a range of materials creatively to design and make products (DfE, 2013, p177).*
Term 1 *Lengths*	**Long-term planning in school**	Year 3 *Drawing*
Week 1 *To compare lengths (m/cm/mm)*	**Medium-term planning**	Term 1 *Drawing using a range of materials*
Individual lesson objective for one session *To compare lengths of objects smaller than 10cm long.*	**Short-term planning**	1st lesson in the sequence of work *To draw from experience using charcoal and chalk.*

What goes into a lesson plan?

For the purposes of this book, I have chosen to concentrate on short-term planning – the most detailed and final planning stage. Long- and medium-term planning are usually carried out well before you arrive for a training placement in school, but these stages will have taken into account many factors, including the school ethos and approach to learning. You will have the opportunity to contribute to these planning stages later in your career.

Common themes can be seen in planning that is presented in different formats, all of which relate to progression in learning. While it is important to be prepared to be flexible with timings and respond to what is going on in the lesson, it is also useful before you start the lesson to have a plan that attempts to ensure that there is neither too much, nor too little going on in a lesson.

The key aspects to consider when planning for progression in pupils' learning are:

- pupils' prior learning;

- the lesson objective;

- success criteria;

- assessment.

Each of these aspects needs to be considered based on knowledge of your class and the different needs of each pupil in your class.

Prior and subsequent learning

Having a secure understanding of pupils' prior learning is crucial in order to ensure that their subsequent learning builds on what they already know so that you can ensure progress. It is sometimes challenging as a trainee to know your class before you plan your first series of lessons, but good mentors will support you in finding this out. Having a secure understanding of the curriculum being taught will also support you so that as you quickly develop the skill of initially assessing pupils' learning and see how they respond to your input, you will be able to adapt your plans for the lesson to ensure that you start from the right point.

As well as discussing the need for teachers to have a good understanding of pupils' prior learning, Hattie (2012) talks about understanding pupils' ways of thinking (as these differ from adults' ways of thinking) and also their motivation to learn; your ability to plan for your class's progress will depend on you developing your understanding of them as learners as well as understanding what they have learned in the past.

It is also useful to consider where you aim for the pupils' learning to progress in subsequent lessons. This will ensure that you keep the learning you are working towards over time at the front of your mind when planning.

 Find out more from ... books

Hattie, J (2012) *Visible Learning for Teachers: Maximising impact on learning.* London: Routledge.

Piaget's work around the stages which pupils' thinking develops can be found in:

Piaget, J and Inhelder, B (2000) *The Psychology of the Child.* New York: Basic Books.

Learning objectives

As Hattie explains, *the more transparent the teacher makes the learning goals, the more likely the student is to engage in the work needed to meet the goal* (2012, p46). These learning goals may be referred to as learning intentions, lesson objectives, learning aims, intended learning or acronyms such as LO (Learning or Lesson Objectives), WALT (We Are Learning To . . .). These terms all refer to the learning that is planned for the lesson.

Learning objectives should:

- be a clear description of what is to be *learned* by end of lesson (not what will be *produced*);
- be achievable in one lesson;
- build on previous learning;
- take account of pupils' prior knowledge;
- be able to be assessed.

Learning objectives are the foundation for all lesson plans and should be based around the skills, knowledge and understanding that pupils will learn during the lesson, rather than the outcome of the lesson (as is sometimes found in trainee lesson plans).

- *Skills* – can be applied in different contexts and often start with 'to be able to' – e.g. to be able to solve multi-step word problems.

- *Knowledge* – pupils know something new; they often start with 'to know' – e.g. to know which materials are thermal insulators.

- *Understanding* – relates to concepts or ideas and often start with 'to understand' – e.g. to understand why Hadrian's Wall was built.

You should avoid linking learning objectives to the context of the learning. This is because assessment is based on the progress of knowledge, skills and understanding, not on specific contexts. If you take the first objective above and add a context, you will be able to see why: *To be able to solve multi-step word problems about the circus.*

We know that pupils make progress at different rates, and that deep learning often takes time, so we know that objectives will need to be revisited. However, there is little chance that you would plan another lesson around circus-related, multi-step problems; you will want to create different learning contexts to engage the pupils and to ensure that they can apply their learning in different contexts to ensure that your learning objectives are not tied to one particular context.

For the same reason, it is best to avoid including what is going to be produced in learning objectives. If we amend the second objective above slightly: *To wrap containers of hot water with different materials to see which keeps water hottest for longest,* we can see that not only does the objective become overly verbose, but also does not allow for the learning to be reinforced, consolidated or applied in other contexts or in other lessons.

It is worth considering at the planning stage when, during the lesson, the learning objective should or could be shared; it might be that initially hiding and later revealing the objective during or at the end of the lesson is more appropriate, although this should be a deliberate pedagogical decision, not an afterthought. Arguably, pupils should be aware of what they are learning in order to learn effectively (Hattie, 2012), but it may be that by sharing the exact nature of the knowledge, skills or understanding in the learning objective at the beginning of the lesson will 'give the game away' and restrict opportunities for learning.

Another useful consideration is that of your choice of language. The plan, as above, is for a different audience from the lesson itself; an adult audience with experience in teaching and education will be able to understand a more complex learning objective than a group of 7-year-olds. Think about this carefully when planning the wording of your learning objective. It may be helpful to include two learning objectives on your lesson plan: one appropriate for adults, and one in 'child-friendly' language.

Success criteria

Success criteria come in different forms. Some teachers see this success criteria as a series of steps to help pupils get to the end goal (or learning objective). Others see success criteria as a measurement against learning outcomes that can support pupils in a deeper understanding of the purpose of the lesson and in evaluating their own success against the learning goal. This is supported by Hattie (2012) who explains that pupils should be aware of the learning objective, and also be able to know whether they have achieved the desired learning.

Teachers often find it beneficial for pupils to be involved in planning their own success criteria. The process of encouraging the pupils to think about their learning, or engaging in metacognition, embeds the teacher's intentions of the learning that will take place in the lesson. However, you should be prepared to steer the pupils in an appropriate direction to ensure that you keep the learning on track, if necessary.

Table 6.3 An example of 'Learning outcome' success criteria and 'Steps to success' success criteria

Learning objective	'Learning outcome' success criteria	'Steps to success' success criteria
To be able to identify odd and even numbers.	I will be able to identify whether a number is odd or even.	Look at the last digit in the number to check the pattern. Divide the number in two to check.
To write an effective characterisation.	Someone who reads it will feel they really know the person.	Use adjectives. Include all or some of the following, with examples: • hobbies and interests; • attitude to others; • what makes that person a friend.

 Reflection and discussion activity

Reflection

Trainee: analyse your learning objectives; think about whether they relate to skills, knowledge or understanding. Also, consider whether context or outcomes appear, and, if so, how will this impact on assessment. Which ones do you now think would benefit from rewording?

Mentor: think about your trainee's learning objectives that you feel were not successful (i.e. resulted in insufficient progress for learners). Why?

Discussion

Considering the less successful learning objectives that you have both identified, rework these.

Also, consider the link between learning objectives and success criteria that you have used. Do they clearly convey the intention of the learning that will take place in the lesson and enable pupils to be aware of what success looks like?

Assessment

Assessment as a concept is discussed more fully in Chapter 7 by Elizabeth Farrar, so this chapter will concentrate on its place within the planning structure.

From a planning perspective, opportunities to assess are vital to ensure that the assessment does happen. As a teacher, it is easy to get carried away with what is going on in the lesson and become as engaged as the pupils with interesting and exciting learning opportunities. However, your role as the teacher depends on you moving pupils' learning forward, and without assessing what is going on right now, you will be unable to plan subsequent learning.

You should plan what you are going to assess (based on the learning objective and success criteria), but also who you are going to assess and how you are going to assess. It is usually unrealistic to attempt to assess all pupils individually during every lesson. In one lesson, it may be that you plan to focus on a small group of individuals with whom you are working; ask your teaching assistant to focus on another group and make initial judgements about the progress of the rest of the class through questioning at various other points in the lesson. Your marking of their work after the lesson will either support in-lesson assessment or highlight misconceptions that have occurred and inform subsequent plans. Over the next lessons, it is advisable that assessment is focused on different groups. However, while this approach makes assessment manageable, it does require careful consideration at the planning stage to ensure that you gain a clear understanding of how each pupil's progress develops over a sequence of lessons.

Differentiation

Carefully consider, based on the different learners in your class, how to group the pupils. Ensure you are responsive and flexible between subjects and within subjects.

 Find out more from ... websites

The internet is a great source of ideas for planning. Make sure you choose what is needed for your pupils in order to progress in their learning, rather than activities that you think they (or you) will enjoy; remember that the learning objective should lead the planning process. The following are useful websites to help you with planning your lessons:

www.tes.com/teaching-resources

www.hamilton-trust.org.uk/

www.stem.org.uk/cross-curricular-topics-resources (accessed 12 November 2019).

Activities

What are you and the pupils going to do in the lesson in order to support their progress towards the learning objective? What *resources, key vocabulary* and *adult support* are going to be used and by whom? What different parts of the lesson will happen when?

Modelling, where pupils learn from things being demonstrated to them, and *scaffolding,* where pupils' learning is supported by another ('more knowledgeable') pupil or an adult are important learning theories to consider when planning activities. Consider where in the sequence of learning the pupils are and what the desired learning is; would it be most appropriate to introduce parts of the lesson through modelling? At what points would scaffolding deepen their understanding?

Find out more from ... educational theorists

Modelling

Bandura told us that: *Most human behaviour is learned observationally through modelling: from observing others, one forms an idea of how new behaviours are performed, and on later occasions this coded information serves as a guide for action* (1977, p22).

Scaffolding

Vygotsky initially discussed the need to learn from *more knowledgeable others,* as part of his work on the Zone of Proximal Development: *The distance between the actual development level as determined by independent problem solving and the level of potential development as determined through problem solving under adult guidance or in collaboration with more capable peers* (1978, p66).

Bruner (1966) built further on this idea and created the term 'scaffolding' to describe learning that would allow pupils to use what they had learned independently through three modes of presentation.

A useful summary of these and other key educational theorists' ideas can be found in:

Aubrey, K and Riley, A (2016) *Understanding and Using Educational Theories.* London: SAGE.

Key questions and vocabulary

In Chapter 8, John Paramore reflects on how questions to simulate dialogue will support your understanding of questioning. Many teachers find that having key questions planned before the start of the lesson enables them to 'keep on track' in terms of the flow of the lesson and the assessment that will take place. You may want to target questions based upon your previous assessment or provide opportunities to further deepen pupils' understanding.

It is also useful to make it clear at the planning stage what subject-specific vocabulary you are going to use in your lesson. This may involve introducing new words and phrases to your pupils, but should also be in the plan as a reminder to you to continue to embed the vocabulary that pupils need in relation to a particular objective, theme or topic.

Resources

It helps to note down on your plan what resources you need to prepare before your lesson as a reminder as you prepare for the day. Thinking this through should be done alongside your planning of activities and also while considering the varying needs of different pupils.

Role of other adults

Planning for other adults should be embedded throughout other aspects of learning. You can read a detailed exploration of working with Teaching Assistants in Chapter 14 by Emma Clarke. However, in terms of planning, you should ensure that other adults are seen as a valuable resource in supporting pupils' progress and, in the light of this, carefully plan for their involvement in learning throughout the lesson.

It is important not only to plan for the use of other adults within each lesson, but also plan for time for you and any additional adults to discuss the lesson beforehand, and also have time to reflect on pupils' progress afterwards to inform your future planning.

Plenary

An evaluation or reflection upon the aims of the lesson supports both the pupils' understanding of their learning and your own assessment of their learning. Plenaries should not simply be a 'show and tell'; think carefully about the learning that each pupil will engage in during this part of the lesson. Mini-plenaries, or little reviews of learning during the lesson are often more beneficial as they give opportunity for you and the pupils to respond immediately to progress in learning. Usually, these are not planned; you need to learn to realise when a mini-plenary should be included, basing your decisions on your ongoing assessment of the pupils' learning.

Plenaries may include the following.

- Following up on questions that pupils have set themselves at the start of the lesson.

- Opportunities for the pupils to peer- and self-assess against success criteria.

- Asking the pupils to reflect on their learning: *What are the three most important things we have learned in this lesson? What rules or tips could we create to help us next time we are . . . ?*

- Providing opportunities for pupils to apply their learning in different contexts, perhaps justifying choices or providing a rationale based on their learning in the lesson.

- Explaining to the pupils where their learning will develop in subsequent lessons; helping them see that their learning is an ongoing process rather than 'stand-alone' sessions.

 Find out more from ... websites

Mike Gershon has produced a huge range of tools to support the planning process. His 'Plenary Producer' may give you some ideas to start you off:

http://mikegershon.com/resources/download-info/the-plenary-producer-ideas-ks2-ks3-powerpoint/ (accessed 12 November 2019).

As you choose questions or activities for plenaries, carefully reflect on *why* the activity is supporting, deepening or embedding pupils' learning.

 Reflection and discussion activity

Reflection

Mentor: it is useful to remember that your trainee may be moving to work within a different school on their next placement, so giving them the opportunity to experiment with different lesson planning formats will support their professional development.

Trainee: depending on your experience, either:

Ask fellow trainees, other teachers, your training provider to share with you different planning formats that they use. Which ones would you feel most confident to use? Choose one or two that you like best and plan lessons using these instead of the format that you have been using so far.

Or:

Create your own planning format. Make use of key aspects (as above, or as seen in many other plans).

Discussion

Consider what worked and what did not work and why, keeping in mind the main purpose: reminding you of the decisions you made to ensure pupil progress in the lesson.

If we add to the diagram that describes the planning process in more depth now, we see that planning is actually an ongoing or spiral process. The process relies upon *flexibility* and *responsiveness*. Beginning trainees often ask, 'Does it matter if I do not do what I have put on my plan?'. The answer, of course, is that it does not matter at all, as long as the changes made are having a positive impact on pupil progress and, in fact, responding to and adapting planning is integral to ensure that the spiral continues within subsequent lessons. Part of your skills as a teacher depends on your ability to respond to the unexpected, and to learn from it (see Chapter 1 on reflection). The secret to the ability of responding flexibly within lessons lies in your subject knowledge, both of the subject that you are teaching and in your understanding of where your teaching fits within the curriculum, along with your knowledge of the pupils' prior learning, and them as learners (Hattie, 2012). This enables you to respond to a pupil's misconceptions, either by taking them to a different stage in the sequence of learning or by discussing their ideas from a different perspective. It is useful to include possible misconceptions within your plan to help you prepare for them.

Figure 6.2 Planning as a spiral process

Where next? Lesson planning beyond training

A trainee teacher once complained to me that the planning of her mentor (a teacher with 20 years' experience) was not 'as detailed as it should be', and asked if I could provide some examples of 'really good' plans written by good and outstanding teachers. Of course, what makes a 'really good' lesson plan varies from teacher to teacher, at different points in their careers and with different groups of pupils. Remember, lesson plans are for you, to support you in planning for pupils to make progress in their learning. Because you are at an early stage in your professional development, your lesson plans may take longer to create and include more detail than your experienced mentor would include in theirs. However, please remember that this should not always be the case. Be reassured that you will not continue to spend so many hours planning in the future; you will very quickly develop your bank of ideas of different ways to approach learning and different ways to engage pupils, and your own subject knowledge will continue to grow.

Do look at Chapter 15 by Sue Lambert which will support your understanding of Well-being and resilience for all.

Find out more from ... government reports

A recent DfE report from a review group who considered teachers' planning workload is available from the DfE website. This report presents findings that support schools encouraging collaborative planning and making use of high-quality, externally produced resources. It also reiterates the point that planning should serve the purpose of supporting learning, rather than be an extensive and time-consuming task.

www.gov.uk/government/uploads/system/uploads/attachment_data/file/511257/Eliminating-unnecessary-workload-around-planning-and-teaching-resources.pdf (accessed 12 November 2019).

Reflection and discussion activity

Collect examples of planning from different teachers in the school and, if possible, plans that were used in the past.

Reflection

Trainee, ensuring that you remain professional, critically analyse the plans of other teachers in the school (taking care to remember their audience when writing their plans - themselves). What appeals to you when thinking about how you would like to organise your own planning format?

Discussion

Mentor, how has your planning changed during your career? What strategies have you discovered to support efficient and effective lesson planning? Discuss this with your trainee.

However, to avoid having to wait years before things slot into place for you, it is useful to consider possible strategies to improve your lesson-planning efficiency now. I have sometimes heard very enthusiastic trainees suggesting that they have prepared a 'plan B' lesson plan. They have recognised a very important point: that having a contingency plan is useful. However, it seems a little excessive and inefficient to go to the effort of producing two in-depth plans; consideration of alternatives within one lesson plan, having good subject and curriculum knowledge, and seeking support from your mentor about the appropriateness of the plan, should be more than sufficient to ensure that you can respond effectively to unforeseen aspects of your lesson.

Other approaches that may help are:

- Team planning

  - Develop supportive relationships with others in school. If there are parallel classes, share planning. However, it should be noted that you will be held accountable for what is taught in your class, so you should amend and adapt other people's plans before you use them if needed.

- Using published planning

  o   Making use of prepared resources can make planning a much more efficient process (Hattie, 2012; DfE, 2016). The main disadvantage of many published schemes is that they are not specific to your class, so as above, you will need to adapt them.

- Familiar activities

  o   Make use of activities that you have used before, but change the context or content. As well as speeding up your planning, this has the added benefit of making more efficient use of lesson time as pupils are able to get on with activities without lengthy explanations.

- Carousels

  o   Consider using a range of activities that can be used for all groups in the class, but just adapted slightly to provide specific support or extension depending on prior attainment.

- Long-term and medium-term planning

  o   As you become more experienced, you will also have more autonomy over long- and medium-term plans. This will give you the opportunity to plan ahead and have greater understanding of where an individual lesson sits within pupils' long-term learning. Spending time on this stage will also improve efficiency in your short-term lesson planning.

 Chapter summary

Some schools and training providers will recommend that you make use of a particular planning format. In this chapter we have considered the rationale behind planning: pupil progress should be central to the planning process, and your lesson plan is a tool to support you to enable pupils' learning and progress. It should be seen as a more valuable and authentic process than a tick-box exercise for mentors or senior leaders in school. Any planning document that you produce should work for you.

The ideas discussed above are common themes seen in many lesson plans and may provide a good basis as you formulate your own approach to planning. You may decide to use the following headings in your lesson-planning format.

- Prior learning

- Subsequent learning

- Lesson objective

- Reference to National Curriculum or EYFS framework

- Success criteria

- Assessment (how, what, who, when)

- Variation/differentiation (how different pupils/groups of pupils' different needs will be met, how individual pupils and/or groups will be supported and challenged, how learning might be extended) including specific reference to pupils with EAL, SEND, specific needs

- Key questions

- Key vocabulary

- Resources (what and how they will be used)

- Plenary

- Timings

- Role of other adults

It is also valuable to annotate your lesson plans during and after the lesson. Again, for the purpose of ensuring pupil progress over time, get into the habit of making quick written notes on your plans that show both:

- Pupil progress in the lessons: your assessment of pupils' learning, perhaps considering individuals or groups. Begin to think about 'what next?' for individuals and groups.

- Implications for your own learning: 'This aspect worked'; 'At this point, I had to make changes because . . . '; 'Here, I could have. . . . ' etc. These comments will be invaluable in informing later 'reflection-on-action' (Schön, 1983).

Keeping at the front of your mind that one of your main responsibilities as a teacher is to ensure that pupils all make progress in every lesson, it is important that you should always be prepared to adapt your lesson plans as they are happening. Accept that your meticulously prepared lesson plan should be flexible and responsive, and do not stick to the plan if you see that pupils are not learning. However, alongside ensuring that your lesson plans are focused on pupil progress, throughout your career, remember also to make use of lesson plans to reflect on and develop your own teaching. Also, remember to develop strategies that help you maintain efficient and manageable approaches to managing your planning workload.

References

Aubrey, K and Riley, A (2016) *Understanding and Using Educational Theories*. London: SAGE.

Bandura, A (1977) *Social Learning Theory*. New York: General Learning Press.

Bruner, J (1966) *Toward a Theory of Instruction*. Cambridge, MA: Harvard University Press.

Department for Education (DfE) (2013) *The National Curriculum for England: Key Stages 1 and 2 Framework Document*. Available at: **www.gov.uk/government/publications/national-curriculum-in-england-primary-curriculum** (accessed 12 November 2019).

Department for Education (DfE) (2016) *Eliminating Unnecessary Workload Around Planning and Teaching Resources: Report of the Independent Teacher Workload Review Group.* Available at: **www.gov.uk/government/uploads/system/uploads/attachment_data/file/511257/Eliminating-unnecessary-workload-around-planning-and-teaching-resources.pdf** (accessed 29 January 2017).

Department for Education (DfE) (2017) *Statutory Framework for Early Years Foundation Stage.* Available at: **www.gov.uk/government/publications/early-years-foundation-stage-framework--2** (accessed 12 November 2019).

Hattie, J (2012) *Visible Learning for Teachers: Maximising impact on learning.* London: Routledge.

Ofsted (2016) *School Inspection Handbook.* Available at: **www.gov.uk/government/publications/school-inspection-handbook-from-september-2015** (accessed 29 January 2017).

Piaget, J and Inhelder, B (2000) *The Psychology of the Child.* New York: Basic Books.

Pound, L (2009) *Contemporary Thinking and Theorists: An overview of contemporary educational and psychological theorists.* London: Practical Pre-School Books.

Schön, D (1983) *The Reflective Practitioner: How professionals think in action.* New York: Basic Books.

Vygotsky, L (1978) *Mind in Society.* Cambridge, MA: Harvard University Press.

7
Assessment
Elizabeth Farrar

 This chapter will

- explore different approaches to assessment to help children make progress;
- consider what formative assessment strategies might look like in the classroom;
- consider how assessment impacts upon learning objectives and success criteria;
- reflect on the part that feedback has to play in ensuring that children understand where they are in their learning and what they need to do next;
- develop your understanding of summative assessment and its place in primary education.

 Links to Teachers' Standards

1   **Set high expectations which inspire, motivate and challenge pupils**, specifically:
    - set goals that stretch and challenge pupils of all backgrounds, abilities and dispositions.

2   **Promote good progress and outcomes by pupils**
    - be accountable for pupils' attainment, progress and outcomes;
    - be aware of pupils' capabilities and their prior knowledge, and plan teaching to build on these;
    - guide pupils to reflect on the progress they have made and their emerging needs;
    - demonstrate knowledge and understanding of how pupils learn and how this impacts on teaching;
    - encourage pupils to take a responsible and conscientious attitude to their own work and study.

(Continued)

(Continued)

6   Make accurate and productive use of assessment

- know and understand how to assess the relevant subject and curriculum areas, including statutory assessment requirements;

- make use of formative and summative assessment to secure pupils' progress;

- use relevant data to monitor progress, set targets, and plan subsequent lessons;

- give pupils regular feedback, both orally and through accurate marking, and encourage pupils to respond to the feedback.

Introduction

As a trainee teacher, you may wonder what part assessment will play in your daily practice. Will it be something that you need to be concerned with at all, or is it something that the pupils will do, maybe at some future point, such as at the end of the unit of work, the term or the year? What does it look like and why do teachers do it? Any of these questions, and probably many more, might have occurred to you. This chapter aims to address some of them.

Assessment in the classroom takes two forms: summative and formative. Summative assessment takes place at the end of a period of learning such as a unit of work, an academic year or a Key Stage, for instance. Pupils are evaluated against a standard or benchmark. SATs and GCSEs are examples of summative assessment which you will probably be familiar with. Summative assessment is carried out for the purpose of reporting the achievement of individual students at a particular time (Harlen and Harlen, 2007). Formative assessment is ongoing and takes place during the learning process, enabling you to evaluate learning needs and progress. It allows teaching and learning to be modified and adapted to better meet these needs. You will find that formative assessment is often referred to as Assessment for Learning (AfL).

Summative and formative assessment are not contradictory or conflicting practices, but can be seen as complementary approaches. Clarke and Hattie (2001) employ a gardening analogy to explain this. If you think of your pupils as plants, then summative assessment would be the process of measuring them. These measurements may be interesting to compare and analyse, but they do not affect the growth of the plants. Formative assessment is the garden equivalent of you feeding and watering your plants, and therefore directly affecting their growth.

 Reflection and discussion activity

Reflection

Trainee: think about pupils you have worked with and lessons you have observed. What adaptations were being made to lessons to cater for pupils who are working 'below' and 'above' their age-related expectations?

Mentor: think about what adaptations you make for pupil progress. Share some of these with the trainee.

Discussion

Mentor and trainee: discuss the impact of the approaches in helping children to make progress that you have both chosen in the reflection.

Summative assessment

Assessment lies at the very heart of teaching, as you need to know what progress your pupils are making in order to know what you need to teach them. It is certainly not the intention to imply that a 'teaching to the test' approach should be taken, but rather that learning needs should be steered to ensure that progress is made towards the age-related expectations as laid out in the National Curriculum and by individual schools. Assessment is, therefore, fundamental to the whole of your practice. There would be little point in going to swimming lessons for a year if the assessment of your progress at the end was related to your proficiency in salsa dancing, for example. Data gathered through assessment can be collated in many different ways, both using commercial schemes and also schools' own adapted assessment systems. There could be any number of ways in which the school you are working at has chosen to assess their pupils, and so it is neither possible nor helpful to try to explain any of these in specific detail in this chapter. However, I can discuss what the assessment system you are working with needs to be able to do.

The requirements that children need to have achieved by the end of Key Stage 1 and Key Stage 2 are specified within the National Curriculum, and so many schools and commercially produced systems have taken these and reduced them to a set of 'non-negotiables' or key skills. These have then been broken down into what children are expected to know by the end of the year. The pupils are assessed against this set of statements to determine whether they are working below, at or above their year group (often referred to as 'age-related') expectations.

Why test?

Summative testing can contribute to learning but, for instance, teaching a skill for the first half term of the year, followed by a successful assessment, cannot be assumed to indicate that your pupils are secure with that skill and that it can be left behind, safely ticked off on your record. To be certain that the skill is secured, it should be revisited throughout the year in a range of forms to ensure that it is embedded thoroughly. To embed knowledge, understanding or skills, you must provide your pupils with enough opportunities to practise, use, revisit, consolidate and apply what you want them to learn, otherwise their long-term memory is bypassed and things are forgotten, no matter how well they seemed to know or understand them at the point of teaching. Using summative testing can be considered to help to revisit and therefore consolidate prior learning. Faragher (2014) notes that schools now operate within a standards-driven assessment culture. The introduction of the National Curriculum, Ofsted inspections, testing and league tables, along with the glut of associated strategies and initiatives, have all been driven by the intention of improving standards on the international stage as well as nationally. Powerful national bodies have taken charge of the curriculum and assessment, with teachers becoming accountable for the achievement of externally set targets. As trainees, it is useful for you to be aware of the accountability that rests with all teachers for their pupils' progress.

 Reflection and discussion activity

Reflection

Trainee: having looked at the school's systems, consider how every child's progress is being effectively tracked and what is done during daily lessons to feed in to this tracking.

Look out for examples of summative assessment being used to revisit and consolidate learning.

Mentor: consider how you can support your trainee in understanding the place of summative assessment and also the ways in which reporting is expected for accountability. Organise some opportunities to look at examples of summative assessment relevant to the age range of the pupils they are teaching - for example, past papers for Year 6 SATs or Year 1 phonics screening.

Discussion

Trainee and mentor: consider summative assessment preparations in your school and discuss strategies that can be used to minimise any negative effects of the pressures that assessment may produce.

Formative assessment

Black and Wiliam were commissioned by the Assessment Reform Group to review the literature around formative assessment. Their findings, published in *Inside the Black Box: Raising standards through classroom assessment* (1998) were presented to the policy makers. They stated that summative assessment dominated, but that formative assessment had the most potential for improving standards of children's learning. Following this, the 'Excellence and Enjoyment' strategy for primary schools, launched by the Secretary of State in 2003, formally introduced Assessment for Learning into the national teaching and learning agenda. The stage was set for formative assessment to become a fundamental part of primary school teaching and learning.

 Taking it further . . . research

You can read *Inside the Black Box* online, available at: **https://weaeducation.typepad.co.uk/files/black box-1.pdf** (accessed 11 November 2019).

Harlen and Harlen (2007) summarise the key components of formative assessment, and these are clearly reflected in the strategies advocated by Clarke (2014). These include pupils:

- understanding their goals;

- knowing what good-quality work looks like;

- being involved in self-assessment;

- taking a role in identifying their next steps in learning;

- communicating understanding and skills facilitated by the teacher's use of open questions;

- taking part in a two-way dialogue with the teacher encouraging reflection on learning;

- being part of a classroom ethos that promotes engagement and employs learner-centred teaching.

However, as reported by Boyle and Charles (2014), research within a large national sample of primary schools showed that there is wide variety in interpretation and understanding of the term 'formative assessment'. Consequently, you will see lots of different approaches in different schools, but all practitioners are focused upon supporting pupils in moving forward with their learning. You can learn a great deal from a variety of practice.

 Reflection and discussion activity

Reflection

Trainee: look at some of the learning objectives you have seen being used; think about whether they reflect what the pupils did learn in that lesson, and how knowing the objectives helped to move the learning forward.

Discussion

Mentor and trainee: discuss together the success criteria for a particular lesson and consider how these have been arrived at.

Discuss the learning objective(s) for a particular lesson and look at the National Curriculum to see where the objectives have been drawn from.

Formative assessment in the classroom

The use of formative assessment strategies can be planned into all lessons, allowing these techniques to become embedded in your practice.

The following are some formative assessment strategies you could include in your planning.

- Ensure that you have factored in time to allow the pupils to have input when possible; a 'knowledge harvest' before planning begins means that you are aware of what the pupils know and would like to know about a particular topic and can then plan with these factors in mind.

- Sharing of the learning objective ensures that pupils are all aware of the expected learning and focus on 'learning' rather than 'doing'.

- Shared success criteria, ideally developed with pupils. This should also include analysis of examples of 'good ones', possibly as compared to 'less good ones' (you will see some schools call this a WAGOLL: What A Good One Looks Like).

- Effective questioning to be used, both to gauge prior knowledge and to check current understanding throughout the lesson; also to elicit misconceptions, which may result in you discovering the need to adapt the lesson for all – groups or individuals.

- Collaborative improvement during the lesson. This can take the form of mini-plenaries (bringing the whole class back together to review learning so far mid-lesson), which allow for modelling by the teacher or redrafting to better achieve the success criteria using an example from a pupil's work, followed by peer assessment carried out by all pupils facilitated by the example shown (this strategy is further explained later in the chapter).

- A plenary that provides time and opportunity for pupils to self-assess, or peer assess, against the learning objective and success criteria, then reflect on their learning and consider their next steps.

Along with the strategies above that occur at certain points before and within the lesson, feedback should happen *throughout* the lesson, with pupils being involved in self- and peer-assessment. as well as adult-led assessment and feedback. All feedback, oral and written, should be directly related to the learning objectives and success criteria.

 Reflection and discussion activity

Reflection

Trainee: think about the strategies listed above. Find some real examples of these strategies.

Think about which ones you could use effectively in the next lesson you teach.

Mentor: look at an observation you have undertaken and consider how you can give focused feedback to your trainee on the strategies listed above.

Discussion

Mentor and trainee: share the outcomes of both your reflection activities and begin to forward plan next steps for developing competency in this area.

Formative assessment techniques cannot simply be imposed upon a class of pupils to achieve instant success. For the strategies to make a positive difference, rather than just become an imposition, the learning environment has to be right.

How do I create a positive learning environment?

The learning environment is created by a wide range of elements. There are the physical aspects, such as the placement of the tables, wall displays, the arrangement of resources and the lighting. There are also the intangible aspects, including the rules, the way in which learning activities are organised, the sounds and the energy in the room. The teacher's attitude also affects the pupils' response to the environment in which they find themselves. Having a teacher who is negative or uninterested (in either the pupils themselves or the subject matter of the lesson) is unlikely to produce a positive emotional environment, no matter how creative and artistic the appearance of the room. A good environment can be seen in pupils' involvement and reaction to the ethos of the school, and in how they conduct themselves, including their courtesy, respect and manners towards each other. It also shows in pupils' respect for the school's amenities and equipment, which includes the presentation of work in books, and their observance of any school uniform policies. A poor learning environment can be signalled by an untidy or chaotic classroom, and also by pupils' lack of engagement and persistent low-level disruption that contribute to reduced learning and progress.

Wall displays deserve a mention here: be careful what you choose to put on the wall. There is a temptation to select the 'best' work, but think about the message this gives to your pupils. Which pupils' work do you value? Is it only the higher attaining pupils' pieces, or do you recognise that some pupils have put in great amounts of effort, despite not having achieved quite the same outcome as others? If you don't demonstrate that you value everyone's efforts, then some pupils may well not try as hard the next time.

It is often a good idea to allow the pupils themselves to be in charge of creating at least one display in the classroom to ensure that they feel involved in the formation of their own learning environment. Working walls are a useful way not only to include everyone's contributions, but also to assist and promote learning. These displays are interactive, and can be used to record, support and visualise learning. They should reflect the teaching sequence and be built up over time, including good examples of work, key vocabulary, targets, success criteria, cross-curricular links and questions. These displays contribute clearly to building a vibrant and welcoming classroom climate that values learning highly.

The classroom environment contributes a central role in helping pupils to be engaged and successful in their learning. As the teacher, you can take control and adapt the environment to achieve these results. Moving the tables around to achieve a better seating plan, or even altering the lighting or the temperature can improve the effectiveness of learning in the classroom.

Clarke (2014) explains how vital it is to achieve the appropriate learning culture, which includes enabling pupils to develop an awareness of their own knowledge and how they learn, as well as having 'growth mindsets' (this concept, introduced by Carol Dweck (2012), is explored in more detail in Chapter 5) and not being grouped by their ability.

Why is a growth mindset important?

The current primary curriculum works on the principle that all pupils can achieve. If the teacher is going to succeed in enabling all the pupils in their class to achieve the necessary requirements for that year group, as set out in the curriculum documents, then it is vital that they believe this is possible for all pupils. With the exception of a small minority (around 2 per cent of children who potentially cannot achieve in line with their peers due to severe learning impairments), all pupils will be able to reach the goals set. Some pupils will need more time and opportunities for practice, may need more input and support for longer, and will definitely have to invest more effort than their peers, but given these, they will succeed. A pupil whose current assessments suggest they are lagging behind in maths may well be level with, or ahead of, their year group in science or art or PE, for example. To have a growth mindset is to believe that all can achieve, that intelligence is not fixed, and to embrace a belief that there is no 'glass ceiling' preventing pupils from achieving. For example, a child who is not in line with their peers in maths this term, or this year, could catch up and exceed peers at a later stage in their maths learning journey. However, there needs to be a belief (by the teacher and the pupil) that this is possible. Hattie and Clarke (2019) note that an environment in which pupils are not afraid to make mistakes must be fostered, so that children understand that learning is hard work, and they will need to accept challenges and persist even when initially they fail. Labelling pupils as 'low ability' is unhelpful and effectively gives them a golden ticket to stop trying, removing their self-belief and damaging their self-esteem so that it becomes a 'self-fulfilling prophecy'. This brings us back to the importance of establishing a growth mindset with both pupils and staff, and, wherever possible, parents too. Hattie suggests that the most powerful influence on pupil achievement is their own opinion regarding their chances of success (2008, p43). This can then become a barrier if pupils only achieve to an expectation they have formed that is lower than their true potential. Bearing this in mind, it is easy to see how important the promotion of a growth mindset and a positive self-belief is in enabling our pupils to succeed.

 Taking it further . . . research

The work of Carol Dweck (2012) challenges the commonly held belief that intelligence is a fixed attribute. Dweck's research suggests that individuals hold implicit views as to where ability comes from and can be placed on a continuum with fixed and growth mindset at the opposing ends. A person exhibiting a fixed mindset will believe that intelligence is set from birth and cannot be changed, therefore any success is based on innate ability. A growth mindset is seen when individuals believe success is attributed to effort, determination, resilience and perseverance. They believe that intelligence is not predetermined but rather fluctuates depending upon the task or subject, and can be developed through personal endeavour. In the classroom, these mindsets are important as they influence the outcomes of challenges and feedback.

Dylan Wiliam (2007) argues that where the classroom culture focuses on rewards, 'gold stars', grades or place-in-the-class ranking, pupils then look for the ways to obtain the best marks rather than at the needs of their learning which these marks ought to reflect. One reported consequence is that where they have any choice, pupils with a fixed mindset will try to avoid difficult tasks, and will also spend time and energy looking for clues to the 'right answer'. Many are reluctant to ask questions out of fear of failure. Pupils who encounter difficulties and poor results are led to believe that they lack ability, and this belief leads them to attribute their difficulties to a defect in themselves about which they cannot do a great deal. They will then begin to avoid investing effort in learning, which could only lead to disappointment, and try to build up their self-esteem in other ways. This can then lead to a pupil displaying innappropriate or disruptive behaviours. While high-achieving pupils can do well in such a culture, the overall result is to enhance the frequency and the extent of under-achievement. Dweck (2000) suggested that there is a tendency for boys to attribute successes to ability and failures to lack of effort or bad luck, while girls tend to attribute success to effort and failures to lack of ability. For both, successive failures produce learned helplessness. The curriculum subject or aspect of that subject where the failure occurred is then viewed as best avoided wherever possible. A growth mindset, conversely, means that more effort will be directed towards subjects perceived as difficult.

As the teacher, we can influence our pupils' mindets. Telling a pupil they are 'clever' produces a fixed mindset, which then leads to a lack of success. Using the term 'clever' in feedback makes the pupil shy away from challenges as they strive to preserve that 'title', trying not to have any inadequacies or errors revealed that would 'demote' them. They will readily disengage from tasks when obstacles occur. It is important to substitute 'You are clever!' with positive comments about their learning or effort. For example, 'Well done, you have worked really hard at learning how to add fractions!' or 'Excellent work – you have learned from your previous mistakes'. Equally, parents have their role to play. Halmovitz and Dweck (2016) found that parents' beliefs about mistakes and failures shaped their children's mindsets. Those who saw failure as something negative and to be avoided tended to have children with fixed mindsets, while those who viewed failure as a learning opportunity promoted a growth mindset in their children.

 Case study

It appeared that Tom was not achieving as well as his peers throughout Key Stage 1. Maths was a particular area where he was underachieving, and he always worked in a group supported by a teaching assistant. He ended Year 2 well below age-related expectations (as a Level 1 on the previous system). His parents were unconcerned, stating that they 'could not do maths' and did not expect him to be any different. During Year 3, the school launched an initiative to promote a growth mindset. Tom was seen to identify himself as a 'poor learner' and during circle time spoke of how he believed that he was 'no good' at maths. When the class discussed growth mindset and the concept of how intelligence was not fixed, but developed like muscles, Tom cried and said that he had not known that he 'could make himself be cleverer' (sic). Over the next two years the class teacher removed ability groupings and ensured that over the course of a half term, every child had worked together. Opportunities were given for self-selection of activities and tasks, and also the long-term absence of the teaching assistant meant that Tom was no longer able to rely on adult support in maths lessons. In Year 5, Tom would choose to work with older pupils on a regular basis and was keen to challenge himself, regarding failure as an opportunity to learn. The mixed-age group class meant that he was often seen tackling Year 6 tasks. His maths SATs result was one mark away from a Level 5 (using the previous old system of levels), which placed him well above age-related expectations, but also meant that his progress since Key Stage 1 was not only the best of the cohort, but well above average nationally.

(Continued)

(Continued)

Reflection

* Think about how you present differentiated/adapted work to children and whether you may be inadvertently putting a 'ceiling' on their learning, or may be giving them permission not to try by signalling low(er) expectations for them than for others in the class.

Learning objectives and success criteria

Children need to know the reasons for the lesson and what is expected of them. The learning objective serves to identify this clearly. By constructing the learning objective at the planning stage, as the teacher you will have had to think through your own expectations of the learning journey you wish the pupils to take. By starting a lesson plan with a precise view of what the outcome needs to be, the planning will be more focused, the purpose of activities and tasks will be clear and, if this is clear in your own mind, then a successful outcome is much more likely. Giving the children access to your own expectations of the learning will keep the lesson focused firmly on the required learning (Briggs *et al.*, 2003, p25).

In Chapter 6, Rebecca Geeson has explored in detail the key aspects of a successful lesson plan and there are some helpful examples of learning objectives. Learning objectives should be carefully constructed to ensure that they focus on the transferable skill. For example, setting the learning objective of 'We are learning to write a poem about snow' overlooks the fact that, by writing the poem, the pupils are learning specific poetry skills which they can then use to write poems about any given topic. The learning objective should not be context based, but must focus on what the transferable skills are that they are expected to learn in that lesson or unit of work (Clarke, 2014, p79).

 Case study

Lucia had planned a lesson for her Year 3 class with the stated learning objective, 'We are learning how to measure how tall we are'. All the children understood what they were expected to do and spent the lesson engaged in the activity, using various methods of measuring each other and recording their heights. Some time later, thinking of this lesson, Lucia planned another lesson for the children to go outside and measure the sunflowers they had grown, along with the goalposts, fences, walls and other objects in the playground. The children's behaviour rapidly deteriorated and Lucia knew that this could not be due to them working outside as this was a regular feature of her lessons. Gathering the children back for a mini-plenary, her open questions soon uncovered the fact that the children were not relating this activity to the lesson about measuring each other and were very confused about what needed to be done. The learning objective was changed to, 'We are learning to measure heights', and the success criteria were focused clearly on how to successfully measure heights of any objects with the children. The links were made with their previous learning and the pupils completed the lesson successfully. Later in the year, Lucia planned another lesson on measuring to allow her to assess the pupils' learning away from the point of teaching, and this demonstrated that the transferable skills required for measuring height had been acquired and retained by most pupils.

Reflection

• Ask pupils what they are learning and see if you get the response you expected. Think about why you might get different responses that are different from what you expected.

The use of success criteria follows on from the creation of learning objectives for lessons or units of work. Having decided on the end result, the success criteria then provide a clear path from the pupil's prior learning, so current level of knowledge, skill or understanding, to where they are required to be by the end. To use a road analogy, you are guiding the pupils from point A to point B on the map and the success criteria act as signposts along the way to ensure that they take the appropriate route. The success criteria help pupils to identify when success has been achieved, or where things have gone awry, and support them in discussing ways of improving (Clarke, 2014, p81). By providing pupils with examples of good (and possibly weaker) work, it is possible for them to consider the features of these and then construct their own success criteria as they analyse what is required to produce the desired outcome.

Questioning

The use of questioning in the classroom is discussed at length elsewhere in this book (see Chapter 8 by John Paramore). However, as Clarke (2014) and Hattie (2008) state, ongoing effective questioning produces the most important feedback, which is *what teachers learn from students*. The responses you get illuminate your knowledge of the pupils' understanding, thus guiding the lesson and allowing you to plan for individual needs.

In respect of assessment for learning, Dylan Wiliam places a great deal of importance upon what he terms *hinge point questions*. He discussed these in his keynote speech given at the 2007 Association for Learning Technology Conference in Nottingham, England. These questions are a diagnostic tool that provide data on your pupils' learning within the lesson and enable you to pinpoint misconceptions so they can be addressed quickly. They are questions that pupils can answer in no more than two minutes, and which the teacher can look at and interpret the responses in less than 30 seconds. Every pupil answers, usually by holding up an individual whiteboard, unless you have access to an electronic voting system, which is ideal for this type of question. These questions and the multiple-choice answers need to be planned carefully to elicit any likely misconceptions. The possible alternative answers need to help the teacher to see the problems some pupils are having with their reasoning.

 Find out more from ... internet clips

Using the following link, listen to Dylan Wiliam speak about hinge point questions: **www.youtube.com/watch?v=Mh5SZZt207k** (accessed 11 November 2019).

Reflection and discussion activity

Reflection

Trainee: choose a lesson you are about to teach and see if you can devise a hinge point question to use. Come up with multiple-choice answers that will demonstrate clearly some possible misconceptions. Check if it is possible for a pupil to get the answer correct using the wrong reasoning.

Discuss the responses you had with your mentor after the lesson. Consider whether the hinge point question helped you to adapt the rest of your lesson to meet the pupils' needs.

Discussion

Trainee and mentor: discuss the thinking that a child has used to arrive at each of the following answers, and what you would do next to address their misconception.

Question: 45 + 9 =

Answers: (a) 459 (b) 56 (c) 54 (d) 5

Question: What do plants need most to survive?

Answers: (a) Light (b) Soil (c) Food (d) Water

Feedback

Throughout the literature about assessment for learning, feedback is consistently viewed as a vital element. Hattie acknowledges that, of all the influences on achievement, feedback seems to be among those that have greatest effect. There is a challenge in establishing what is precisely meant by the term 'feedback', and equally many types of it are to be found (2008, p173). Hattie's findings suggest that the most powerful feedback is when it is from the pupil to the teacher, as this helps make learning 'visible'.

Feedback is defined as *a consequence of performance* (2008, p174). Feedback given by the teacher needs to result in improvement, and if it does not, then it has been a waste of time and effort on the part of those producing it. Some types, such as the celebratory 'Well done!' and 'Good work!', give no indication to the learner as to what was good, or why they are deemed to have done well. If the feedback you are giving does not indicate what to do next to improve the work, then it serves little purpose other than to demonstrate to someone (parents or carers, line manager, headteacher, inspector) that the pupil's work has been read. Accountability means that teachers do often feel obliged to write copious amounts in books which will not have an impact on learning, but is there to just show that it has been done. When marking is done well, comments will identify what has been done successfully, what needs improvement and how to go about making that improvement. Do be aware that the addition of a mark or grade has been suggested to take pupils' attention away from any comments, and in the case of lower ability children to demotivate them (Black *et al.*, 2003, p43). As noted in the current Ofsted *School Inspection Handbook* (2019, p45): *When used effectively, assessment helps pupils to embed knowledge and use it fluently, and assists teachers in producing clear next steps for pupils.* However, this does not mean that it should be a burdensome task. As schools tackle teacher workload issues, some have implemented so-called 'no marking' policies, whilse others use 'in flight feedback' or 'live marking'. In practice, these all mean that marking and feedback happens during the course of the lesson, giving pupils immediate information regarding their progress and next steps. This means that not only are teachers freed from facing a large pile of books to mark after the lesson has finished, but also that pupils can act on the feedback from the teacher while they are still actively engaged in their learning. It isn't hard to see that this is a great improvement with benefits for all concerned.

It should be noted that feedback alone is not the magic wand that it is perhaps sometimes touted to be. Hattie and Clarke (2019) make the point that how effective feedback is depends upon how the students interpret and use it. They also assert that it needs to be combined with effective teaching and learning strategies to promote the best progress in pupils.

 Find out more from . . . internet clips, websites

Dylan Wiliam conducted an experiment looking at the use of grades. He found out some interesting things about whether grades lead to improvements (which usually they do not) and how pupils respond to a lack of grading (which initially they did not like). In the following video clips there are also examples of assessment strategies in action (in a secondary school). See his work using the following link (this is the second episode where teachers use comments not grades): **www.youtube.com/watch?v=1iD6Zadhq4M** (accessed 11 November 2019).

Remember that the key indicator that feedback has been successful is when students have responded to it and made the necessary improvements to their work. If the same mistake is being made continually and teacher comments are repeated, then this is likely to be picked up during book scrutinies and the effectiveness of feedback will, quite rightly, be called into question. Feedback must produce progress.

 Reflection and discussion activity

Reflection

Trainee: make sure that you are familiar with the school's feedback and marking policy. Consider examples of where you have seen this policy being implemented and look at these to see if you can identify improvements that have appeared as a result.

(Continued)

(Continued)

Discussion

Trainee and mentor: find and discuss some examples of feedback in books that have had a clear impact on learning. Compare these with some examples of feedback the trainee has produced and see if you can identify any ways the trainee teacher could make their feedback more effective.

You need to give your pupils opportunities to employ self-assessment and peer-assessment during lessons. Collaborative improvement is a strategy advocated by Clarke (2014) in which the use of the visualiser enables pupils' work to be displayed at any point in the lesson and improved collaboratively. Success criteria are used to provide a framework for the assessment, so your pupils can identify effective parts and explain why they are positive. Improvements can then be suggested for the work. After this modelling process, pupils can work in pairs to find good points and to make improvements. The sharing of ideas should be promoted and this co-operative feedback will produce a quality of discussion that is often absent from just swapping books (2014, p123). The reflection on learning that this process enables is an important element of AfL: it promotes independent learning, communication and support in the classroom. This can start from the Foundation Stage where there should be an emphasis on building an open, reflective climate in which adults model appropriate language and behaviour. It should then be developed throughout the primary phase with peer- and self-assessment and evaluation, which start off as oral comments in the Foundation Stage and then extend to include written comments as pupils move up through the Key Stages. This assessment cycle enables children to reflect on what has been learned and, when appropriate, judge it against a set of criteria. Evaluation describes the process that children use to gain an understanding of how they are learning. Both are equally important for your pupils' development and should be ongoing within your daily teaching.

 Case study

Natalie was becoming frustrated with the lack of progress her Year 5 pupils were showing with their writing skills. She spent many hours writing extensive amounts of feedback into their books, but it was apparent that little improvement was resulting from it. Her school provided her with a visualiser and explained the concept of collaborative improvement. She showed the class examples of writing that had been produced by a previous Year 5 class and asked them to identify the good points. They constructed a list of success criteria and the class began to draft their own work. At various points during this process, Natalie selected a pupil through her random 'lollipop stick' system (this is where all pupils' names are on lollipop sticks and the teacher pulls out names to respond to questions) and together the class assessed the work so far. As it was clear to the pupils that this was a draft, they were happy to share ideas and accept suggestions for improvement. These were marked on the work using the interactive whiteboard and then copies were printed off and circulated around the room for reference. Good parts were highlighted in pink and points to redraft were highlighted in green. The pupils then worked in pairs to replicate the process themselves. Although initially the improvement in the standard of writing was quite limited, Natalie persevered until the way of working was embedded and the pupils would actively request an 'improvement stop'. The feedback became very precisely related to the success criteria and the standard of writing rose rapidly across the entire class. Natalie reduced her own marking to specifically commenting on the criteria, to suggest an improvement and to model an example of what she required. Time was then put aside each week when the pupils would respond to the marking and demonstrate the required improvement.

Reflection

- Consider whether your marking is related to the success criteria of your lesson, and whether you are giving your pupils time to read and respond to any marking you do.

What have we found out?

In conclusion, you have seen that you need to collect information at the start, at the end and throughout the lesson. Opportunities to discover misconceptions need to be planned for and you need to have a range of options ready to rectify these. The information must be used to enable you to adapt lessons and decide how best to cater for your pupils' learning needs. If there are problems – and pupils are not making the expected progress – explaining it all again, but louder, may not be the best solution Alternative strategies could include the provision of more examples, giving concrete apparatus, if appropriate, giving opportunities for reteaching another child, asking for an explanation of their thinking or giving more time for practice. To be effective, you need to structure your lessons to incorporate all the key elements of the assessment cycle that have been discussed in this chapter. With the framework of formative assessment in place, including the use of learning objectives and success criteria, which are fully understood along with feedback directly related to these, delivered in a suitable learning environment, you should find that positive outcomes are accessible for all of your pupils.

References

Black, P and Wiliam, D (1998) *Inside the Black Box: Raising standards through classroom assessment*. London: School of Education, King's College London.

Black, P, Harrison, C, Lee, C, Marshall, B, and Wiliam, D (2003) *Assessment for Learning: Putting it into practice*. Maidenhead: Open University Press.

Boyle, B and Charles, M (2014) *Formative Assessment for Teaching and Learning*. Los Angeles, CA: SAGE.

Briggs, MS, Woodfield, A, Martin, CD and Swatton, PJ (2003) *Assessment for Learning and Teaching in Primary Schools: Meeting the professional standards framework for QTS (Achieving QTS)*. Exeter: Learning Matters.

Clarke, S (2014) *Outstanding Formative Assessment: Culture and practice*. London: Hodder Education.

Clarke, S and Hattie, J (2001) *Unlocking Formative Assessment: Practical strategies for enhancing pupils' learning in the primary classroom*. London: Hodder & Stoughton Educational.

Dweck, CS (2000) *Self Theories: Their role in motivation, personality and development*. London: Taylor & Francis.

Dweck, CS (2012) *Mindset*. London: Robinson.

Faragher, S (2014) *Understanding Assessment in Primary education*. London: SAGE.

Halmovitz, K and Dweck, CS (2016) What predicts children's fixed and growth intelligence mindsets? Not their parents' view of intelligence but their parents' view of failure. *Psychological Science*, 27(6): 859–69.

Harlen, W and Harlen, PW (2007) *Assessment of Learning*. London: SAGE.

Hattie, JAC (2008) *Visible Learning: A synthesis of over 800 meta-analyses relating to achievement*. London: Routledge.

Hattie, JAC and Clarke, S (2019) *Visible Learning: Feedback*. Abingdon: Routledge.

Ofsted (2019) *School Inspection Handbook*. Available at: **https://assets.publishing.service.gov.uk/government/uploads/system/uploads/attachment_data/file/828469/School_inspection_handbook_-_section_5.pdf** (accessed 10 October 2019).

Wiliam, D (2007) *Assessment, Learning and Technology: Prospects at the periphery of control*. Available at: **www.alt.ac.uk/sites/default/files/assets_editor_uploads/documents/altc2007_dylan_wiliam_keynote_transcript.pdf** (accessed 29 January 2017).

8

Questioning to stimulate dialogue

John Paramore

 This chapter will

- analyse and understand the motives for asking questions;
- examine the sorts of questions that teachers ask;
- begin to understand how opportunities to extend dialogue can be exploited or missed;
- develop your understanding of the key requirements for asking effective questions.

 Links to Teachers' Standards

1 **Set high expectations which inspire, motivate and challenge pupils**, specifically:
- set goals that stretch and challenge pupils of all backgrounds, abilities and dispositions.

2 **Promote good progress and outcomes by pupils**, specifically:
- accountable for pupils' attainment, progress and outcomes;
- be aware of pupils' capabilities and their prior knowledge, and plan teaching to build on these;
- guide pupils to reflect on the progress they have made and their emerging needs;
- demonstrate knowledge and understanding of how pupils learn and how this impacts on teaching.

(Continued)

(Continued)

3   Demonstrate good subject and curriculum knowledge, specifically:

- have a secure knowledge of the relevant subject(s) and curriculum areas, foster and maintain pupils' interest in the subject, and address misunderstandings;

- demonstrate a critical understanding of developments in the subject and curriculum areas, and promote the value of scholarship;

- demonstrate an understanding of and take responsibility for promoting high standards of literacy, articulacy and the correct use of standard English, whatever the teacher's specialist subject.

4   Plan and teach well structured lessons, specifically:

- impart knowledge and develop understanding through effective use of lesson time;

- promote a love of learning and children's intellectual curiosity;

- reflect systematically on the effectiveness of lessons and approaches to teaching;

- contribute to the design and provision of an engaging curriculum within the relevant subject area(s).

Introduction

There is plenty of useful advice available for teachers on questions and questioning as there is on the development of a dialogic classroom. Such practical advice is, necessarily, underpinned by theories or beliefs about how pupils learn and how you, as teachers, can best facilitate that process.

Questioning seems the natural thing for teachers to do, so much so that you probably do a lot of it without thinking too deeply. Consequently, when you reflect on lessons – as teachers or observers – it may be that you don't always give a great deal of detailed attention to the effect that asking particular questions may have on the learning, and how a different question may have altered the course of the learning. The quality and balance of questioning exhibited by a trainee teacher is a clear indicator of the difference between authentic professional practice and superficial mimicry. If we're not asking questions for the sake of it, what are you asking questions for? In other words, what might your motives for questioning be?

At this stage, it should be noted that you won't be considering the sort of managerial and rhetorical questions that you often use when you're busy 'organising' everything and everyone – 'why did you do that?' or 'would you like chips or mash?', for example. Here, you will focus exclusively on questions and answers that are connected with the learning intentions of a lesson/session.

It might be worthwhile pointing out, therefore, what this chapter does and does not set out to achieve. There have been many attempts down the years to classify and categorise questioning and some of those classifications are more useful than others. Indeed, you will look briefly at the 'grand-daddy' of them all, Bloom's taxonomy, below. I will, inevitably, draw on some of these ideas with what I'm offering here, but the aim is to simplify matters rather than offer a comprehensive synthesis of everything that is out there at this time. In so doing, I will, hopefully, offer some focus and clarity for trainees not necessarily available elsewhere. The point of this chapter, therefore, is not simply to present a rehash of all the different questions you might ask and entreat with you to ensure that there is a balance between such questions in your teaching. The point is to enable you to link the questions you ask to what you're trying to achieve learning-wise in the classroom. To do this, you will start by unpicking why you would want to ask questions in the first place and link that to the effect of asking different sorts of questions. You will look closely at what is considered to be just as crucial as asking a good or appropriate question in the first place – that is, what you do with the response(s) you get. This is the start of making the connection between the beginnings of dialogue and dialogic teaching and questioning.

That said, there is a long-standing and ongoing problem with the balance of questioning in teaching in that teachers are consistently told, by research, that they still dominate classroom talk and ask too many closed questions. However, planning to ask higher order or open questions is all well and good and, indeed, you would be well advised to do this as a trainee, but, in the long run, this approach can feel a little stilted and unresponsive unless the level and balance of your questioning becomes almost second nature. The development of this skill is dependent on three interconnected requirements, illustrated in Figure 8.1, below, which will be returned to in the summary. First, the depth of your subject knowledge is crucial to your ability to ask good questions, as is your knowledge of individual pupils as learners. In addition, you need to be as highly engaged with the content of your teaching as you would want your pupils to be. Thus, you need to ask yourself, as you go along, as many questions as you actually ask out loud – such as 'How might I model/scaffold this differently to overcome Lucy's misconception?' or 'Does Sam really understand that? – I'll ask him to explain how he did it'. In other words, you should be actively engaged in making sense of the pupils' understanding of their learning, and it is as important to develop this disposition as it is to be aware of the sorts of questions available to you. Some call the practice that characterises this attentiveness 'reflection-in-action' (*see* Schön, 1991) but others would say, more simply, that you need to be 'switched on' and 'in the zone'.

Incidentally, in the classroom, the evidence of your deployment of these three requirements is what will distinguish you as a professional. Nowhere is your professional autonomy more apparent than when you're in the heat of the action making informed decisions, about how you might best progress the pupils' learning: day-by-day, hour-by-hour, minute-by-minute.

 Reflection and discussion activity

Mentor: think about a trainee who has struggled to make progress. To what extent, in your experience, did gaps in the requirements for effective questioning in Figure 8.1 contribute to that lack of progress? Discuss this with your trainee to explore the importance of effective questioning and what will help a trainee to develop effective questioning?

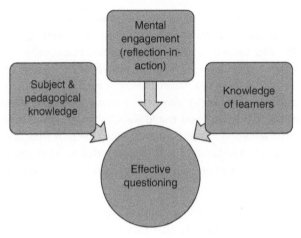

Figure 8.1 Requirements for effective questioning

Motives for asking questions

 Reflection and discussion activity

Trainee: what do you think the teacher wants or is trying to achieve by asking each of these questions? How do the questions differ in their purpose?

- When was the Great Fire of London?

- Can you explain how you did that?

- In your investigation, what have you found out about triangles?

- What did you find difficult about that?

- Do you like this painting? How could it be improved?

As implied above, the question that teachers don't ask often enough is what might be called the 'meta-question' – i.e. you don't ask enough questions about our questions. The importance of questioning is acknowledged and, in an attempt to become more effective and add a veneer of sophistication questioning, you may dip into, say, Bloom's taxonomy (sketched out below), to locate where and how you might throw some higher order questions into your repertoire. The talk, in educational contexts, is often quite loosely about 'open' and 'closed' questions, 'high-order' and 'low-order' questions without spending a great deal of time unpicking what these ideas mean. As is usual in the professional academic sphere, you can go to the literature and unearth any number of articles unpicking questioning in a sophisticated way. But, in reality, teachers don't spend a great deal of time brushing up on definitions of a variety of relevant concepts before heading off to work in a morning. Thus, you tend to use terms that denote concepts in an 'everyday' simple sense and make necessary assumptions about what your audiences (the people you are talking to and emailing, etc.) are going to understand by them.

To illustrate this point, 56 postgraduate trainee teachers were asked informally how they understood the four terms mentioned above. 'Closed' questions are generally taken by trainees to be ones that require one correct and mostly 'one word' answer, whereas 'open' questions either have 'more than one right answer' or answers that are 'a matter of opinion'. Low-order questions tend to be equated with closed questions and high-order questions are either synonymous with open questions and/or they are questions that 'make you think', or ones that require the use of 'complex reasoning skills'. Trainees also recognise that for some (generally lower order questions) 'you either know the answer or you don't' and for others (i.e. the ones that require 'complex reasoning'), you can construct a response on the spot by synthesising information you already have or that you have been provided with. For questions that boil down to a 'matter of opinion', including questions with a moral dimension, people ideally use the information they already have to hand to make a balanced judgement. However, if you are particularly prejudiced in a certain way, then you may have already made up your mind on some questions, despite evidence to the contrary.

Trainees and qualified teachers are often guided towards the categorisation already mentioned called Bloom's taxonomy, and/or its subsequent revisions, as an aid for developing their own questioning techniques. The taxonomy is, basically, a hierarchical classification of cognitive (and other) processes which, at its most basic level, involves us 'remembering' certain knowledge and, at its zenith, sees us synthesising or 'creating' new knowledge. As you can see on the left-hand side of Table 8.1, there are four other levels of cognitive activity in between – i.e. 'evaluating', 'analysing', 'applying' and 'understanding'. These are easier to understand in relation to questioning if each level is related to a set of verbs and a particular question.

Over its very long lifespan, the taxonomy has been tweaked a little, but the basic structure is still recognisable and it is strongly recommend to anyone interested in unlocking the true power and potential of questioning in a dialogic classroom. There are much more comprehensive (and colourful) guides to this taxonomy available in books and via the internet which give a far greater range of verbs and associated questions and activities. However, many of these, useful though they are, can be rather too much to take in at once – particularly in the context of all the other new information that trainees have to assimilate in a short space of time.

You don't just ask 'higher order' questions for the sake of it. Here, there is a simpler categorisation of questioning based upon your motives for wanting to ask those questions in the first place. So, instead of giving you a copy of Bloom's taxonomy and letting you decide how you apply it to what you want to achieve in the classroom, this will begin with the things commonly done in the classrooms and link those to the sorts of questions that might be asked. Furthermore, in this chapter, you need to think about what you do in the crucial moments *after* you've asked a question. (See Anderson and Krathwohl (2001) for further reading.)

Table 8.1 *The basic structure of Bloom's taxonomy*

Category	Key verbs	Examples of questions
Synthesising (creating)	adapt, predict, design, imagine	How could you adapt and improve on this design?
Evaluating	judge, weigh up, assess, test	What do you like about this painting and why?
Analysing	sort, organise, classify	What have these shapes got in common?
Applying	show, represent, demonstrate	Can you give me an example of how evaporation can be helpful to us?
Understanding	explain, compare, contrast, rephrase	Can you explain what happens if you put salt into water?
Remembering	show, tell, recall, recite	What are the colours of the rainbow?

Here, for simplicity's sake, I will argue that our motives for using questioning tend to fall into three broad categories that I've termed 'motives'. First, we might want to acquire information on the current state of pupils' learning; second, we might want to use questioning as an opportunity to develop that learning further; third, we might want pupils to evaluate the knowledge they already have, both about themselves and the wider world. Either way, responses to questions should provide you and your pupils with information about what to do next. If you now go back to the reflection box at the end of the introduction, can you see how the questions given reflect one or more of these three motives? You may or may not have thought of other reasons to ask questions, but they ought to fall into the very broad areas I've described. Table 8.2 summarises *the three motives* and the educational purpose which they serve.

Motive 1: to test and probe knowledge and understanding

By asking questions with this motive in mind, you are collecting useful assessment information (see Chapter 7) on what knowledge pupils have already got or have acquired as a result of your inspirational teaching. Learning in this context is often observed as the replication of a desired behaviour or, in other words, via the supply of a correct answer. This information could, if you do anything with it, help you to decide who needs further help and who is ready to take the next steps you've planned for their learning. In this sense, you are *testing* their knowledge. You might decide, as a result of your testing, that some of the answers, although correct, didn't give you enough information to satisfy you that the respondents really did know their stuff. Or, in other cases, you might have received a completely wrong answer. Either way, you might then engage in asking *probing* questions in order to ascertain the depth of their knowledge or the nature of their misconception.

Table 8.2 Motives for questioning: a summary

Motive: I want . . .	Purpose: in order . . .	Questions: by asking . . .
1. Questioning to test and probe knowledge and understanding		
. . . to **test** pupils' knowledge and explore reasoning through 'probing' understanding . . .	. . . to plan the next steps accurately and identify gaps in knowledge. This is an opportunity for pupils to recall previous learning at beginning of a lesson or recap as part of plenary or mini-plenary. Probing is necessary to elicit clarification and to enable pupils to cement their understanding through articulation.	What is the name of . . . ? Where/What/When . . . ? Can you remember . . . ? Can you explain why . . . ?
. . . to enable pupils to **apply** given knowledge in a new situation in order to solve problems . . .	. . . to give pupils the opportunity to demonstrate that they can apply technical skills and knowledge in a new context. Demonstration of this ability is indicative of independent working and pupils' level of understanding.	Can you use what you know about X in order to solve Y? What does this tell you about . . . ? Can you explain that using these words in your answer?
. . . to enable pupils to **analyse** phenomena (e.g. numbers, words/ texts, objects, sounds) based on given/ defined properties . . .	. . . to ensure that pupils are able to recognise and sort members of particular groups (e.g. even numbers, mammals, fiction, planets). At this level, the teacher defines the criteria for sorting ('Can you show me all the yellow ones?') or does the sorting herself ('What have these got in common?'). Here we establish the 'ground rules' that can enable success in the next section. For example, we need to recognise the key characteristics of a haiku or a piano symphony before we can create our own by applying the technical skills we are developing.	Can you sort these objects according to these characteristics? What have these got in common? Why is X an example of Y? Can you *find another* example of X?

(Continued)

Table 8.2 (Continued)

Motive: I want . . .	Purpose: in order . . .	Questions: by asking . . .
2. Questioning to generate knowledge		
. . . to help pupils to generate/**create** (i.e. **synthesise**) their own classifications and/or examples of phenomena . . .	. . . to enable pupils to make choices and use their **judgement** so that they can: - explore and choose appropriate alternatives; - reject inappropriate choices; - explore connections between and among groups; - generate their own examples.	Can you *find a better example* of X (e.g. an adjective, an appropriate material) and explain why it is better? Can you create *another or different* example of X (e.g. a haiku, a waterproof shelter, a number sequence)?
. . . to lead pupils to **investigate** a range of alternative possibilities and draw conclusions from their findings (**i.e. test hypotheses**)	. . . to hand the questioning over to the pupils so they can discover things for themselves. Investigations across the curriculum where pupils and teachers ask the question '**What if I change this?**' or '**What is the effect of doing (or not doing) that?**' are possibly the most powerful questions in the generation of new knowledge.	What if I change X? What can you tell me about . . . ? How have you come to that conclusion?
3. Questioning to problematise knowledge		
. . . to enable pupils to **self-evaluate** and reflect on the learning process as well as the content . . .	. . . to promote independence through the development of pupils' self-awareness as learners. . . . for pupils to become aware of their strengths and areas for improvement. They should be encouraged to articulate their needs as learners. They need to be clear when they have met the learning intentions.	What did I find hard about that? How do I know I've met the success criteria? What could you (or I) do better next time?
. . . to enable pupils to **interpret** and weigh up contradictory evidence	. . . to explore issues where there are differing points of view can be explored and resolved through *dialogue* (as opposed to debate).	Why do you think . . . ? What is the evidence for . . . ? What is your opinion on . . . ?
. . . to enable pupils to make **judgements** based on moral reasoning.	. . . to promote moral development. This can be overlooked and is a topic in itself. Pupils should be given opportunities to understand that 'right' and 'wrong' are not absolutes or givens, but are negotiated in social and cultural contexts.	What would you do in this situation? Is it right that . . . ?

- When you are asking 'testing' questions, ensure that you also ask children, where appropriate, to explain how they arrived at their answers – i.e. don't forget to 'probe'.

  o At other times, you might want to explore the pupils' ability to select and apply the knowledge you're reasonably confident they have through giving them a *problem to solve*. Here, you could either expect children to respond in a particular way, or you could accept more creative solutions. The ability to select and *apply* knowledge and resources in a new context is a powerful indication of understanding. Pupils need to make the connection between knowledge and skill acquired in relatively abstract circumstances, and how such learning may be applied to solve 'real-life' problems.

- When you are asking questions that demonstrate the ability to apply knowledge, ensure that you have also helped pupils to develop strategies for problem solving in a range of contexts.

  o The application of knowledge can also be extended to classification activities where pupils sort objects or phenomena into groups according to identifiable characteristics. For example, they might have learned that triangles are shapes with three sides and you might ask them to extract all the triangles from a group of polygons. However . . .

- When asking pupils to engage in classification activity, be clear, with yourself, what the purpose of the exercise is.

  o This is because the motivation for asking pupils to classify could be to get them to apply what they have already learned ('Can you find all the triangles?'), it could be to lead them towards a specific conclusion ('What have these got in common?' 'Can you sort these into two groups?' 'Which is the odd one out?', etc.), or it could be to generate new knowledge by giving pupils the responsibility for the sorting criteria ('Can you explain how you sorted these?').

Motive 2: to generate knowledge

Do note here, then, that there is not an absolutely clear cut-off between probing knowledge, extending knowledge and generating new knowledge as your questions may have the effect of facilitating all three at once – just be clear about what you want your questions to achieve. Your prime motivation for questioning in this category is to develop critical learning that has already taken place or to promote completely new learning altogether. Learning here is seen as a process of intra-mental activity (i.e. thinking on your own to make sense of the world) and/or inter-mental activity (i.e. things shared among groups of learners who learn from each other). Thus, in the fullness of time, pupils should be asking others and themselves at least as many questions (both out loud and 'inside their heads') as they are asked in the course of their learning.

When basic factual knowledge has been established and probed, pupils can be encouraged to become creative with it and extend it further – that is to say, when they are beginning to know where 'things fit' through classification activities, our further questions can help them to:

- explore and choose appropriate alternatives – e.g. choosing the right materials for a project;

- reject inappropriate choices – e.g. substituting one word for a better one;

- explore connections between and among groups – e.g. food webs, nouns and adjectives;

- generate their own examples – e.g. now you know how a torch works, can you design and make your own?

Such activities are connected with the development of particular technical skills, which are crucial if creative activity is going to produce anything with purpose and value.

Thus, the implication in using questioning to extend and generate knowledge is that teachers do not simply (in the words of the Teachers' Standards) *impart knowledge* and then test it, but that, through our questioning, we *facilitate* an environment where pupils can co-construct 'new' knowledge among themselves. Investigations are potentially the most powerful activity for the creation of this new knowledge and the most powerful question of all questions supports this motivation – the one that starts with *'What if . . . ?'*

A *'What if . . . ?'* question is applicable across all curricula, for all age groups and is one that learners should be given the opportunity to ask themselves and each other regularly. It relates, in terms of Bloom's taxonomy, most closely to the idea of 'synthesis' and the creation of new knowledge. *'What if . . . ?'* questions are also connected with 'exploratory talk' where pupils are not afraid to tentatively explore their own and others' ideas where, in addition to *'What if . . . ?'* they also, typically, use language (or exploratory actions associated with such language), for example:

- *'I wonder if it would be better to do it like this?', 'Perhaps we could try . . . ?', 'Could we add another . . . ?'* or *'What about using . . . ?', for example.*

Investigating is associated with *possibility*, which, in itself, is associated with *changing variables*. Most obviously, this applies to maths or science investigations where we might be encouraged to ask such questions as:

- *'What if I change the amount of X?'* or *'What if I flip the shape over?'*

But it applies across the whole curriculum. In English we might ask:

- *'What if the story didn't end like this?'* or *'What if I use a different adjective here?'*

Or, in music:

- *'What if we use a tambourine to represent the wind?'*

Of course, there is more to extending and generating knowledge than asking, or getting pupils to ask, *'What if . . . ?'* questions. However, the incorporation of authentic opportunities for pupils to engage in investigative exploration has the power to unleash the potential of creativity and independence that is so often missed when teachers simply 'impart knowledge', test it and move on.

Motive 3: to problematise knowledge

Discovering new things about the world through investigation, even when supported by high-order questioning, can still be about right and wrong answers. There is nothing wrong with that, but you may, from time to time, require children to *make a reasoned decision or judgement* on a question that does not, necessarily, have a right or a wrong answer. Here, you are asking children to engage with knowledge as *contingent*. This means understanding (or beginning to understand) that your beliefs about aspects of the world are dependent upon what you know at any one time and that, with new knowledge, those beliefs are open to change. This idea is linked closely with moral development. Also, the previous section mentioned pupils engaging in 'exploratory' talk, but here, for the first time, you meet the idea of learning as a sociocultural process being driven exclusively through dialogue. 'Dialogue', which will be considered in the next section, in a social context, should enable pupils to form and re-form their ideas through listening to and taking into account the ideas of others. 'Others' might be 'experts', those directly affected by the issues in question or neutral observers. Whoever they are in dialogue with, you should provide opportunities for pupils to interpret contradictory evidence on issues, particularly issues important to them, by asking:

- *What would you like to happen here?, Why do you think . . . ?, What is the evidence for . . . ?, What is your opinion on . . . ?, Is it right that . . . ?*

You should also give pupils the opportunity to begin to make *moral judgements*. They should be enabled to understand that, ultimately 'right' and 'wrong' are not absolutes or givens, but are negotiated in social and cultural contexts. To answer the question, *'Why is it wrong to run in the corridor?'* the respondent could either refer to a higher authority and reply *'Because Mrs X says so'* or *'Because it's against the rules [which were given to us by Mrs X]'* or they might deploy some reasoning as to why this might not be a good idea. Although *'Because I say so'* is an expedient justification in certain circumstances, how would you want educated citizens to weigh up more controversial issues such as abortion, gay marriage, assisted dying, the death penalty, etc.? Would you want them to have carefully considered the arguments from all sides, or would you be content for them to defer completely to the 'higher' authority – for example, the law as it stands, politicians, elders, religious and community leaders?

Alongside this process, you need to enable pupils to *self-evaluate* and reflect on the learning process as well as the content. Children need to be aware of their own strengths and areas for improvement. They should be encouraged to articulate their needs as learners and they need to be clear about when they have met the learning intentions. In other words, we should encourage children to ask themselves questions such as:

- *'What did I find hard about that?', 'How do I know I have met the success criteria?'* or *'What could I do to improve?'*

Asking the right questions for the right reasons and at the right time is crucial, but what happens next, after a question has been asked, is at least as important and deserves similar attention. The next section will explore the opportunities and pitfalls associated with promoting dialogue in the classroom.

Find out more from . . . reading

Alexander, RJ (2015) *Towards Dialogic Teaching: Rethinking classroom talk* (4th edn). York: Dialogos.

This book explores dialogic teaching and learning and why it is an important approach.

Taking it further . . . research

Dialogic Teaching Report: improving talk for teaching and learning

The Education Endowment Foundation conducted a dialogic teaching research project which was designed to improve the quality of classroom talk as a means of increasing pupils' engagement, learning, and attainment . . . . It emphasised dialogue through which pupils learn to reason, discuss, argue and explain, in order to develop their higher order thinking and articulacy. The report also provides useful background information about dialogic teaching.

https://educationendowmentfoundation.org.uk/public/files/Projects/Evaluation_Reports/Dialogic_ Teaching_Evaluation_Report.pdf (accessed 11 November 2019).

Responding to answers: supporting exploratory talk and dialogue

One issue that can emerge as the result of a barrage of quick-fire *Motive 1: questioning* (which can appear to the casual observer as a pacey, engaging, interactive episode) is that the opportunity for extending learning is closed right down or neglected altogether. In an attempt to get 'coverage' and full participation, you might forget to probe pupils' understanding and their ability to apply it. It would be much better, and potentially more effective for everyone, if you spent longer exploring individual responses and giving pupils a chance to reason. In recent years, many teachers have increased 'wait time' for pupils to respond to questions and have also used 'talk/response partners' to help children to do their reasoning with each other *before* they respond. Thus, the time given with questions tends to be 'front-loaded' in the sense that much of the reasoning is meant to take place before the response is given. There are, however, problems with this approach, especially when it is taken by trainees. First, if the question requires a right/wrong answer or a one-word answer (such as 'What is 3 x 4?' or 'Can you give me an example of an adjective?'), there is, potentially, not a lot there to talk about. Second, and linked to the first problem, when one partner supplies the answer immediately because they 'just know it', then again, there is not a lot to talk about.

- Don't be a slave to coverage – having lollipop sticks with names on to make sure you have asked everyone a question is fine, as is the idea of 'talk partners' – but don't let uncritical use of these techniques get in the way of learning.

This section will refer to two sorts of talk (although there are, arguably, more) that we may engage children in. 'Exploratory talk' has already been mentioned; this is where pupils play with ideas, think out loud and make suggestions, etc. This sort of talk becomes 'dialogic' when there is a *reciprocal* aspect to it. This means that dialogue is a two-way street of *contribution* and *accommodation*. As such, not only should those engaged in dialogue be contributing their ideas and thinking to the talk, they should also be accommodating, or, at least, open to accommodating ideas shared by the other(s).

Dialogue, then, is more than mere talk or conversation, and it is quite difficult to facilitate. However, if it is equated with 'talk' (as tends to happen), then you are not likely to ask questions that can lead to productive dialogue. First, think before asking a question – how or where is the answer coming from?

- Is it already there in some way (i.e. something you assume/hope they've already learned)?

- Are you looking for open-ended, exploratory talk, leading to the creation of a new idea?

- Does it demand reasoning, and, if so, present an opportunity for dialogue?

- Or are you just 'fishing' and/or will guessing be the order of the day?

This thinking will determine the 'mileage' you are going to get out of your questions in terms of dialogue and learning through dialogue. However, dialogue is also difficult because of the assumptions it makes about those engaged in it. There is an implication that all parties will have something to contribute and all parties will take on board new knowledge as a result of the interaction. The focus here is going to concentrate on those moments after a question has been posed and how you might facilitate, rather than stifle, extended talk and reasoning as a gentle way into a dialogic approach. For a start, take the following conversation (the children have been learning about the seasons).

Teacher: *Tom, what's your favourite time of year?*

Tom: *Christmas.*

Teacher: *Why do you like Christmas?*

Tom: *Presents.*

Teacher: *OK, Tom. Laura, what's your favourite time of year?*

Laura: *Christmas.*

Teacher: *Hands-up if your favourite time of year is Christmas.*

[Everyone puts their hand up]

Although the teacher attempted to get Tom to share his reasons, his focus on Christmas and the subsequent, rather unproductive conversation meant that a learning opportunity was closed down rather quickly. The teacher's role has been quite passive, Tom has (quite innocently) usurped the agenda and the opportunity for productive talk has closed right down. Realistically, we do need to *engineer* and *steer* classroom talk towards productive enquiry – or, in other words, *dialogue*. Below is an example of how the talk might have facilitated reciprocity:

Teacher: *Tom, remember we have been learning about the seasons – look at the posters we've been using. So, Tom, what's your favourite time of year – what's your favourite season?*

Tom: *Winter.*

Teacher: *Laura, what's your favourite season?*

Laura: *I like the autumn.*

Teacher: *Tom, explain to Laura all the things you like about winter. When you've done that, Tom, Laura will explain to you why she likes the autumn and what's special about it.*

          [A couple of minutes later]

Teacher: *Laura, what did Tom tell you about the winter? Did you agree with him?*

There is no dialogue per se evident in this extract, but the important thing to note is how the teacher has taken the time to set up the possibility of reciprocity – i.e. an exchange and modification of views. In order to do this, she has:

* recapped previous learning briefly to jog memories and give a focus/context;

* anticipated deviation or blind-alleys by clarifying the subject matter;

* provided opportunity for pupils to share their personal knowledge and opinions derived from that knowledge;

* provided opportunity for pupils to go on to share reasoning and, possibly, learn or consolidate something and modify a previously held viewpoint.

This example gives children the opportunity to *analyse* the information they already have and *synthesise* it with new information provided by their partner. Thus, Laura could, potentially, remind Tom or even introduce him to aspects of autumn that cause him to *re-evaluate* his view of it. As such, the teacher's motive for setting up this exchange sits across the categories of 'extending' and 'evaluating' knowledge described above.

Although it is more difficult to achieve, dialogue can also generate completely new, factual knowledge about the world, particularly if pupils are engaged, initially, in exploratory talk using the *'What if . . . ?'* approach.

 Reflection and discussion activity

Reflection

Which of these *facts* (i.e. none of these things are a matter of opinion) about the world could, in theory, be *discovered* by primary-age pupils through practical activity and dialogue?

- The need to move from non-standard to standardised measures in maths.

- The relationship between the circumference and diameter of a circle.

- The workings of a volcano.

- The number and fate of Henry VIII's wives.

- How to mix orange paint.

The first two examples in the reflection and discussion activity have been done, successfully, in Key Stage 2. The third example would probably require doctoral level science/geology and enormous resources, although there's nothing wrong with asking 'How do you think this works?' The answer to the fourth item is never going to emerge through the power of reason alone – it simply requires a book or a broadband connection. Learning to mix orange paint is certainly exploratory in nature, but whether you would promote extended dialogue through it is debatable.

Establishing factual/practical knowledge through dialogue can be a relatively lengthy process and, for many, too risky and haphazard. For example, giving children a ruler and getting them to measure things in centimetres will get much quicker results than setting up a dialogical scenario where, eventually, children need to come to the conclusion that we need to standardise our measuring system. As professionals, you have to make choices. But do be aware, as mentioned at the beginning of this section, of the difference between *interactive pace* (i.e. how much seems to be getting done in the classroom) and *cognitive pace* or how thoroughly things are getting done.

 Chapter summary

This chapter has related the sorts of questions you can ask and our motives for asking those questions. These motives are based upon the educational opportunities you wish to promote in your classrooms. However, merely asking the right questions does not necessarily maximise these opportunities, so how you are able to follow up on children's responses becomes just as crucial. Below is a summary of some of the obstacles trainees can face when trying to promote learning through questioning and extended talk, and how they might be overcome. It is clear that to surmount some of these obstacles you will require skills developed through life-long learning and experience – but this is a good place to start.

My pupils are reluctant to contribute

Spend time developing the right classroom climate for open talk by:

(Continued)

(Continued)

- modelling yourself as a learner/co-learner;

- promoting enquiry-based learning – plan to take the opportunities described in this chapter;

- actively encouraging contributions – take all of them seriously and model respect;

- giving time for pupils to answer *and* ask questions.

They do contribute, but are not very good at explaining their answers

- Know when you're merely testing knowledge already acquired – and get a balance. Pupils will not develop this ability if they are not given the opportunity.

- Be clear exactly what you want from questioning and classroom talk: is it dialogue you're after and, if so, think how your questions facilitate (or inhibit) dialogic talk?

I sometimes don't know how to respond to a misconception effectively

There is no getting round the fact that, to be effective in your questioning, you need good subject knowledge, beyond the level at which you're teaching. This will develop in time but, in the meantime:

- research the subject matter you are going to be engaging with – don't 'wing it';

- be ready with alternative resources to model, scaffold or present ideas in different ways.

But, beware! Supposedly knowing (or not knowing) your stuff can lead to a one-dimensional approach driven by your own 'superior' knowledge of the subject and where *you* think the pupils need to go. Some pupils will see things in different, yet legitimate, ways.

My pupils seem to 'go off at a tangent' when answering questions and investigating

We often close opportunities down – from the pressures that are on us to 'move on', but also from our own insecurity (see previous points on misconceptions): what can seem to be off-topic or plain 'wrong' contributions.

- Always ask pupils to explain themselves – they might even know more than you!

- Take time to 'tune in' and explore where the respondent is 'coming from' and run with their line of thinking – keep an open mind-set.

- Be as engaged with the thinking process as you expect your pupils to be.

You need to develop the ability to think on your feet. There is only a certain extent to which questioning and dialogue can be pre-planned. The key to this whole chapter has been *recognising and exploiting opportunities*. Hopefully, you will, in your practice, begin to recognise more and miss fewer.

Find out more from ... reading

Alexander, RJ (2015) Dialogic teaching and the study of classroom talk: a developmental bibliography.

Available online at: **www.robinalexander.org.uk/wp-content/uploads/2012/10/Alexander-dialogic-teaching-bibliography1.pdf** (accessed 11 November 2017).

Dawes, L (2014) Organising effective classroom talk. In Cremin, T and Arthur, J (eds) *Learning to Teach in the Primary School* (3rd edn). London: Routledge.

Eaude, T (2015) *New Perspectives on Young Children's Moral Education: Developing character through a virtue ethics approach*. London: Bloomsbury.

References

Anderson, LW and Krathwohl, DR (2001) *A Taxonomy for Learning, Teaching, and Assessing* (abridged edn). Boston, MA: Allyn & Bacon.

Schön, D (1991) *The Reflective Practitioner*. Aldershot: Ashgate Publishing.

9
Behaviour

Emma Clarke and Steve McNichol

This chapter will

- consider the expectations set out in the Teachers' Standards (2012) relevant to managing pupils' behaviour (Standard 7);

- support you in developing an understanding of how to establish a 'framework for discipline' using a structure for establishing a safe classroom environment through rules, rewards and sanctions to manage pupils' behaviour effectively;

- challenge you to consider alternative perspectives, by exploring the benefits of adopting restorative and solution-focused approaches to managing behaviour.

Links to the Teachers' Standards

1   **Set high expectations which inspire, motivate and challenge pupils**, specifically

- establish a safe and stimulating environment for pupils, rooted in mutual respect.

7   **Manage behaviour effectively to ensure a good and safe learning environment,** specifically:

- have clear rules and routines for behaviour in classrooms, and take responsibility for promoting good and courteous behaviour both in classrooms and around the school, in accordance with the school's behaviour policy;

- have high expectations of behaviour, and establish a framework for discipline with a range of strategies, using praise, sanctions and rewards consistently and fairly;

- manage classes effectively, using approaches which are appropriate to pupils' needs in order to involve and motivate them;

- maintain good relationships with pupils, exercise appropriate authority, and act decisively when necessary.

Introduction

Promoting positive behaviours within the classroom has been a priority for many years in education. In fact, it is something that new teachers state as an aspect they worry about when starting with a new class. Teachers must create a classroom in which pupils feel safe and learning can take place effectively. When considering success in achieving this, much is determined by how you *manage* the behaviour of the pupils within the classroom, keeping disruption to a minimum and on-task behaviour to a maximum. This chapter will introduce some main approaches to achieving this, taking into account both theory and practice.

The chapter will address how you, the trainee teacher, can work towards meeting the requirements of the Teachers' Standards in terms of behaviour management and how school mentors can support you. It will identify key themes and explore how these can be developed so that you can demonstrate competence and confidence in this area to support your journey towards becoming an effective teacher.

Establishing a 'framework for discipline'

One of the requirements of the Teachers' Standards (2012) states that teachers must *establish a framework for discipline with a range of strategies, using praise, sanctions and rewards consistently and fairly* (Standard 7). This is very much in line with a behaviourist approach (discussed briefly in Chapters 3 and 4), often seen in practice through Canter's Assertive Discipline approach. This approach was first published by Marlene and Lee Canter in 1976 and has become firmly established as the most common systematic approach to behaviour management in schools, based on a structure of creating rules, rewarding pupils for following these rules, and applying sanctions to any pupil who breaks the rules.

 Reflection and discussion activity

Reflection

Trainee: read your school's behaviour policy. What aspects of a rewards and sanctions approach are used in your school? How important are rewards and sanctions as a way of managing behaviour in your school?

Mentor: consider the different behaviour policies you have seen throughout your career and whether rewards and sanctions have been the foundation of the approach. Which reward systems seemed to be most motivational for pupils?

Discussion

Trainee and mentor: focus on the rewards system in the class. When is this mostly used? Are there any times in lessons when rewards are used less often? Do you think there is a reason for this?

Find out more from ... books

Canter, L (2010) *Lee Canter's Assertive Discipline: Positive behavior management for today's classroom* (4th edn). Bloomington, IN: Solution Tree Press.

Rules

Often, schools can seem full of rules. Classroom rules, whole-school rules, playground rules, lunchtime rules and uniform rules are often all found in one school. But who decides the rules? How should the rules be worded so that they are clearly understood? How many rules should there be?

The first thing to decide upon when writing school rules is who should be involved in the process. Essentially, this comes down to two choices – do you, as the teacher, take full control, or are the pupils involved?

The framework of Assertive Discipline very much encourages the use of *teacher-formulated* rules on the basis that pupils need to know what expectations you have of them. These rules should then be communicated to pupils with no potential for alteration or adaptation. Tom Bennett, recently the chair of the ITT Behaviour Working Group and government-appointed 'behaviour tsar', also supports this approach on the basis that *I know [as the teacher] what they need because I am an adult. This is not a democracy* (Bennett, 2016). However, in many schools, teachers are now encouraged to involve pupils in the writing of class rules to support and encourage their contribution to the classroom environment. It can be argued that when pupils are involved in creating the rules, they are more likely to comply with them. Often, this leads to a renaming of expectations from 'rules' to 'class agreement' or 'code of conduct', to reflect the fact that pupil voice has been taken into account when setting class expectations. It is for the teacher to decide how they choose to approach the process of setting rules when they have their own classroom in which to do so, but it is worth giving consideration to how other teachers in the school go about this and which approach you feel is most appropriate.

Case study

Sabina is a School Direct trainee teacher who has a Key Stage 2 class. On her first day with the pupils, she asks them to write down key words to describe the kind of behaviour they think makes coming to school enjoyable. When Sabina collects the pupil's ideas, words such as kind, helpful, considerate, polite, honest, respectful, careful and gentle feature prominently. As a result, Sabina uses these words to write a 'class agreement' on a large piece of gold paper:

(Continued)

(Continued)

We are gentle.

We are kind and considerate.

We respect other people and all property.

We are honest and always tell the truth.

We help other people.

We are always polite.

The next day, Sabina asks each pupil in the class to paint their thumb and print on to the class agreement as a sign that they agree to follow this.

When writing classroom rules or agreements, it is important to consider how these are going to be worded. There are two main ways of wording rules: *positively* (things you want the pupils to do) or *negatively* (things you don't want the pupils to do). For example, 'be kind to others' (positive) could also be phrased 'do not be mean' (negative). Assertive Discipline encourages the use of both positively stated and negatively stated rules, such as 'follow directions' (positive), 'no teasing or name calling' (negative) and 'no swearing' (negative) (Canter, 2010, p23). Others claim that rules should always be *phrased in a positive rather than a negative way* (Cowley, 2014, p158) as negative rules instruct pupils what *not* to do, rather than what *to* do. This is more likely to lead you to over-use sanctions rather than promote positive interactions with pupils. Because your primary responsibility involves the creation of positive behaviour, rather than the elimination of negative behaviour, it is therefore our opinion that it is preferable to use positively stated rules.

 Reflection and discussion activity

Reflection

Trainee: look at the rules in the classroom. Are they stated positively or negatively?

Mentor: when you observe trainees and comment on behaviour management, do you focus on moral or procedural rules?

Discussion

Discuss the rules you feel are most important in the classroom and in the school as a whole. How can you communicate this to pupils in the class? How can a trainee teacher model and reinforce expectations during lessons?

Find out more from . . . books

Rogers, WA (2012) *You Know the Fair Rule: Effective behaviour management in schools* (3rd edn). London: Pearson Education.

Taking it further . . . research

Goodman, JF (2006) School discipline in moral disarray. *Journal of Moral Education*, 35: 213-30.

Rewards

As with rules, often schools have many different rewards systems that aim to promote and reinforce good behaviour. Often these include a mixture of:

- *Individual rewards* such as merits, stickers and individual 'points'. Often these are collected and prizes given to pupils who reach set amounts. However, one-off rewards such as certificates (perhaps called 'Star of the Week') are also commonly used. Other reward systems rely on a raffle, with pupils earning individual tickets for a set period of time and the winning pupil earning the prize when the raffle is drawn.

- *Group rewards* such as table points, whole-class rewards and whole-school house systems. Often, these are collected by pupils and combined together, with a prize being given to a winning team at a certain point in time (usually at the end of a term) or when a set amount is achieved.

As much as all of these reward systems may appear to be promoting good behaviour, they have to be carefully considered as they can have a detrimental impact on behaviour if they are not used thoughtfully. Indeed, the concepts behind some of the systems are inherently flawed. For example, pupils quickly realise that raffle-ticket reward systems rely more on luck at the point of the draw than on their behaviour, and that in a class the probability of winning is extremely low. Likewise, group rewards can often cause resentment among pupils. First, group reward systems reward pupils who may not have earned any of the points. Second, group reward systems fail to reward pupils who have earned a significant number of points but are not in the winning team. This often makes group reward systems unfair in the eyes of pupils.

Find out more from . . . books

Dix, P (2017 *When the Adults Change, Everything Changes.* Carmerthon: Independent Thinking Press.

Case study

Kingfisher Primary School uses a reward system based on merits. All pupils have a merit card which has 50 small boxes inside. Each time a pupil demonstrates behaviour that is above and beyond the expectation, staff sign one of the boxes. When all the pupil's boxes have been signed, they earn a badge that they are able to pin on their school uniform or take home, which is presented in a whole-school assembly.

Over their time in school, pupils build up their merits and badges.

Table 9.1 Building up merits and badges

Number of merits	Badge
50	Bronze Shield
100	Bronze Star
150	Silver Shield
200	Silver Star
250	Gold Shield
300	Gold Star

This system motivates the pupils to strive for the next badge and maintain good standards of behaviour.

However, rewards must be managed carefully. First, it is important not to over-reward. If too many rewards are given out, they quickly lose value and pupils will come to expect to be rewarded for simply doing what is normally expected. It is also important to give a reward only when a pupil shows behaviour *above and beyond* what would normally be expected of them. Second, over-rewarding poses the very real risk of stifling pupils' intrinsic motivation. If pupils are only behaving positively in order to achieve a reward, once the reward is removed, so the inclination to behave in this manner might also disappear. Of course, under-rewarding is also detrimental, as pupils will soon give up if they feel the rewards are unlikely to be given even when they display positive behaviour. Getting the balance right is the key to a reward system, but there is no hard-and-fast rule that can be applied, as no two groups of pupils are the same.

A common, non-tangible reward is that of pupil praise. This is the main reward that pupils actually experience in school (Cowley, 2014) and it is well established that teacher praise can have a positive impact on behaviour (Floress and Jenkins, 2015). As with tangible rewards, it is claimed that positive praise will motivate pupils to repeat appropriate behaviour and so reduce disruption (Porter, 2014). However, as with tangible rewards, it is important not to praise too frequently as this can soon become undervalued, less powerful and therefore less likely to impact on behaviour. Similarly, it is important not to exaggerate praise ('Wow, you are sitting on that chair brilliantly! Amazing! Fantastic! I have never seen anyone sit on a chair as well as that in my life!'), as pupils will soon realise that your praise is false and, therefore, will not value it.

In conclusion, reward systems and praise can be a powerful tool in promoting positive behaviour in the classroom. However, choosing the correct system and getting the balance right in terms of tangible rewards and praise is the key to success in this area.

 Reflection and discussion activity

Reflection

Trainee: observe your mentor (or another teacher).

How do pupils react when they are praised or given a reward?

Ask some pupils how much they value the rewards they are given.

Look at the reward system on the following link: **www.classdojo.com** (accessed 11 November 2019). Do you think this is an effective reward system?

Mentor: observe the trainee and record the frequency of rewards and praise used. Do you think the balance was right? What was the impact of the rewards and praise on pupil learning?

Discussion

Trainee: talk to your mentor about how you felt pupils reacted to earning a reward or being praised.

Mentor: discuss with the trainee the impact that rewards and praise had on pupils during the lesson you observed.

 Taking it further . . . research

Payne, R (2014) Using rewards and sanctions in the classroom: pupils' perceptions of their own responses to current behaviour management strategies. *Educational Review*, 67: 483-504.

Robins, G (2012) *Praise, Motivation, and the Child.* New York: Routledge.

Sanctions

The final element to the 'framework for discipline' (Standard 7) in most schools is that of sanctions – enforcing negative consequences when a pupil breaks the rules with the aim of deterring them (and others) from doing so again. As with rewards, there are a number of different systems used by schools to apply sanctions to pupils who breach the rules. The two main systems are:

- a hierarchical system, where the severity of the sanction depends on the seriousness of the pupil's behaviour;

- a cumulative system, where the severity of the sanction increases each time a pupil displays unwanted behaviour (this is favoured by many schools).

Whichever system is used, the first important element to any sanctions system is that you communicate it clearly to pupils and parents. The aim of this is to avoid any notion that some pupils are sanctioned differently from others and therefore prevent any perceived unfairness in the system. Pupils need to know what the sanctions system is and what the consequence of poor behaviour will be prior to it being imposed. One way to do this is to publish the system in advance, such as the one suggested by Canter's *Assertive Discipline* that outlines the sanctions used in a cumulative system:

First time: *Warning.*

Second time: *Five-minute time out away from other students.*

Third time: *Miss free choice time.*

Fourth time: *Call parents.*

Fifth time: *Send to office.*

(2010, p35)

Once the sanctions have been communicated to pupils and parents, it is then important that you approach implementing them with fairness and consistency. Pupils will soon notice if some are sanctioned for certain behaviour and others are not. This can quickly breed resentment and damage teacher–pupil relationships. However, in the desire to be seen to be fair, teachers can often fall into the trap of public sanctioning. The original 1976 edition of Canter and Canter's *Assertive Discipline* encouraged teachers to write the names of pupils on the board when they displayed unwanted behaviour, putting a 'cross' next to their name for each time the pupils subsequently repeated the behaviour (or behaved in another unwanted manner). However, it was soon noticed that this public sanctioning often led to more conflict and damaged pupil–teacher relationships, and the following edition of *Assertive Discipline* in 1992 advised teachers to keep track of this privately rather than publicly. It is also important to avoid group or whole-class sanctions. Punishing innocent individuals for the behaviour of a minority (or even the majority) of pupils is inherently unfair and is one of the quickest ways to damage relationships with pupils.

As with rewards, there are potential pitfalls to sanctions. If they are issued too often for minor breaches of procedural rules, there is a risk of creating a negative classroom atmosphere that is not conducive to learning. There is also the likelihood that pupils will begin to resent the teacher, leading to an increase in undesirable behaviour and perhaps even provoking retaliation against the teacher (Porter, 2014). However, allowing pupils to display increasingly poor behaviour and failing to intervene by applying any sanctions is likely to lead very quickly to a further deterioration in behaviour. Once again, the key is in choosing a system that is appropriate for each class of pupils and implementing this fairly and consistently.

Reflection and discussion activity

Reflection

Trainee: observe your mentor (or another teacher). What informal strategies do they use to deal with minor misbehaviour so that they do not have to use formal sanctions?

Mentor: how can you support your trainee to develop informal strategies for dealing with low-level behaviour?

Discussion

Mentor and trainee: discuss the strategies that can be used to address minor misbehaviour without using formal sanctions. What type of behaviour can be dealt with using informal strategies? What type of behaviour should always be dealt with using formal sanctions?

 Find out more from ... books

Cowley, S (2014) *Getting the Buggers to Behave* (2nd edn). London: Bloomsbury.

Preventing and responding to low-level disruption

What is low-level disruption?

The term 'low-level disruption' is often used to describe minor but problematic pupil behaviour that occurs within the classroom that negatively impacts on the delivery of the lesson by the teacher and the learning of the pupils. Ofsted's *Below the Radar: Low-level disruption in the country's classrooms* report emphasised the need for this kind of disruptive behaviour to be addressed as it can have a detrimental impact on the life chances of pupils (Ofsted, 2014). As a general rule, low-level disruption in primary classrooms tends to involve behaviours such as:

- calling out;

- talking and chatting (when this is not supposed to be happening);

- disturbing other pupils;

- not getting on with work;

- fidgeting or fiddling with equipment or other objects;

- making noises, such as humming, whistling or 'pen clicking';

- swinging on chairs.

It can be tempting to ignore these behaviours and hope they will stop. However, this is not usually the case. Low-level disruption can quickly 'spread' from one child to another in the class and, as a result, become more disruptive and even more difficult to stop.

Prevention is better than cure

Tom Bennett's 2017 independent review of behaviour in schools, *Creating a Culture*, repeatedly found that the best teachers prevented low-level disruption as much as possible. Given that the most common forms of low-level disruption can be predicted and anticipated, there are steps that can be taken by the teacher to prevent this kind of behaviour from occurring in the classroom. Using Table 9.2 below as a guide, consider what you could do to prevent each type of low-level disruption from happening.

Table 9.2 Preventing low-level disruption

Example of behaviour	Strategies for prevention
Calling out	
Talking and chatting	
Disturbing other children	
Not getting on with work	
Fidgeting or fiddling with equipment or objects	
Making noises	
Swinging on chairs	

The aim of the activity you have just completed is to begin to consider the specific strategies for the prevention of low-level disruption within the context of your own classroom or setting. Many of the strategies you considered may have involved setting clear expectations in the form of class 'rules' (as discussed in a previous section of this chapter), making changes to the classroom environment, the organisation of equipment, pupil seating plans, and your own and other adults' positioning in the classroom. By considering and implementing specific strategies to prevent low-level disruption, this reduces the opportunity for this to occur and, as such, maximises teaching and learning time in every lesson.

Low-level responses to low-level disruption

Although you can consider and implement strategies for preventing low-level disruption as much as possible, it is very unlikely that you will be able to prevent it entirely. While there can be a temptation to ignore low-level disruption, there is also the temptation to over-react to this kind of behaviour when it occurs.

As with the previous activity, it is worth considering how you will respond to the different types of low-level disruption that are most likely to occur in your classroom. Using Table 9.3 below as a guide, consider the ways in which you could respond to each example of low-level disruption, trying to avoid sanctions (or the threat of sanctions) that may damage your relationship with the pupils who are displaying the disputive behaviour.

Table 9.3 Low-level responses to low-level disruption

Example of behaviour	Teacher response
Calling out	
Talking and chatting	
Disturbing other children	
Not getting on with work	
Fidgeting or fiddling with equipment or objects	
Making noises	
Swinging on chairs	

The aim of the activity you have just completed is to consider the specific strategies for responding to low-level disruption within the context of your own classroom or setting. Some of the strategies you considered may have involved non-verbal communication, refocusing the pupils on their learning, giving 'whole-class reminders' (as opposed to highlighting the behaviour of individuals), praising pupils who are displaying the correct behaviour (with the hope that any pupil causing low-level disruption will 'get the hint'), using humour or changing your own or other adults' position in the room in response to a pupil's behaviour. However, you may have also considered other responses that might suit your own classroom or setting that may be effective for responding to low-level disruption.

So far, this chapter has outlined the use of rules, rewards and sanctions, and has also introduced some aspects of the system of Assertive Discipline. The approaches discussed above form the 'bread and butter' of strategies for managing behaviour that you will undoubtedly have seen, used or even remember having experienced. However, despite continued support from the government, issues have been raised regarding these types of approaches. Criticisms include the lack of focus on emotions and the emphasis on teacher power. Although these approaches can be helpful to teachers in the short term as they provide a very clear framework, they have been criticised for their oversimplification and mechanistic views of behaviour.

It is also very easy, particularly if you are nervous or have a challenging class or pupil, to quickly fall into the trap of focusing on sanctions rather than praise. It is all too easy to focus on what pupils are doing 'wrong' rather than notice the pupils who are doing exactly what they have been asked. Because of the issues with a rewards and sanctions approach, some schools have begun to manage behaviour in a way that takes some account of feelings and emotions. These approaches support pupils in developing the skills they need to manage their own behaviour and, therefore, shift the emphasis away from teacher control. The review of Initial Teacher Training (Bennett, 2016) suggested that *It is imperative that new teachers have a full and varied toolkit of strategies at their disposal*. This highlights the need for a wide range of approaches to take into account the diverse needs of pupils and the issues with a 'one-size-fits-all' approach to managing behaviour. Sproson (2004) described a 'behaviour suitcase' that all teachers needed, from which they were able to use mixed and varied strategies. He believed that pupils fill their own 'suitcases' and begin to manage their own behaviour through watching the teacher model different strategies. However, if behaviour is managed using only rewards and sanctions, some pupils will have very empty suitcases.

Two very different approaches will now be discussed: restorative approaches and solution-focused approaches. Both of these shift the emphasis away from teacher control, which has been shown to reduce self-esteem and intrinsic motivation (Kohn, 1993), and towards empowerment, for both pupils and teachers.

Restorative approaches

Restorative approaches (RA, or restorative justice as it is also known) are used by the police, probation service and youth workers as well as schools. Hansberry (2016) suggested that restorative approaches distinguish between 'managing behaviour' and 'managing relationships'. At the core of RA is not modifying behaviour but changing the way pupils see and feel about each other, which in turn influences their behaviour. The focus of RA is through pupils 'putting things right', rather than simply being punished as might happen in a rewards and punishment-based approach. However, using RA to manage behaviour is not something which you can do in isolation: it needs to be built into a whole-school plan and ethos. However, once it has been established, it can be used with individuals, groups or even whole classes.

Table 9.4 Contrasting authoritarian and restorative approaches

Authoritarian approaches	Restorative approaches
The focus is on:	*The focus is on:*
Rule-breaking	Harm done to individuals
Blame or guilt	Responsibility and problem-solving
Adversarial processes	Dialogue and negotiation
Punishment to deter	Repair, apology and reparation
Impersonal processes	Interpersonal processes
and, as a result:	*and, as a result:*
The needs of those affected are often ignored	The needs of those affected are addressed
The unmet needs behind the behaviour are ignored	The unmet needs behind the behaviour are addressed
Accountability = being punished	*Accountability = putting things right*

Source: Adapted from Hendry et al. (2011).

 Reflection and discussion activity

Reflection

Trainee: what skills do you think you would need to support pupils in 'putting things right'? What skills do you think pupils would need to develop? How can that be encouraged in the classroom?

Mentor: consider how you can support the trainee in developing short PHSCE sessions or Philosophy for Children (P4C) activities that will encourage the development of the skills identified.

Discussion

What might be the advantage of pupils repairing the problem, rather than adults punishing? Are there any issues with this type of approach?

Hendry *et al.* (2011) stated that RA were based on several key tenets, which made it distinct from other approaches. These include: genuineness, valuing people, empathy, responsibility, accountability and optimism. You can see that these qualities could help to develop pupils' self-actualisation and skills for life, and are quite distinct from the focus on 'controlling' pupils' behaviour that you may have seen in other approaches. RA helps to develop skills in both pupils and teachers, including:

- active listening;

- emotional literacy;

- patience;

- objectivity;

- anger management;

- dealing with difficult situations.

In practice, these skills are nurtured and accountability is provided through 'restorative conversations' or 'restorative meetings', as opposed to rewards and sanctions. The meetings are based on a scripted series of questions that provide support for both the teacher running the meeting and the pupil attending. The meetings (also known as conferences) or conversations can be large or small, formal or informal, but they rely on all staff using the process consistently. The same questions are asked to both the pupil who has caused the 'harm' and to the pupil who has been 'harmed'.

- *Can you tell us about what happened and how you became involved?*

- *If necessary: What happened next and/or what else? (Ask this until their story unfolds.)*

- *What were you thinking at the time this happened?*

- *What have your thoughts been since?*

- *Who has been affected/upset by this and in what way?*

- *What has been the hardest thing for you?*

(www.restorativejustice4schools.co.uk)

At the conference, when the questions have been asked and answered, a conference agreement is drawn up. This is a record of the initial problem or incident, what has been agreed between the pupils at the conference, as well as possibly a section detailing what will happen if the agreement is broken or the incident happens again. An important next step is to set a time to review the agreement to make sure it is suitable and working. This important step helps to develop and maintain what Hansberry (2016) terms *the 3 Es: engagement, explanation and expectation*. These ensure that pupils are actively involved in the process and understand what they need to do, as well as being clear on any new expectations for their behaviour.

To summarise, RA is a whole-school approach based on respect, responsibility, repair and reintegration. Research (Kokotsaki, 2013) shows that the approach has advantages, specifically:

- pupils feel their teachers are fair, show care and respect;

- pupils feel safer and more comfortable at school;

- attendance improves;

- reduction in low-level disruption;

- particular benefits for vulnerable children and those with social, emotional and behavioural difficulties (SEBD);

- higher levels of participation and engagement in lessons;

- improved attainment.

However, like all approaches, research (Howard, 2009) suggests that there are also some issues, which include:

- Senior Leadership Team (SLT) support is crucial;

- remaining neutral can be an issue for some teachers;

- restorative approaches need to be embedded in the school's ethos and values;

- it is not a 'quick fix';

- restorative interventions are voluntary for all those involved (both an advantage and a disadvantage).

 Reflection and discussion activity

Reflection

Trainee: what do you think the advantages of RA might be? Are there any aspects which you could implement in your classroom?

Mentor: have you used RA in the past? Do you foresee any other issues with this approach or any other advantages?

Discussion

Look at the list of issues with RA. How could they be addressed? Consider specifically the voluntary aspect of RA. How could this be both an advantage and disadvantage? Are there opportunities in your practice for restorative conversations?

Find out more from ... websites and books

A very brief overview of RA in school - a great beginner's guide: **www.educ.cam.ac.uk/research/projects/ restorativeapproaches/RA-in-the-UK.pdf** (accessed 11 November 2019).

Detailed websites, both with a section of free downloadable resources:

www.restorativejustice4schools.co.uk/wp/?page_id=45

https://transformingconflict.org/restorative-approaches/ (accessed 11 November 2019).

A very comprehensive book: Hansberry, B (2016) *A Practical Introduction to Restorative Practice in Schools: Theory, skills and guidance*. London: Jessica Kingsley.

Solution-focused approaches

Another strategy to positively manage behaviour, which also contrasts with the traditional rewards and sanctions approach, is that of solution-focused approaches (SFA). SFA has its roots in counselling and therapeutic approaches, and, unlike the traditional view of managing behaviour or the notion of 'harm' which exists in RA, SFA is a purely positive forward-thinking strategy. SFA can be used to work with individual pupils or the whole class. Unlike other strategies for managing behaviour where the 'problem' is within the child which can lead to labelling, SFA is predicated on the notion that pupils have their own ideas and strengths, and are able to decide what best works for them, which removes the need for some form of treatment or intervention from outside adults. Within SFA, teachers work alongside pupils and, like aspects of RA, is 'done with' rather than 'done to' pupils.

Reflection and discussion activity

Reflection

Trainee: how many labels or categorisations have you seen or heard so far in schools? What are the advantages of 'categorising' or labelling pupils? Are there any disadvantages?

Mentor: consider some of the labels which you use in your class or school. How are they helpful for teachers? Do they place any limits on teachers or pupils? How are these overcome?

Discussion

Share your thoughts from the reflection activity.

Try to be mindful of the labels you use in your own practice. What would happen if we stopped labelling pupils?

A key difference between SFA, and other classroom practices, which may sound surprising, is that the problem is not important. Here, you are *too busy helping pupils find solutions to difficulties* to be investigating the problem itself (Milner and Bateman, 2011, p17). That is quite a switch in thinking for many teachers. Milner and Bateman (2011, p17) found that children *may not wish to, or feel unable to explore the reasons why they are struggling*. They suggest that *digging into the problem* even when our intentions are to help can be *disrespectful and possibly painful* for the pupil. However, if a pupil wanted to share a problem, you would obviously be available and listen. The idea of not forcing the pupil to discuss the problem also links to the bigger view in SFA that you as the teacher are neither the expert in, nor responsible for, finding a solution to the problem. Again, both of these are radical shifts in most teachers' practice, particularly the traditional methods of managing behaviour where teachers often tell pupils what their 'problem' is – i.e. 'you can't sit still', 'you can't concentrate', 'you can't stop talking', and then make themselves the holder of the solution – i.e. 'you need to move seats', 'stand up', 'stay in at playtime', and so on.

With SFA, the solutions to the problem and the best way forward are all the responsibility of the pupil; your job is to support them in finding a solution. Here the pupil (rather than teacher, educational psychologist, doctor, etc.) is the 'expert' in their own lives and possesses all the skills and knowledge they need to arrive at the solution. Your job is to develop supportive conversations that allow pupils to use their own knowledge, strengths, skills and abilities to work towards a solution.

> *The philosophy underpinning SFA includes an unwavering belief in children's capacities to find their own solutions – the guiding principle is if it works, do more of it. If it doesn't work, do something different.*

> (Milner and Bateman, 2011, p25)

Reflection and discussion activity

Reflection

Trainee: what skills might you need to facilitate these types of conversations? Can you see any advantages or disadvantages to this type of approach?

Mentor: reflect upon your own experiences of being an 'expert' in the pupil's problem and providing solutions. Are there times when this hasn't worked well?

Discussion

Before you continue reading, how does this approach make you feel? How and why is it different from a traditional 'authoritarian' approach?

Like RA, SFA is a very structured approach that provides you with a 'security blanket' when using strategies that are new. SFA can be used with both children and adults, focusing on the 'light at the end of the tunnel' rather than on the oncoming train. The process is very easy to do and requires no expensive or specific resources, only a pen, paper and time. The first step is to consider the pupils' long-term goals by asking them structured questions, sometimes referred to as the 'miracle question'. James's (2016, p151) version of this is simply: *Suppose things are going to get better, what would you notice that's different?*

The more comprehensive 'miracle question' is:

> *Suppose that while you are sleeping tonight, a miracle happened. The miracle is that the problem you have is solved. However, because you are sleeping, you don't know the miracle has happened. So when you wake up tomorrow morning what will be different that will tell you that the miracle has happened and the problem is solved?*

(Milner and Bateman, 2011, p51)

You can see that both of these questions focus on the solution rather than the problem. Simply asking a pupil to envisage a time when things are better immediately has a positive effect. It might then be necessary to narrow down their answer a little, possibly by asking questions that focus on what they will be doing. For example, if, after giving the pupil time to think and absorb the question, they say 'I'll be happy', you might need to make it more specific by asking them, as Milner and Bateman (2011, p52) suggest, *What are you doing when you're happy?*, *How do other people know when you're happy?*. Focus on what the pupil will 'see' and 'do', which helps to make the goal more concrete and less abstract. Again, simply picturing themselves doing these things will positively affect a pupil. These types of questions can be used with individuals, groups and even a whole class.

As part of this process, you can ask pupils an 'exception' question. For example, if the pupil suggests that when things are going well they will not be shouting out, ask them if they can think of a time they were about to or could have shouted out but did not. Pupils often find this tricky, so you can support them by reinforcing that it is a really difficult question and that 'I don't know' is an acceptable first answer, but don't settle for this. Keep encouraging the pupil to think of one occasion where they did not shout out etc. This exception then shows pupils that they are actually already making progress towards their goal.

The next step in the process is scaling, where the pupil, group or class will scale themselves between 1 and 10. This is very helpful as it provides a visual reminder to pupils about how much progress they are making and it can be done as often as necessary (at the end of every lesson, morning, day, week or whatever is required). Once explained, it only takes moments to do, so is easy to fit into a busy school day. On the scale, 1 represents no achievement towards their goal and 10 represents meeting their goal. This strategy is for the pupil – the teacher cannot impose their views. For example, if the pupil feels they are a 5, the teacher cannot step in and say, 'but you're shouting out, you're only a 2!' As the pupils rate themselves, you can continue to support them by asking further questions – for example, 'I see you are a 3 now. What will you be doing at 4? What will that look like?'. A great way to end an SFA conversation is with a compliment: this might be related to some changes in the pupil's behaviour, about progress they have made, or the way they are engaging with the process. As the pupil develops, you could even see if they can give themselves a compliment.

It can be seen that the whole emphasis on SFA is about positively moving forward, focusing on progress, what has worked and future developments. This can often start a virtuous cycle, rather than the vicious cycle of sanctions, and make the classroom a much happier and brighter place to be.

 Reflection and discussion activity

Reflection

Trainee: use the miracle question to consider an aspect of teaching you are currently anxious about. For example, if managing behaviour is an issue that concerns you (as it is for the majority of new and trainee teachers) ask yourself some of these 'miracle question prompts' from Milner and Bateman (2011).

When you are meeting your specific goal in managing behaviour:

- *What will you notice?*

- *What will you see?*

- *What will be different?*

- *What will other people and your class notice about you?*

- *What sort of things are you saying to yourself at the end of the day?*

Has this already made you feel a bit more hopeful and positive? Try scaling now: mark 1-10 on a piece of paper. Think about your best possible hope for managing behaviour. Where are you now? Mark it and date it.

Follow this up as regularly as necessary, at least daily for a couple of weeks to track the progress you are making.

Mentor: think about how you can engage in a solution-focused conversation with the trainee about their scaling chart. Encourage them to articulate what the next step on the scale would look like. Can you give them a compliment and encourage them to compliment themselves?

Discussion

Have the solution-focused conversation together in a mentor meeting.

How does this approach make you feel? Which aspects do you feel you could use now? What aspects would you like to find out more about?

 Find out more from . . . books

A very readable and practical text:

James, G (2016) *Transforming Behaviour in the Classroom: A solution-focused guide for new teachers.* London: SAGE.

A very accessible and comprehensive text with many case studies:

Milner, J and Bateman, J (2011) *Working with Children and Teenagers Using Solution Focused Approaches: Enabling children to overcome challenges and achieve their potential.* London: Jessica Kingsley.

 Taking it further . . . research

Although the strategies you use to manage behaviour will be informed by your own values, beliefs, experience and the school's own behaviour policy, Visser (2002) devised a list of *eternal verities* based on his time supporting pupils with challenging behaviour. He believed that these eternal verities were features of good practice in classroom management. They included:

- a shared understanding of labels;
- inclusive practice;
- a belief that behaviour can change;
- prevention is better than intervention;
- acceptable behaviour needs explicit modelling;

(Continued)

(Continued)

- communication;

- empathy;

- boundaries and challenges are set;

- relationships are positive;

and finally,

- humour.

 Reflection and discussion activity

Trainee: how might these 'verities' look in practice? Can you illustrate what your mentor might see if they walked into the classroom and these were enacted? How many of these have you seen in action? Are there any that you think are more important than the rest? How many exist in your current practice and the practice you have observed?

Discussion

What strategies discussed in this chapter can help foster these 'eternal verities' in classrooms?

 Chapter summary

Hopefully, through this chapter you will have seen that there is a wide range of strategies for managing behaviour. Often, many aspiring and new teachers are specifically concerned with issues in relation to managing behaviour. However, careful and considered proactive management of behaviour can do a lot to ameliorate those worries. It is also very important to remember that behaviour does not occur in a vacuum, and a myriad of factors, including how well-planned, resourced and engaging your teaching is, will all impact on the behaviour your pupils display.

References

Bennett, T (2016) Challenging behaviour. In Association of Teachers and Lecturers Changing Behaviour. *Report Magazine*, January.

Bennett, T (2017) *Creating a Culture: How school leaders can optimise behaviour*. London: Department for Education.

Canter, L (2010) *Lee Canter's Assertive Discipline: Positive behavior management for today's classroom* (4th edn). Bloomington, IN: Solution Tree Press.

Canter, L and Canter, M (1976) *Assertive Discipline: A take-charge approach for today's educator*. Santa Monica, CA: Lee Canter & Associates.

Canter, L and Canter, M (1992) *Assertive Discipline: Positive behavior management for today's classroom* (2nd edn). Santa Monica, CA: Lee Canter & Associates.

Cowley, S (2014) *Getting the Buggers to Behave* (2nd edn). London: Bloomsbury.

Department for Education (2012) *Teachers' Standards*. London: HMSO.

Floress, M and Jenkins, L (2015) A preliminary investigation of kindergarten teachers' use of praise in general education classrooms. *Preventing School Failure*, 59: 253–62.

Hansberry, B (2016) *A Practical Introduction to Restorative Practice in Schools: Theory, skills and guidance*. London: Jessica Kingsley Publishers.

Hendry, R, Hopkins, B and Steele, B (2011) *Restorative Approaches in Schools in the UK*. Swindon: ESRC.

Howard, P (2009) *Restorative Practice in Schools*. Available at: **www.cfbt.com/en-GB/Research/…/r-restorative-practice-in-schools-2009**

Kokotsaki, D (2013) *A Review of the Implementation of Restorative Approaches and its Outcomes within Durham Local Authority*. Durham: CEM.

Kohn, A (1993) *Punished by Rewards: The Trouble with Gold Stars, Incentive Plans, A's, Praise, and Other Bribes*. Boston: Houghton Mifflin.

James, G (2016) *Transforming Behaviour in the Classroom: A solution-focused guide for new teachers*. London: SAGE.

Milner, J and Bateman, J (2011) *Working with Children and Teenagers Using Solution Focused Approaches: Enabling children to overcome challenges and achieve their potential*. London: Jessica Kingsley Publishers.

Office for Standards in Education (Ofsted) (2014) *Below the Radar: Low-level disruption in the country's classrooms*. Manchester: HMSO.

Porter, L (2014) *Behaviour in Schools: Theory and practice for teachers* (4th edn). Maidenhead: Open University Press.

Shreeve, A, Boddington, D, Bernard, B, Brown, K, Clarke, K, Dean, L, Elkins, T, Kemp, S, Lees, J, Millar, D, Oakley, J and Shiret, D (2002) Student perceptions of rewards and sanctions. *Pedagogy, Culture & Society*, 10: 239–56.

Sproson, B (2004) Some do and don't: teacher effectiveness in managing behavior. In Wearmouth, J, Glynn, T, Richmond, R and Berryman, M (eds) *Inclusion and Behaviour Management in Schools: Issues and challenges*. London: David Fulton, pp311–21.

Visser, J (2005) Key factors that enable the successful management of difficult behaviour in schools and classrooms. *Education 3–13*, 33(1): 26–31.

10
Vulnerable groups
Shaun Thompson

 This chapter will

- develop your understanding of different vulnerable groups and begin to identify the barriers to learning, which may impact upon progress of these pupils;
- consider distinctive approaches to planning, teaching and learning in order to engage and support vulnerable pupils;
- develop your understanding of a range of support and interventions for vulnerable learners and consider how to maximise progress for these pupils;
- engage with monitoring and tracking the progress of vulnerable groups in order to evaluate the impact of your practice;
- reflect upon the needs of vulnerable learners within your class and consider a variety of approaches to enhance your practice.

 Links to Teachers' Standards

A teacher must:

5   Adapt teaching to respond to the strengths and needs of all pupils, specifically:

- know when and how to differentiate appropriately, using approaches which enable pupils to be taught effectively;
- have a secure understanding of how a range of factors can inhibit pupils' ability to learn, and how best to overcome these;

(Continued)

(Continued)

- demonstrate an awareness of the physical, social and intellectual development of children, and know how to adapt teaching to support pupils' education at different stages of development;

- have a clear understanding of the needs of all pupils, including those with special educational needs; those of high ability; those with English as an additional language; those with disabilities; and be able to use and evaluate distinctive teaching approaches to engage and support them.

There are also strong links to all the Teachers' Standards, but particularly Standards 1, 2, 4, 6, 7 and 8, and Part 2.

Introduction

In Ofsted (2013) terms, vulnerable children are among those groups that may need additional support or intervention in order to make optimum progress.

Many children, at some point, may be described as 'vulnerable' due to their exposure to social or personal factors. However, certain groups of children are more likely to be at a greater risk of requiring targeted support, due to factors that may impact upon their learning and progress, such as specific learning needs, behavioural difficulties, issues surrounding attendance at school, family circumstances and poverty. While care must be taken not to automatically apply labels to children and make assumptions about their ability based on their specific needs or circumstances, it is essential that you have an understanding of the potential barriers to learning, which may be a consequence of such factors.

It is also important to remember that when considering vulnerable children, it may not only be related to those individuals who find learning challenging. Those pupils who are very able or the higher attainers may also be considered as 'vulnerable'. If sufficient challenge and strategies to enable these individuals to enhance their knowledge and skills further are not considered carefully in planning, teaching and assessment by the teacher, the impact upon progress may well be substantial.

It is often much simpler to identify those individuals who are already presenting difficulties or who have by now been 'labelled' or become known to other agencies. However, as a teacher, it is also of great importance to be aware of those pupils who may be 'at risk' of doing so, in order to ensure that support and intervention may be put in place early. You may begin to notice small behavioural changes, be aware of a change in circumstance at home, or simply notice specific areas of difficulty or anxiety among individuals. Identifying and targeting such individuals early on may enable prevention of difficulties later on.

 Reflection and discussion activity

Reflection

Trainee:

- Consider any individuals within your class who have specific learning needs already identified. Discuss with your mentor how this may impact upon their learning.

- Are there other individuals within your class who may be considered as 'vulnerable'? Use one of your mentor meetings to share this discussion with your mentor and to explore the impact this may have upon your own classroom practice.

- Discuss with your mentor any individuals who you may consider to be 'at risk' within your class. What is your evidence for this? Reflect upon your observations of these individuals and how this may impact upon your practice.

Mentor:

- Consider your trainee's understanding or awareness of any 'vulnerable' individuals within the class.

- Encourage your trainee to reflect upon the individual learning needs and circumstances surrounding specific pupils within the class, which may impact upon their teaching.

- Discuss with your trainee any specific barriers to learning, which may be present for individuals within the class, and support them in reflecting on these implications for their planning and teaching.

- Discuss with your trainee those pupils who are making less than or at risk of making less than expected progress within the class. Support your trainee by identifying these individuals and how this may impact upon their planning and teaching.

Special Educational Needs and Disabilities (SEND) and Inclusion

According to DfE (2015) guidance, a child or young person (up to the age of 25) has SEN if they have:

- a learning difficulty or disability that calls for special educational provision to be made for him or her;

- a significantly greater difficulty in learning than the majority of others of the same age, or

- a disability that prevents or hinders him or her from making use of facilities of a kind generally provided for others of the same age in mainstream schools or mainstream post-16 institutions.

Note that some children may not have a SEN, but may have a disability, and are therefore covered under the SEND *Code of Practice* (DfE, 2015).

Many children and young people who have SEN may have a disability under the Equality Act 2010 – that is:

a physical or mental impairment which is long term and (has) substantial adverse effect on their ability to carry out normal day-today activities. The definition includes sensory impairments, such as those affecting sight or hearing, and long term health conditions such as asthma, diabetes, epilepsy, and cancer.

(DfE, 2015)

With this definition in mind, teachers' focus should be on *inclusion* for these individuals. According to Booth *et al.* (2000, p13):

> *Inclusion is seen to involve the identification and minimising of barriers to learning and participation and the maximising of resources to support learning and participation and as Slee (2001) points out, 'Inclusion starts with ourselves' [as teachers].*

Teacher expectations can play a significant role here: low expectations can breed low aspirations. The focus should not be on what pupils cannot do, but what the barriers are, which are preventing them from accessing the learning.

The *Code of Practice* (DfE, 2015, p17) emphasises the fact that schools (and therefore teachers):

- **must** *make reasonable adjustments, including the provision of auxiliary aids and services, to ensure that disabled children and young people are not at a substantial disadvantage compared with their peers.*

There will most likely be individuals within your class who have been identified as having specific learning needs or disabilities. With regard to these pupils, consider what the barriers to learning may be. Typical barriers to learning may include:

- difficulty in concentrating;

- organisational difficulties;

- behavioural difficulties;

- difficulties in accessing learning materials;

- challenges with expressive or receptive language;

- anxiety or frustration when faced with tasks.

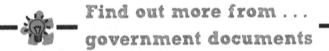

Find out more from ... government documents

www.gov.uk/government/uploads/system/uploads/attachment_data/file/398815/SEND_Code_of_Practice_January_2015.pdf (accessed 12 November 2019).

Implications for planning

Being aware of the potential barriers faced by individuals within the class will enable you to plan appropriately so as to minimise or remove these barriers to learning. As Black-Hawkins *et al.* (2007, p31) state: *if feelings such as fear, humiliation, failure, intolerance and anger are ignored then barriers to inclusion and achievement are strengthened.* In order to reduce or remove these barriers to learning, when planning your lessons, consider the following:

- Have you provided opportunities (including reasonable adjustments) for these pupils to succeed?

- Is the task structured into manageable 'chunks'?

- Are there resources available, which may support the learning for these pupils – e.g. concrete apparatus, visual cues, word banks, key vocabulary, etc.?

- Are your expectations high, yet achievable?

- Could you make use of peer support or additional adult support (if available)?

- What is your role in supporting these learners?

- Do you need additional resources/items to overcome any organisational issues?

- Have you planned for key questions, which you know these individuals will be able to answer, in order to increase their confidence?

- Have you considered the likely misconceptions or difficulties based on previous assessment/lessons, which may impede the learning of these individuals?

Some pupils within your classroom may have a support plan in place – this may be an Education Health Care Plan (EHCP). If this is the case, ensure that you consider this when planning your lessons – you may find that specific resources and strategies for teaching and learning are referred to within the plan. The EHCP should include the *views, wishes and feelings of the child (or young person) and their parents* (DfE, 2015, p19). If an EHCP is in place for a child, or children, in your class, discuss this with your mentor and the SENDCo (Special Educational Needs and Disabilities Coordinator).

When considering the support offered to children with SEND, the 'graduated approach' should be used. The *Code of Practice* (DfE, 2015) defines a 'graduated approach' as: *a model of action and intervention in early education settings, schools and colleges to help children and young people who have special educational needs.*

The graduated approach is a four-stage cycle of Assess–Plan–Do–Review, which should be considered throughout your teaching and learning. If high-quality inclusive teaching within the general classroom is not supporting the individual to make expected progress, then the graduated approach to teaching and learning should be applied. This cycle should be constantly revisited, making small tweaks each time, enabling support and interventions to become more and more narrowly focused on the individual pupil's needs. It is important to remember that if an intervention is unsuccessful, there is no point in repeating this. As the teacher, you need to consider why it may have been unsuccessful (or the parts of it which were) and refocus the support or intervention for the next cycle. As Figure 10.1 shows, communication with the SENDCo and parents are crucial within this process. Evidence that you have followed this approach and implemented a range of interventions, support and strategies are crucial as part of the EHCP process – without this evidence, it is unlikely that a child will be able to gain an EHCP.

The Graduated Approach

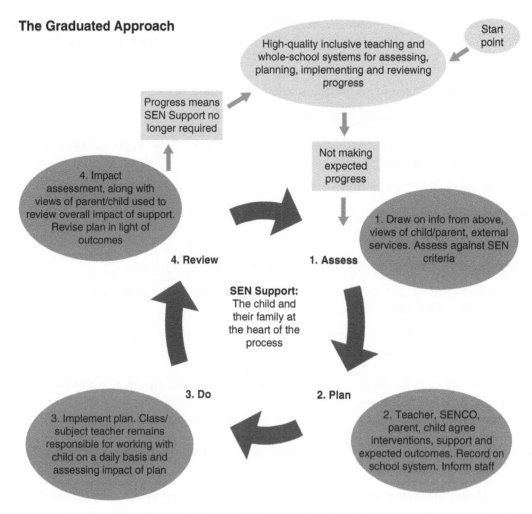

Figure 10.1 The graduated approach to supporting learners with SEND (The Code of Practice, 2015)

Application to practice

By focusing on removing the barriers to pupils' learning, along with careful planning, you may also wish to consider the physical environment of your classroom. Ensure that your planning clearly considers the needs of these specific pupils in your class and how you intend to support their learning/reduce the barriers to learning.

 Reflection and discussion activity

Think about the individual needs of learners within your class and consider the physical environment of the classroom.

Mentor and trainee: think about the questions below and reflect on how you are meeting the needs of all the children.

- How do the displays support learning?

- Are there visual cues to support learning?

- Is a range of children's work displayed to ensure they feel valued?

- Do the seating arrangements take into account individual pupils' needs (e.g. distractions, peer groups, access, etc.)?

- Do individuals need to be positioned nearer the front/back of the classroom? If so, are they?

- Can all learners clearly see you and your modelling?

- How are you implementing the graduated approach for specific learners within your classroom? What interventions or strategies have you already tried and what will you do next?

During your teaching, it is important to remember the aspects within your planning to removing barriers. For example, if resources are useful to support individuals, ensure that you model how to use these resources effectively – remember, children need to be taught the skills of how to use them.

If you have additional adult support within your lesson, consider carefully their role during your teaching. How can they be best utilised during this time to support learning? Trainees sometimes fall into the trap of utilising adult support effectively when the children are working independently, but often fail to consider their support during the teaching input. Additional adults may be used to support learning in a variety of ways – for example, managing behavioural issues, reinforcing learning through additional modelling or questioning, supporting teaching with additional resources, and so on. The key here is effective communication with your additional adults: do they know what is expected of them throughout *all* parts of the lesson? However, additional adults should not solely be assigned to working with those pupils with SEND (unless this is an entitlement of the EHCP), so you must consider carefully *your* role as the teacher. There is more about the role of other adults in the classroom in Chapter 14.

 Case study

Anna has a poor attention span and often struggles to understand concepts demonstrated by the teacher when she is on the carpet. She becomes easily distracted and disengaged from learning. The teaching assistant often sits with her to try to maintain her focus. When she returns to her table to carry out her work, the teaching assistant usually begins by remodelling the tasks with her and then supporting her with her work. While Anna has the teaching assistant with her, she is usually able to complete her tasks well. However, as soon as she is left alone, she goes off task and usually explains to the teacher that she does not understand and that the work is too hard.

Reflection and discussion activity

Mentor and trainee: think about this case study. Before reading on, discuss whether you think this support is actually promoting the best opportunities for Anna's learning throughout the whole lesson. How might you adapt this? What might some of the issues be here?

In the case study above, Anna has been receiving support within lessons to help her with her concentration and understanding. It has become usual practice for the teaching assistant to follow this routine most of the time. By sitting with her on the carpet and maintaining her concentration, the teaching assistant may be managing her behaviour more than supporting her learning. Also, Anna may well be used to the teaching assistant working with her on her tasks and continually modelling and reassuring her, whereas in reality, it may be that Anna's independent skills are being hindered as a result of over-reliance on this support.

The teacher may wish to reconsider how the teaching assistant could be successfully deployed to support Anna's learning throughout the whole lesson. Rather than sitting with her on the carpet to maintain her attention, perhaps she could reinforce the learning through small group modelling with Anna (and other children if appropriate) in parallel with the teacher, enabling her to engage with learning right from the start. By doing this, it may be that Anna is then confident to tackle one or two questions or examples independently, before the teaching assistant or teacher returns to check on her understanding and move her learning on to the next step.

Children such as Anna can easily become dependent on additional support, especially if that is what they are used to. By the teacher effectively communicating with the teaching assistant beforehand to enable her to mirror the teaching input with Anna and therefore support her learning from the start, hopefully Anna will gradually begin to apply her learning independently. This can then be gradually increased over a period of time, enabling Anna to develop her independent learning skills.

Support from other professionals

Working with pupils with SEND can be both rewarding and challenging. A key part of your professional role is to work alongside other professionals in order to achieve the best outcomes for pupils (Teachers' Standards 8). There may be a wide variety of professionals, both internally and externally, who are involved with specific pupils within the class. These may include the SENDCo, learning mentors, behavioural support staff, speech and language therapists (SALT), educational psychologists, physiotherapists, school nurse, and so on. These professionals are experts: remember, they are there to support you as well as the individual pupil.

Parents and carers play an integral role in all pupils' learning. However, for pupils with SEND, it is essential that they are also involved at all stages with their child's education. Effective communication with parents and carers can often alleviate anxiety and concerns and can prove beneficial in terms of sharing successful strategies or triggers for certain behaviours for their children. Good communication with parents/carers may provide you with valuable information about the child's specific interests, difficulties and behaviours.

Reflection and discussion activity

Reflection

Trainee:

- Are you familiar with any EHCPs for individual pupils within your class? How will these impact upon your planning and teaching? What adaptations do you need to make in order to meet the needs set out in the EHCP?

- What are the specific barriers to learning for individual pupils within your class? What strategies may be effective in reducing or minimising these barriers?

- Reflect on your expectations for all pupils within the class and consider whether your expectations are high for all pupils, including those with SEND. Consider how you demonstrate this within your planning and teaching.

- Consider how can you best utilise any additional adult support you may have within your lessons and what the desired impact upon pupils' learning is (at *all* stages of the lesson).

- Arrange to meet with the SENDCo to discuss their role and the support they can offer. Discuss with them how they support individual pupils and colleagues throughout the school and how they coordinate support from external agencies and parents and carers. You may also wish to discuss the EHCP process with the SENDCo.

Discussion

Mentor:

- Discuss with your trainee how they are considering inclusive approaches within their planning.

- Encourage and help your trainee to explore available support and resources throughout the school to support the learning of pupils with SEND as part of their professional development.

- Consider the trainee's planning and observations you have carried out to encourage them to reflect upon their deployment of additional adults within all parts of their lessons. Encourage your trainee to consider whether additional adults are supporting learning at all points of the lesson.

Higher attaining pupils and inclusion

The terms 'gifted' and 'talented' are sometimes still used within classrooms today – 'gifted' referring to the most-able pupils academically and 'talented' to those most-able pupils creatively or artistically. For the purposes of this book, we will consider those pupils who are deemed 'more' or 'most-able' or those who are identified as the higher attainers. So who are they? According to work by Koshy *et al.* (2012) and much of the DfE guidance, these pupils form the top 5–10 per cent of the pupils within the class or school.

In terms of identification of these pupils, it is those pupils who are consistently working significantly above their age-related expectation within a particular subject. This is not always easy to identify. Again, you must proceed with caution here, as your responsibility as a classroom practitioner is to set high expectations for all pupils and provide an environment that will enable all children to thrive. You must ensure that you do not get caught up too much with labels. Nevertheless, those higher attaining pupils within classrooms are all too often overlooked in terms of their development and thus their progress.

Monitoring the progress of these pupils is essential in order to ensure that they continue to make expected or better progress over time and not simply 'coast' along. A common mistake, often made by trainee teachers (and some experienced teachers), is to simply provide more of the same for these pupils as an extension task or to simply move them on to the objectives of the following year group. The National Curriculum (2013) does not endorse this. It states: *[teachers] should plan stretching work for pupils whose attainment is significantly above the expected standard*. With such pupils in mind, as a teacher, you need consider developing the depth and breadth of pupils' learning and understanding, rather than simply continuing on to the next year's objectives. This links in closely with teaching for mastery, discussed further in Chapter 5. Consideration should be given to the pupils' application of the knowledge and skills taught to a wide variety of contexts such as problem solving and investigation in mathematics.

 Reflection and discussion activity

Reflection

Mentor and trainee: using the school's tracking system, look at the pupils within your class. Who appears to be working consistently above their age-related expectations in reading, writing and/or maths?

Discussion

Are they the same pupils or are there differences between subjects? How is this taken account of when planning for differentiation within these lessons or grouping of these children in certain lessons?

Barriers to learning

While some pupils will quite happily plough on through pages of calculations in maths, or produce lengthy, well-structured pieces of writing in literacy with ease, for many, this simplistic approach to their work can cause boredom. This in itself may well lead to other unwanted behaviours such as distractions to others, lack of effort or interest, production of poor quality work, and perhaps even very little or no progress whatsoever. Who could blame them? Your responsibility for teaching these pupils needs to ensure that you have high expectations for them, which may be further challenged once they have achieved the objective of the lesson.

Implications for planning and teaching

As previously discussed, knowing who these higher attaining pupils are within different subjects is essential. You need to be responsive to their needs. Consider how to stretch these individuals through carefully planned activities and teaching – remember, it is about broadening and deepening their knowledge within subjects, not simply more of the same or moving on to the next year's objectives.

 Reflection and discussion activity

Reflection

Trainee, in terms of lesson planning, consider the following questions:

* What do the higher attaining pupils already know?

* What do you want them to achieve by the end of the lesson?

* How will you move their learning on?

* Will they work independently or be guided by an adult?

* How can you embed the objective in order to deepen and broaden their knowledge and skills?

Discussion

Mentor: can you share some useful examples with the trainee about how you support the higher attaining children in different areas of the curriculum?

Adult support should not just be limited to those pupils who find learning more challenging: higher attaining pupils need to be taught how to apply their knowledge and skills, and to deepen their understanding through accurate and clear modelling. Consideration should also be given to vocabulary development. Can these pupils explain their mathematical reasoning clearly or explain why a particular approach is more beneficial than others? Can they further develop the vocabulary they are using within their written work? Do they understand this vocabulary? It is not enough for them simply to include subordinate clauses within their writing because that is what you have taught them, but can they understand why and when they are used? Can they use them effectively to modify their writing?

You may also want to consider the questions you are asking during the lesson to these pupils. Can they explain why a particular concept works or how improvements can be made? It is not about trying to catch these individuals out or to give them unachievable goals, but to teach them how to reflect upon their work, how to improve, how to challenge and be critical, and deepen their understanding. Chapter 8 about questioning and dialogue will help you to think about the different questions you might want to ask to challenge and encourage higher order thinking.

Reflection and discussion activity

Reflection

Trainee: look through one of your lesson plans from earlier in the week and consider, through discussion with your mentor, how you have catered for those highest attaining pupils within the class. You may wish to choose a focus child or a group to reflect upon when discussing these questions.

- Are these pupils identified within your planning?

- Did you use questioning as a tool for extending their learning?

- Did you use adult support to extend and challenge these pupils or did they learn independently?

- Did you provide a clear model to enable these pupils to apply or develop their skills?

- What could they do by the end of the lesson that they couldn't do at the start?

- Did they make progress? How do you know?

Free school meals/pupil premium grant

Free school meals (FSM) were first introduced under the 1944 Education Act in order to ensure that children from the lowest income working families would have access to at least one good meal a day. This scheme continues to be in place for children from families meeting certain criteria today, namely, those in receipt of:

- *Income Support;*

- *income-based Jobseeker's Allowance;*

- *income-based Employment and Support Allowance;*

- *support under Part VI of the Immigration and Asylum Act 1999;*

- *the guaranteed element of Pension Credit;*

- *Child Tax Credit (provided you're not also entitled to Working Tax Credit and have an annual gross income of no more than £16,190);*

- *Working Tax Credit run-on – paid for 4 weeks after you stop qualifying for Working Tax Credit;*

- *Universal Credit.*

(DfE, 2016)

Children who are eligible for FSM enable the school to qualify for additional funding to support these learners, known as the pupil premium grant (PPG). In addition to those children currently in receipt of FSM, eligibility for the school to receive PPG funding also includes those pupils:

- recorded in the January 2016 school census who are known to have been eligible for free school meals since May 2010, as well as those first known to be eligible at January 2016 (known as Ever FSM 6);

- who are or have previously been looked after in care (LAC);

- who are from families where one or more parents are serving in the armed forces (known as service children).

Allocation of these funds to mainstream schools is generated from data collected in the January school census. Those schools, which are academies, will receive their funding directly from the Education Funding Agency (EFA).

Find out more from . . . your school or academy

Your institution will hold a central record of all pupils who are currently eligible for PPG.

Barriers to learning

According to Field (2010), a young person living in poverty at 16 has an increased risk of still living in poverty in their thirties and older. The socioeconomic status of the family may significantly impact upon a child's educational achievements. Various researchers (Sylva *et al.*, 2010) have identified how parental aspirations and engagement with their children's learning may give rise to what Bourdieu (1976) described as a 'cumulative effect' for pupils who are overall lower attainers, as he suggests that they must be even more successful than some of their peers in order for their families or teachers to recognise this success and encourage further study. Bourdieu (1976) goes on to discuss how influences from family life and backgrounds, particularly with respect to success or failure at school, may give rise to a self-perpetuating notion of low aspirations as they may have witnessed first-hand the objective chances of social mobility through education.

Implications for planning: planning for inclusion

Within their revised National Curriculum documentation, the DfE (2013) place great emphasis on the requirement of teachers to *set high expectations for every pupil* (p8) (Teachers' Standards 1). As discussed earlier in the chapter, caution must be applied to ensure that assumptions or labels are not used to create stereotypes. However, it is important that you are aware of these individuals within your class and ensure that you plan your lessons carefully to overcome any barriers to learning. By considering Bourdieu's (1976) theory, you must ensure that you do not contribute to the 'cumulative effect' of underachievement for these pupils by disregarding the need for high expectations. According to Ofsted (2013), high-quality teaching is seen to be the most effective element in the redistribution of equality. Careful planning, along with the school's strategic approach for spending the PPG funding to support learning, may involve activities such as:

- additional classroom resources to aid learning;

- additional adult support to enhance teaching and learning within the classroom;

- the use of additional adult support to provide teaching and learning support outside of the classroom (interventions);

- financial support for families to enable their children to engage in educational visits of enrichment opportunities.

 Reflection and discussion activity

Reflection

Consider the children within your class who are eligible for the PPG. Reflect upon the following questions and then discuss them with your mentor.

- Are there any specific barriers to learning that you can identify for these children?

- What is the impact of these barriers upon their learning?

- What can you do to overcome these barriers?

- Are your expectations high for *all* learners within your lessons?

- Is it clear in your planning and teaching how you are supporting these learners to overcome their barriers to learning?

Discussion

What else could you do to enhance their educational achievement?

Many of the strategies discussed earlier relating to supporting children with additional needs are still relevant for these pupils. You may wish to consider the following:

- Is the learning environment within your classroom conducive to promoting high self-esteem and high expectations?

- Do you promote inclusive attitudes within your classroom through activities such as circle time, supporting the development of relationships and peer working?

- Do you help to ensure positive relationships with parents and carers through effective communication and contact?

Some schools may have a designated member of staff to support with pupils who are eligible for PPG. This may be a specific role assigned to them or may be part of the role of the SENDCo. Who is this in your school?

Other vulnerable groups

In addition to the specific groups already discussed within this chapter, there may be other factors that can contribute to children becoming vulnerable. These may be related to attendance, both long- and short-term. Children who have poor attendance at school are likely to be vulnerable to low educational achievement due to gaps in their knowledge. Poor attendance may be due to a variety of reasons: frequent need for medical appointments, family issues, cultural factors – e.g. children from traveller families. It is important that you are aware of any children with issues surrounding attendance and to attempt to understand why this may be.

Find out more from . . . your local authority or academy chain

They will have information and specific formats for recording targeted support through the 'Team Around the Child' (TAC).

Reflection and discussion activity

Are there any children within your class who have (or are known to have) poor attendance? If so, find out what the reasons for this may be. Arrange to discuss with your class teacher/mentor or other members of staff (SENDCo, PPG Co-ordinator, family liaison worker) about issues surrounding attendance. How does the school support families and individuals where attendance may be an issue?

There may, of course, be other reasons why individuals may be considered 'vulnerable'. It could be that there are concerns surrounding safeguarding or specific child protection issues relating to a child in your class. If this is the case, it is important that you are aware of these, but remain sensitive to the needs of the child and family concerned. Remember, confidentiality is a key professional attribute. Chapter 13 explores more about your role in safeguarding.

Support and intervention

When considering any of the vulnerable groups discussed in this chapter, your role as a teacher is to ensure the best access to high-quality teaching and learning for these children through applying your knowledge and understanding of the barriers to learning within your own practice. Many strategies have already been discussed, but you may wish to consider the following questions when reflecting on your classroom practice:

- Do you provide opportunities for peer support/mentors within your lessons to enhance peer relationships and promote high expectations?

- Are there any external agencies involved with individual pupils within your class? If so, have you liaised with them and followed their guidance?

- Have you drawn on the expertise of other members of staff within the school to support you in your own practice? For example, perhaps there is a teacher who demonstrates excellent behaviour management – have you arranged to observe them?

 Find out more from ... online documents

Department for Education (2010) *Intervening to Improve Outcomes for Vulnerable Young People: A review of the evidence.* Available at: **www.gov.uk/government/uploads/system/uploads/attachment_data/file/182255/DFE-RR078.pdf** (accessed 12 November 2019).

When considering interventions to support individuals or groups of pupils, ensure that the intervention is appropriate. It is important that you match up the needs of the individuals with the specific interventions being delivered. This may well link in to your formative and summative assessment in the classroom – if there are specific gaps in pupils' knowledge or understanding, ensure that the intervention is matched to address these. A common method of delivering interventions is after a sequence of teaching. While this can be very effective, consider alternatives – would it be beneficial to provide intervention or support before teaching a particular sequence or aspect? Read the case study about Mark, below, and consider how you might provide support before your lesson.

 Case study

Mark has specific difficulties with expressive and receptive language. He struggles with recalling specific facts and grasping new vocabulary when it is first introduced to him. As a result, he has become very quiet and lacks confidence in many lessons, particularly when new concepts or vocabulary are introduced. He will frequently become upset and frustrated when faced with work, which requires him to apply new concepts or use vocabulary which is new to him.

Mark's mother frequently visits the school to discuss her concerns with his difficulties. She has a good relationship with the class teacher and support staff and is always wanting to know how she can help him at home.

Reflection and discussion activity

Think about a topic you know is coming up soon, in science or history, for example. Considering Mark in the case study above. What support might you be able to provide before you begin to teach the new topic? What key vocabulary will you be introducing in this topic? Discuss how you might provide some support to Mark in becoming familiar with this key vocabulary before you introduce the topic. What activities could you advise his mother to do with him in order to support him before you introduce the new topic?

 Chapter summary

Within this chapter, some examples of vulnerable groups have been discussed, along with some of the barriers to learning which may present themselves. Caution around labelling and stereotyping 'vulnerable groups' has also been discussed throughout the chapter. A range of strategies have been explored in order to support your own classroom and professional practice when considering 'vulnerable groups'. An emphasis on identifying and reflecting upon the barriers faced by these children has been identified as crucial in terms of planning and teaching to effectively support these pupils. By reflecting on your own practice and discussing with your mentor and other key members of staff within the school, you will continue to develop and enhance your own practice. Maintaining high expectations for all pupils and supporting them through specific interventions, both prior to and following your lessons, is an effective technique in helping them to overcome their barriers to learning. By having a clear understanding of the steps needed to succeed and the next steps in developing pupils' knowledge and understanding, you will contribute to ensuring expected or better progress for these pupils. This chapter has also highlighted the importance of effective planning of lessons in order to consider the resources or teaching strategies required to ensure the best outcomes for all children. Chapters 5, 6, 7, 8 and 15 will also be helpful for reflecting about planning and teaching for vulnerable groups.

References

Black-Hawkins, K, Florian, L and Rouse, M (2007) *Achievement and Inclusion in Schools*. Oxford: Routledge.

Booth, T, Ainscow, M, Black-Hawkins, K, Vaughan, M and Shaw, L (2000) *Index for Inclusion*. Bristol: Centre for Inclusive Studies in Education.

Bourdieu, P (1976) The school as a conservative force: scholastic and cultural inequalities. In Dale, R, Esland, G and MacDonald, M (eds) *Schooling and Capitalism*. London: Routledge & Kegan Paul, pp110–17.

Department for Education (DfE) (2013) *Key Stages 1 and 2: Framework Document* (DFE-00178-2013). Available at: **https://assets.publishing.service.gov.uk/government/uploads/system/uploads/attachment_data/file/425601/PRIMARY_national_curriculum.pdf** (accessed 3 March 2020)

Department for Education (DfE) (2015) *Special Educational Needs and Disability Code of Practice: 0 to 25 years. Statutory guidance for organisations which work with and support children and young people who have special educational needs or disabilities.* Available at: **www.gov.uk/government/publications/send-code-of-practice-0-to-25** (accessed 3 March 2020).

Department for Education (DfE) (2016) *Pupil Premium 2016 to 2017: Conditions of grant.* Available at: **www.gov.uk/government/publications/pupil-premium-conditions-of-grant-2016-to-2017** (accessed 3 March 2020).

Education Act 1944 Available at: **http://www.educationengland.org.uk/documents/acts/1944-education-act.html** (accessed 20 April 2020).

Field, F (2010) *The Foundation Years: Preventing poor children becoming poor adults.* Report of the Independent Review on Poverty and Life Chances. London: Cabinet Office.

Koshy, V, Pinheiro-Torres, C and Portman-Smith, C (2012) The landscape of gifted and talented education in England and Wales: how are teachers implementing policy? *Research Papers in Education*, 27(2): 167–86.

Ofsted (2013) *Unseen Children: Access and achievement 20 years on.* Report ref: 130155. Available at: **www.gov.uk/government/publications/unseen-children-access-and-achievement-20-years** (accessed 3 March 2020).

Slee, R (2001) Inclusion in practice: does practice make perfect? *Educational Review*, 53(2): 113–23.

Sylva, K, Melhuish, E, Sammons, P, Siraj-Blatchford, I and Taggart, B (2010) *Early Childhood Matters: Evidence from the effective pre-school and primary education project.* London: Routledge.

11

Supporting learners with English as an Additional Language (EAL)

Ami Montgomery

This chapter will

- support you in reflecting upon how teachers can:
  - support bilingual learners;
  - support language development for all learners with EAL including learners at various stages of second language acquisition (SLA);
  - support all learners for a life in a multilingual world;
- provide you with the opportunity for engaging in discussion around issues relevant to EAL and diversity in the primary classroom;
- introduce you to practical and accessible resources and a range of strategies for developing language proficiency for learners with EAL;
- provide theoretical explanations for English language support and provision.

Links to the Teachers' Standards

5   **Adapt teaching to respond to the strengths and needs of all pupils**, specifically:

- know when and how to differentiate appropriately, using approaches which enable pupils to be taught effectively;

(Continued)

(Continued)

- have a secure understanding of how a range of factors can inhibit pupils' ability to learn, and how best to overcome these;
- demonstrate an awareness of the physical, social and intellectual development of children, and know how to adapt teaching to support pupils' education at different stages of development;
- have a clear understanding of the needs of all pupils, including those with special educational needs; those of high ability; those with English as an additional language; those with disabilities; and be able to use and evaluate distinctive teaching approaches to engage and support them.

Introduction: language diversity and understanding EAL

In this chapter, the term 'learner with English as an additional language (EAL)' will be used to refer to pupils whose first language is other than English: *First language is the language to which the child was initially exposed during early development and continue to use in the home and community* (DfE, 2007).

Throughout this chapter I will argue that for effective EAL provision to be in place in your primary classroom, you need to connect the issues of language, literacy and culture in a more practical way (explored later in the chapter). Up until now, these issues have generally been considered to exist largely detached from one another, both in research and in practice. Traditionally, educators would consider culture as distinct from language, except in the most superficial of ways. By this I mean that learning the English language for a pupil with English as an Additional Language would appear *divorced from the influence of native culture on learning* (Nieto, 2010, p1). However, it is now evident that language, literacy and culture are connected in many ways and you should hold an awareness of how these aspects will affect your pupils' education. A deeper understanding of race, culture and ethnicity is vital to effective EAL provision and practice.

The number of learners with EAL entering English-speaking education systems is globally increasing. Current statistics in UK mainstream classrooms alone indicate a considerable growth in pupils learning English as a second, third or even fourth language, with increasing numbers of pupils entering the primary classroom with little or no English. Most teachers now have experience of working with pupils at varying levels of EAL, whether newly arrived or from resident families who are bilingual. This may be something you have experienced yourself when out on placement or during work experience in the primary classroom. To prepare yourself for this in the future, it is important for you to have secure awareness of the English language, to understand the different stages of language development, and to acknowledge the benefits and barriers of bilingualism/multilingualism.

 Reflection and discussion activity

Reflection: benefits of bilingualism and multilingualism

Trainee: before reading the next part of the chapter, reflect upon the following:

Either think about someone you know who is bilingual or multilingual or watch this clip of learners in a multilingual classroom.

Case Study: The Bilingual Stream - preparing the children for the world of tomorrow: **www.youtube.com/watch?v=xO2dg8KLYJY** (accessed 11 October 2019).

Think about what pupils benefit from when there are a range of languages in the classroom.

- What do you think encourages positive attitudes towards community languages? This can be based from what you have seen from around school, talking with other colleagues or from the clip above.

- What barriers could you face in a bilingual/multilingual classroom?

Mentor: reflect on your own experiences of working with bilingual and multilingual pupils.
Think about some of the possible barriers to meeting the pupils' diverse needs. How do you promote positive attitudes towards other languages within the classroom?

Discussion

Mentor and trainee: share your ideas from the reflection. Are there similarities and differences?

 Find out more from . . . internet clips

Further information can be found in 'The benefits of a bilingual brain' by Mia Nacamulli (2015). Available at: **www.youtube.com/watch?v=MMmOLN5zBLY&t=202s** (accessed 11 October 2019).

What does it mean to be a learner with EAL?

When considering this question, it is helpful to acknowledge a few initial assertions. First, a large and growing number of EAL learners who attend UK primary schools face the dual challenge of reaching proficiency in spoken English while grasping the curriculum and developing their written language skills in English simultaneously.

Second, within the literature, the current definition of EAL covers a wide range of pupils with varying needs and outcomes, learners who do not have English as their first language, including bilingual pupils who are fluent English speakers and new migrants who may not speak any English. This challenges the misconception of EAL being only those pupils newly arrived in schools. Hayden (2006) highlights that there are approximately 1.5 billion users of English in the world and predicted *by 2015 half of the world's population (approximately 3.5 billion) will be speaking or learning English* (Hayden, 2006, p163).

EAL learners' umbrella

All learners with EAL possess diverse experiences and a breadth of knowledge of languages, literacies, cultures and schooling which they bring to their new classroom, linguistic and cultural resources that they can use during their English language learning journey. Consequently, learners with EAL often require different approaches and techniques within the primary provision. Irrespective of their level of English, a learner with EAL will require ongoing and long-term support. As highlighted in the work of Cummins and Nakajima (1987), it often takes an average of five to seven years to become fully competent in a second language. This can vary from one individual to another. However, some non-native speakers of the English language can develop conversational competency and often native-like fluency within only two years. You need to be aware that although their spoken English may be very good, the learner will still require ongoing language support, possibly for several years. Teachers have the initial responsibility of creating a safe environment for new arrivals and for ensuring that all learners feel valued and included. Newly arrived learners with EAL face many barriers: being unable to speak any English at all results in the learner with EAL feeling particularly shy and worried about how to communicate with others. They often want to be on their own with limited interaction with peers and teachers. After all, one of the most difficult and frustrating things is the inability to communicate with others and to tell them how they feel or what they want.

Table 11.1 Definitions of EAL

Advanced bilingual learners	2nd and 3rd generations of settled ethnic minority.
New to English learners	Recent arrivals new to English, little or no experience of schooling and others who are literate in first language.
Refugee and asylum-seekers EAL learners	Education has been disrupted because of war/other traumatic experiences.
Isolated EAL learners	In school settings with little prior experience of bilingual pupils.
Sojourner EAL learners	Parents are working and studying and in England for short period of time.

 Case study

Isabel is the youngest of three siblings. They were all born in the UK. However, their family only speak Portuguese at home, despite the fact that they all speak English fluently. Isabel's grandparents moved to the UK for work. Isabel attends a local Portuguese Supplementary School at the weekends in addition to studying at her local primary school from Monday to Friday.

Asad was born in Somalia but he left with his family when he was a young child. For many years, Asad lived in Saudi Arabia until his family came to England when he was seven. They lived in temporary accommodation at first and Asad did not immediately find a school place.

Nadia is a Year 5 pupil who attends a small primary school in a small village in England. She has been living in the UK for three years. However, she hasn't always been at her current primary school. Previously, Nadia attended a large multicultural school in the south of England where there were other native speakers of Arabic who Nadia spent time with in and outside of school. However, due to work commitments, Nadia's family have relocated to an area where they are isolated.

Reflection activity

Trainee: read the case studies above and use the definitions in Table 11.1 to identify which group of EAL learners these pupils belong to.

In the case studies above, you were introduced to three EAL learners and asked to use Table 11.1 to identify which group they belong to. Each of these pupils (Isabel, an advanced bilingual learner; Asad, a refugee learner new to English; and Nadia, an isolated learner) have particular experiences and knowledge, and linguistic and cultural resources, which can be seen as strengths and benefits to the primary classroom, or weaknesses and barriers to learning.

Being aware of these different categories of EAL is especially important for preparing and providing for those more vulnerable learners with EAL, who are experiencing emotional difficulties due to experiences of war, loss or trauma. It is the educational rebuilding of worlds, along with economic and sociocultural support, which above all will determine the long-term well-being of millions of child survivors of war. Conteh (2019) identifies refugee and asylum seekers as an additional group who require further consideration and thought due to their diverse backgrounds, and the fact that their previous education may have been disputed. This group of learners with EAL is a particularly diverse group. While some children may arrive in the UK with both parents or being cared for by only one parent, others may live with older siblings, relatives or friends, or even arrive alone and unaccompanied. Schools and teachers play a vital role in promoting the well-being of refugee children, helping them to rebuild their self-esteem and friendships, and to fully achieve their full potential.

Discussion activity

Mentor: talk to your trainee about pupils you have taught who might fit into any of the following categories.

Learners who are:

- second and third generation members of settled ethnic minority communities (advanced bilingual learners);

- recent arrivals and new to English with little prior schooling;

- recent arrivals and new to English who are literate in their first language/s;

- asylum seekers or refugees whose education has been disrupted due to war or other traumatic experiences;

- isolated learners in school settings with little prior experience of bilingual learners;

- Roma and Gypsy pupils;

- children of parents who are studying or working for a short period of time.

(Conteh, 2019)

From your experience, what may be the strengths and possible needs of these pupils?

Any new arrival entering the English mainstream classroom will require access to the English language as quickly as possible, referred to by Cummins (1979) as Basic Interpersonal Communication Skills (BICS). These are the skills required for developing the appropriate language for the given social context and for oral fluency. This level of linguistic competence is required before they can access Cognitive Academic Language Proficiency (CALP), which is the linguistic knowledge and literacy skills required for full academic proficiency. This means that before pupils can access more complex language, including academic language used in learning, they need to be competent in basic language.

How do learners with EAL acquire the English language?

Second language acquisition

Many factors need careful consideration when exploring second-language acquisition for learners with EAL. First, let us consider the stages in which a language is learned for a bilingual learner. As set out by Tabors (1997, p39), the first of the four stages of acquisition includes a period of time where the learner of EAL will continue to use their home language in the second-language learning environment, or may even enter a 'silent period'. It is important that the learner with EAL feels able to do this and that their home culture is recognised and celebrated.

During the second stage of early acquisition, a learner with EAL may also enter a non-verbal period as they start to collect information about the linguistic characteristics of the new language and experiment with new sounds. For the duration of the 'silent period', learners with EAL will familiarise themselves with the similarities and differences in the sounds of their native language and the English language. Throughout this early stage of acquisition, it is important to ensure that learners with EAL have access to good models of the English language and also have access to the survival language required for their daily routines. Survival language is that key vocabulary your EAL learner will need on a daily basis; this includes key classroom vocabulary, language to assist with communicating with friends in and out of the classroom and language for daily routines.

 Reflection and discussion activity

Reflection

Mentor and trainee: consider some of the suggested strategies below for assisting EAL learners when in a non-verbal phase of second language acquisition (SLA).

- Continue to talk, even when the learner does not respond.

- Collaborative learning: continue to include the learner in small groups with other pupils.

- Use a variety of question types to draw answers and contributions.

- Include other pupils as the focus in the conversation.

- Drawing on the learner's linguistic and cultural resources, promote the use of their first language (L1).

- Accept non-verbal responses from the learner.

- Praise the learner for limited or minimal contribution.

- Set clear expectations which include the need for the learner to respond with repeated words and/or counting.

- Communicative practice: structure lessons and activities which encourage child-to-child interaction.

- Provide activities which reinforce language practice through role play.

(Clarke, 1992, pp17-18)

Discussion

Mentor and trainee: discuss these ideas. Would they all work well in your classroom? How might these vary depending on the situation? Why might having a variety of approaches be useful?

Subsequent to the experimentation of sounds phase, where your learners with EAL will be familiarising themselves with the similarities and differences in sounds of their new additional language, your EAL learners will start to use individual words and phrases in the new language. This is often in the form of *repetition and language play, use of formulae, routine and single words* (Drury, 2007, p37). They use formulae and language chunks as ready-made phrases for specific routine situations that allow the EAL learners to interact with others. These language chunks often include memorised sequences of routine language used within the setting, which include answering the register, asking to go to the toilet, or language in rhymes and stories. It is essential during this time that your learner with EAL is immersed in a language-rich environment with good models of the English language.

Eventually, learners with EAL begin to develop a more productive use of the second language which marks the beginning of developing more efficient and complex uses of the English language. They may combine some of the language chunks they have acquired in earlier stages and begin to produce longer and more complex sentences which approximate more closely to the intended meaning.

Many theoretical frameworks attempt to understand which method would be most effective when approaching teaching English, and place different values on the role of interaction in second-language acquisition (SLA).

Krashen's (1985) theory, which became a predominant influence in both second language teaching practice and later theories, proposes that SLA is determined by the amount of understandable and comprehensible input, at a level just beyond the current linguistic competence of the learner. Similar to Vygotsky's *zone of proximal development* (1962) – the difference between what a learner can do without help and what they can do with help – Krashen's scaffolding theory maintains that a second language is acquired unconsciously in a manner similar to the acquisition of a first language. He further highlights how acquiring language is predicated upon the concept of receiving messages that learners can understand. Teachers can make language input comprehensible through a variety of strategies, such as linguistic simplification, and the use of visuals, pictures, graphic organisers, and other strategies used with learners with EAL.

Table 11.2 Theoretical frameworks for second language acquisition

Pre-20th century	Early 1900s	1940s, 1950s	1960s, 1970s	1980s, 1990s	1990s-present
Grammar, translation	Audiolingual, direct method	Behaviourist, S-R-R*	Universal grammar, LAD**	Information processing models	Social interactionism
	Bloomfield, Fries	Skinner	Chomsky, Krashen	Anderson, MaLaughlin	Vygotsky, Snow

* Stimulus Reponse Reinforcement

** Language Acquisition Device

Other theoretical frameworks take an interactionist position and acknowledge the role of two-way communication. Pica (1994), Long (1985) and others emphasise that conversational interaction facilitates SLA under certain conditions, *in meaningful activities learners are compelled to negotiate for meaning . . . to express and clarify their intentions, thoughts, opinions . . . which permits them to arrive at a mutual understanding* (Lightbrown and Spada, 2013, p122).

 Reflective activity

As you continue to work through the activities in this chapter, refer back to the following statements and think about whether you agree or disagree with them.

1. Learning a second language is just like learning a first language.

2. Parents should be told to promote the use of English at home to ensure their child acquires the English language sooner.

3. Learners with EAL who are born in England will acquire the English language before starting school.

4. A pupil's first language gets in the way of their learning of English.

5. It is not important for teachers to concern themselves with the EAL learner's first language and culture, just to ensure they deliver the curriculum.

6. Younger learners with EAL will acquire the English language quicker than older EAL learners.

7. Learners with EAL need to learn the basics and simple English language structures first before they can be immersed in the mainstream classrooms and curriculum.

8. Learners with EAL speak English just like monolingual native English pupils.

9. Learners with EAL have an adverse impact on attainment and depress standards in schools.

Practical approaches for promoting language learning for learners with EAL

Preparing for new arrivals: essential conditions for learning and emotional well-being

When preparing for the arrival of an EAL learner, it is important to consider essential conditions for learning. Pupils need to feel safe, settled, valued and secure, and have a sense of belonging, where learning builds on what the learner knows and what they can do. Schools should recognise the positive contribution that new arrivals can make to the school, and it is important for new arrivals to see their language and culture positively reflected in school: *young children need to have their languages valued and their home experiences affirmed in order to feel secure enough to venture into the language and culture of their early years setting* (Siraj-Blatchford et al., 2003). No pupil should be expected to cast off the language and culture of home as they cross the school threshold.

There are numerous external and internal factors that influence the rate at which a learner with EAL acquires English. External factors include a learner's attitude, gender, age, social class, ethnic identity and language input, influenced by their new learning environment (Ellis, 1994). It is essential that you understand the importance of getting to know your EAL learner and their background, to promote their emotional well-being and to successfully prepare the essential conditions for learning.

To do this, you need to consider the new arrivals' cultural and language background. Consider if they:

- have had schooling in the UK or other country – full, interrupted or none;

- have specific cultural, religious, national and linguistic backgrounds which need catering for;

- are literate in one or more languages;

- are highly motivated to learn;

- are higher attaining pupils;

- have learning difficulties;

- are living with adults who themselves are experiencing emotional difficulties or withdrawal;

- are experiencing cultural disorientation, as well as feelings of loss, grief and isolation.

Find out more from ... websites

Read Nonchev and Tagarov's (2012) handbook on integrating refugee and asylum-seeking children in educational systems, giving support in preparing for EAL learners from backgrounds of war. Available at: **https://csd.bg/publications/publication/integrating-refugee-and-asylum-seeking-children-in-the-educational-systems-of-eu-member-states/** (accessed 11 October 2019).

The multicultural classroom and the importance of multicultural education

Multicultural classrooms must thrive on the differences and uniqueness of their pupils and use them as an underpinning for development and growth. Diversity and differences command work, resolution, openness and understanding, and for those teachers who address and embed this into their practice, they will succeed in creating a learning environment that will advance the educational goals of all pupils.

As a teacher, you are required to identify, differentiate and understand what it means to teach in a classroom which is multicultural and to understand that this includes, but is much more than, content integration. Content integration deals with the extent to which you use examples and content from a variety of cultures and groups to illustrate key concepts, principles, generalisations and theories. This is often seen as only benefiting learners who are of ethnic minority. However, it becomes clear with practice that this has benefits for all.

A range of nationalities in a primary classroom is an asset: pupils bring with them different backgrounds, cultures, faiths and language. This is something we should celebrate. Differing cultural perspectives provide a dynamic and vivid opportunity for debate and the need for mutual respect adds to the general dignity of the environment.

The immersive language classroom

Many theoretical frameworks attempt to understand which method would be most effective when approaching teaching English as a second language. However the communicative approach has been identified as particularly important in SLA (Pica, 1998; Canale and Swain, 1980). Oral communication becomes the most important component because it allows the learner to possess the basic knowledge of the second language that is necessary before grammatical rules can be applied. An inclusive setting, where the learner is fully immersed in the native language, is seen to be most beneficial because it allows the learner with second-language difficulty to practise with their native peers and those who are fluent in the English language. Within this context, both first and second languages are used and are a source of inspiration for any activity. An example of this is when learners are asked to engage in a writing activity and are given the opportunity to complete part of the activity in their first language. The main ideas that the learner wishes to convey are in their first language and then the written account is produced in their second language, which can be with the assistance of what Vygotsky would call a *more knowledgeable other*.

The communicative approach additionally allows for collaborative learning, which is extremely important for language teaching and learning as it is language-focused and EAL friendly. With three main areas of focus – empowerment, access and exploratory talk – collaborative learning is a situation in which two or more people learn or attempt to learn something together, where they capitalise on one another's resources and skills.

- **Empowerment** Building on and valuing a pupil's prior knowledge and understanding and encouraging pupils to share ideas confidently.

- **Access** Ensuring that pupils have access to difficult concepts/areas of learning. This is often done through the use of visuals and tries to move the learners from the concrete concept to abstract ideas.

- **Exploratory talk** Encouraging peer talk to aid and assist learning as opposed to the increased use of teacher talk.

Teaching communicative competencies across the curriculum can benefit all pupils in a group of learners, not just those who are bilingual/multilingual.

Find out more from . . . websites

Information about collaborative learning and access to further learning resources can be found at: **www. collaborativelearning.org/** (accessed 11 October 2019).

How to assess and monitor learners with EAL

Differences in educational, social and linguistic experience will mean that EAL learners of the same age and same length of residency in the UK might be at very different stages of EAL development with regard to the four skills and in the various areas of language. A useful EAL assessment system should measure development in speaking, listening, reading and writing; link to the language needed in the curriculum; be age-related; and support teachers to plan for effective teaching and learning. To successfully map the development of your learners with EAL, especially in the early stages of acquiring English, it is essential that formative assessments are implemented effectively. However, initial formal assessments have been judged negatively as they can often lead to false conclusions, which may be highly damaging to the progress of the pupil, particularly if results place the pupil in a lower ability group. The need for early monitoring and careful tracking of your EAL learner's development is highlighted in recent school performance tables and statistics which show that by the end of the Early Years and Foundation Stage (EYFS) only 44 per cent of learners with EAL are at a good level of development (GLD).

A Language in Common (2000), produced by the Quality and Curriculum Authority (QCA), provides an overview of some of the language focuses for formative assessment for learners with EAL and offers some helpful guidance on how to record language development and progress. A further example of early formative assessments which can be incorporated to map the progression of your EAL learners is the *Assessment Framework* of NASSEA (Northern Association of Support Services for Equality and Achievement). This framework provides an overview of the stages and steps in language progression, outlines key descriptors for each of the four language skills, and provides case studies to assist with identifying these descriptors for your EAL learners and planning for progression templates.

However, more recent research commissioned by The Bell Foundation has been conducted in response to the DfE's introduction of EAL English language proficiency scales (2017) and their aim to collect data on the English proficiency of EAL pupils to inform educational policy. This move was rooted in the basic rationale that current data on EAL pupils does not distinguish between pupils who lack a basic command of the English language versus those who are bilingual and have mastered English sufficiently to access the curriculum.

The English proficiency statistics for the first time provide important national statistics on the characteristics of this particular group of learners. This allows the department to measure whether the individual pupils, or the schools they attend, face additional educational challenges.

Reflection and discussion activity

Reflection

Prior to undertaking this task, you will need to familiarise yourself with the DfE's *English Language Proficiency Scales* (2016), The Bell Foundation's *EAL Assessment Framework* (2019), the QCA's *A Language in Common* (2000), NASSEA's *EAL Assessment Framework* (2016) and/or other possible assessment methods used in the school.

Trainee: identify two EAL learners in the school: one new to English and the other an advanced EAL learner.

Observe both EAL learners, in a wide range of settings, if possible, to find out the following information.

- What language(s) do the two pupils understand, speak, read and write in?

- Do they attend supplementary or community language classes? If possible, try to find out which language(s) are used when and for what purposes.

- Were they born in England or abroad? If they were born abroad, how long have they been in England and what was their pattern of migration?

- How long have they been in this school?

- Do they have the opportunity to use their first language(s) with other pupils in the school or with staff? If so, how often and when? How do they feel about this?

- Use either The Bell Foundation's assessment framework, or the NASSEA EAL *Assessment Framework* (2016) system to identify their stages of EAL acquisition for speaking, listening, reading and writing. Then identify specific areas for development for each pupil in each of the four skills.

Discussion

Trainee and mentor: compare your findings with regard to the assessment stages for each of the four language skills: speaking, listening, reading and writing. Discuss what their EAL needs are and how these are met in the context of the mainstream primary classroom.

How to plan for learners with EAL in your class

Planning for your learners with EAL can be a daunting task, but it does not need to be. When planning for learners with EAL in the primary classroom, there are several principles which you need to keep in mind. First, it is essential that you develop a positive ethos for learners with EAL, which reflects the language and cultures of all pupils in your class, and that you provide the opportunity for learners to use their first language in everyday activities. This offers further opportunity for your multilingual learners to *affirm their identity* (Conteh, 2019, p70) and to learn in a safe and secure learning environment. Another vital principle you need to consider when planning for your EAL learners is the importance of talk, and the opportunity for them to be able to explore their ideas and concepts orally with others, in addition to extensive opportunities for more practical and hands-on activities that enhance language learning. These are especially important before extended writing activities. Remember the important of message abundancy; present similar information in a variety of different ways, amplify rather than simplify.

To plan effectively for your EAL learners, you need to consider the balance between teaching the curriculum content in an interesting and challenging way, while making sure that you are supporting their specific English language needs. When planning, you need to consider what you are expecting your EAL learners to do with the language they are learning and the kinds of language they will require to access the learning (Conteh, 2019, p75).

 Reflection and discussion activity

Reflection

Read the following examples of classroom practice and consider the questions below.

In an RE lesson, the two newly arrived pupils are working together supported by a teaching assistant and are colouring in a picture of a mosque. The rest of the class are working on an activity to identify the names and function of each section of the mosque.

Leticia is a new arrival in Year 5 and a beginner in English. Her school reports from Colombia show that she has good literacy skills in Spanish. The class teacher gives her some English grammar worksheets to complete while the other pupils are doing extended writing.

Discussion

- Is there any good practice here?
- How could practice be improved?

Trainee and mentor: now compare your ideas and discuss the similarities and differences in your responses.

Using your assessment data for one of your learners with EAL, discuss how you could use Tower Hamlet's *Progression in Language Structures* (2009) to effectively plan for your next lesson.

There are a number of approaches to engage learners with EAL. Some of these are presented in the work of Nichiols (2010):

- A whole brain approach to learning that incorporates the theory that learners have different preferred ways of learning and acquiring information.

- Uses a variety of training techniques and activities that appeal to multiple intelligences and that of a wide variety of learners.

- Creates a stress-free environment for learners that promotes the idea of learning being powerful and fun.

- Reduces the time spent in the classroom as well as designing learning programmes due to the activity.

Find out more from ... websites

Follow the links below to listen to Cummins's talking about his five principles of supporting EAL learners.

1. Identify language and content objectives.

2. Frontload the lesson.

3. Provide input.

4. Enable language production (oral and written).

5. Assess language and content objectives.

www.youtube.com/watch?v=Zu-6V3N5RHI

www.youtube.com/watch?v=XjABYSrRGu8

What current teaching practice is taking place?

The Education Endowment Foundation (EEF) and The Bell Foundation have recently commissioned two reports to analyse the evidence on the achievement of pupils with EAL. Together, these ground-breaking reports present a comprehensive overview of the issues relating to EAL facing schools today. Subsequent reports commissioned by The Bell Foundation continue to highlight the importance of research surrounding learners with EAL and include particular focuses on Policy, Pedagogy and Pupil Perceptions, EAL and Initial Teacher Training and educational outcomes for learners with EAL (Anderson et al., 2016).

Taking it further ... research

In Strand's report (Strand, 2015) there is a presentation of an in-depth analysis of the most recent England National Pupil Database (NPD) from 2013 addressing the question 'Who are the most at-risk groups of EAL learners and what are the predictors of low attainment for these learners?'. Murphy's report is a systematic review of international research into interventions designed to improve their English language and literacy in order to identify the most promising programmes and interventions (Murphy, 2015). In Strand and Hessel's 2017 report, they present findings from their study surrounding the English language proficiency of learners with EAL and their overall attainment and achievement by local authority.

You can find the reports at:

Strand, 2015: **https://v1.educationendowmentfoundation.org.uk/uploads/pdf/EAL_and_educational_achieve ment2.pdf** (accessed 11 October 2019).

Murphy, 2015: **www.unboundphilanthropy.org/sites/default/files/EAL_Systematic_review1.pdf** (accessed 11 October 2019).

Strand and Hessel, 2017: **www.bell-foundation.org.uk/research-report/english-as-an-additional-language-proficiency-in-english-and-pupils-educational-achievement-an-analysis-of-local-authority-data/** (accessed 11 October 2019).

All other research reports commissioned by The Bell Foundation mentioned above can be found at:

www.bell-foundation.org.uk/research-reports/eal-programme/ (accessed 11 October 2019).

The current standards for teachers emphasise the provision required for learners with EAL in Teachers' Standards 5: *Teachers must take account of the needs of pupils whose first language is not English* and recognise *their ability to take part may be in advance of their communication skills in English* (DfE, 2012). This raises the question of how we effectively challenge curriculum learning while language development is still in the very early stages. The literacy skills that develop in primary school go on to serve as the foundation upon which further academic learning proceeds at secondary education.

Sometimes teachers may be misguided by misconceptions of language learning and further myths when learning a new language.

 Discussion activity

Look at the misconceptions below. Discuss together why some teachers might have these misconceptions and how you can avoid this happening in your teaching.

1. Languages should be kept separate or learners become confused - interference.
2. Pupils will pick up English naturally in the classroom, they don't need teaching - immersion.
3. Language diversity is a problem and better if pupils speak English at all times.
4. It is impossible, or very difficult, to learn a new language beyond a young age - the critical period.

Focused language knowledge is required by all. Language is our tool for all learning, an *inextricable part of our personal and social lives, the cultures we live in, and who we are* (Conteh, 2019, p33). Many primary school pupils with EAL struggle with the more passive and receptive language skills, listening and reading comprehension in particular (McKendry and Murphy, 2011). Therefore, it is critical that you have a thorough understanding of the development of language and literacy skills in order to be able to develop appropriate and effective pedagogical support. Every child is capable of learning, but in very different ways; you will need to understand how to mediate all other factors, social, cultural, emotional, affective and cognitive resources, political and historical, which contribute to or hinder their learning experience.

A further possible misunderstanding for teachers is the confusion between EAL and SEN. Language needs should not be perceived as learning needs and a learner with EAL must not be categorised as having special educational needs per se.

 Find out more from . . . research

Cummins (2001) argues that the misconception surrounding the crossover with EAL and SEN (Special Educational Needs) can have negative academic outcomes. It can lead to learners with EAL being assessed as having learning needs and placed within SEN groups when actually their needs are specifically language needs. They require specific language support to assist with developing across the four skills – speaking, listening, reading and writing – especially if they are to be able to cope with the demands of the primary curriculum. Cummins's theoretical models will help you develop an understanding of the different ways in which your EAL learners' experience language learning.

 Chapter summary

Within this chapter you have thought about the diversity in the range of experience and knowledge that multilingual and EAL learners bring to your classroom and strategies to help new arrivals embrace their new cultural experiences. You have also discussed the importance of recognising and reflecting on your experiences of language diversity and ethnicity for your own professional development.

You have looked at some research in the first part of the chapter which suggests some effective approaches to second language acquisition, and how theoretical approaches can develop your own awareness and understanding of how language and learning are linked. Additionally, you have further considered practical approaches for EAL learners and promoting language learning through effective assessment and planning. Within this section you have been introduced to the importance of speaking and listening for learning, collaborative learning, and developed your understanding of how to plan and teach to promote language learning across the curriculum.

Finally, you have explored what current provision and teaching practice is taking place in our primary classrooms and offered practical suggestions that will assist with language learning for your EAL learners.

Throughout the chapter you were challenged to think about how primary classrooms must thrive on the uniqueness of all learners. Diversity and differences command work, resolution, openness and understanding. Through this you will be able to create a learning environment that will advance the educational goals of all pupils.

References

Bell Educational Trust, The (operating as The Bell Foundation) (2017) EAL assessment framework for schools: introduction. Available at: **https://www.bell-foundation.org.uk/eal-programme/teaching-resources/eal-assessment-framework/** (accessed 3 March 2020).

Anderson, C, Foley, Y, Sangster, P, Edwards, V, Rassool, N (2016) *Policy Pedagogy and Pupil Perceptions: EAL in Scotland and England.* Available at: **https://www.bell-foundation.org.uk/app/uploads/2017/05/Policy-Pedagogy-and-Pupil-Perceptions-Final-full-report-Web-Version-pdf.pdf** (accessed 3 March 2020).

Canale, M and Swain, M (1980) Theoretical bases of communicative approaches to second language teaching and testing. *Applied Linguistics*, 1(1): 1–47.

Clarke, P (1992) *English as a 2nd Language in Early Childhood.* FKA Multicultural Resources Centre. Richmond: Victoria, Australia.

Conteh, J (2019) *The EAL Teaching Book.* London: SAGE.

Cummins, J (1979) Cognitive/academic language proficiency, linguistic interdependence, the optimum age question and some other matters. *Working Papers on Bilingualism*, 19: 121–9.

Cummins, J (2001) *An Introductory Reader to the Writings of Jim Cummins.* Clevedon: Multilingual Matters.

Cummins, J and Nakajima, K (1987) Age of arrival, length of residence, and interdependence of literacy skills among Japanese immigrant students. In Harley, B, Allen, P, Cummins, J and Swain, M (eds) *The Development of Bilingual Proficiency: Final report.* Toronto: Modern Language Centre, OISE.

Department for Education (DfE) (2007) *Ensuring the Attainment of Pupils Learning English as an Additional Language: A management guide.* Ref: DfES 00011-2007. Available at: **https://www.naldic.org.uk/Resources/NALDIC/Teaching%20and%20Learning/ks3_ws_eal_mgmt_gd_sch_strat.pdf** (accessed 3 March 2020).

Department for Education (DfE) (2007) *New Arrivals Excellence Programme Guidance.* Ref: 00650-2007BKT-EN.

Department for Education (DfE) (2011) *Teachers' Standards.* Available at: **https://www.gov.uk/government/publications/teachers-standards** (accessed 3 March 2020).

Department for Education (DfE) (2016) Available at: **https://ealresources.bell-foundation.org.uk/sites/default/files/document-files/DfE%20school%20census%20proficiency%20in%20English%20scale.pdf** (accessed 3 March 2020)

Department for Education (DfE) (2017) *Collection of Data on Pupil Nationality, Country of Birth and Proficiency in English: Summary Report.* DfE 00316-2017. London: Department for Education.

Department for Education (DfE) (2019) *Schools, Pupils, and their Characteristics.* London: Department for Education. Available at: **https://www.gov.uk/government/statistics/schools-pupils-and-their-characteristics-january-2019** (accessed 3 March 2020)

Drury, R (2007) *Young Bilingual Learners at Home and School.* Stoke-on-Trent: Trentham.

Ellis, R (1994) *The Study of Second Language Acquisition.* Oxford: Oxford University Press.

Hayden, M (2006) *Introduction to International Education: International schools and their communities.* London: SAGE.

Krashen, S (1985) *The Input Hypothesis*. Beverly Hills, CA: Laredo Publishing Company.

Lightbrown, PM and Spada, N (2013) *How Languages are Learned*. Oxford: Oxford University Press.

Long, MH (1985) Input and second language acquisition theory. In Gass, S and Madden, C (eds) *Input in Second Language Acquisition*. Rowley, MA: Newbury House, pp377–83.

McKendry, M and Murphy, VA (2011) A comparative study of listening comprehension measures in English as an additional language and native English-speaking primary school children. *Evaluation and Research in Education*, 24: 17–40.

Murphy, V (2015) *A Systematic Review of Intervention Research Examining English Language and Literacy Development in Children with English as an Additional Language (EAL)*. Oxford: Oxford University Press.

Nichiols, G (2010) Accelerated learning and elearning: an overview. IT6930, Internship in Information and Learning Technologies.

Nieto, S (2010) *Language, Culture, and Teaching: Critical perspectives*. New York: Routledge.

Nonchev, A and Tagarov, N (2012) Integrating refugee and asylum-seeking children in the educational systems of EU member states. Bulgaria: Center for the Study of Democracy.

Northern Association of Support Services for Equality and Achievement (NASSEA) (2016) EAL *Assessment Framework*. Bury: NASSEA.

Pica, T (1994) Research on negotiation: what does it reveal about second language learning conditions, processes and outcomes? *Language Learning*, 44: 493–527.

Pica, T (1998) Second language learning through interaction: multiple perspectives. In Regan, V (ed.) *Contemporary Approaches to Second Language Acquisition in Social 13–14 Contexts: Crosslinguistic perspectives*. Dublin: University College Dublin Press, pp9–31.

Quality and Curriculum Authority (QCA) (2000) *A Language in Common: Assessing English as an additional language*. London: QCA Publications.

Siraj-Blatchford, I, Sylva, K, Taggart, B, Melhuish, E, Sammons, P and Elliot, K (2003) *The Effective Provision of Pre-School Education (EPPE) Project: Technical Paper 10 'Intensive Case Studies of Practice Across the Foundation Stage'* (DfES Research Brief, RBX 16-03). Available at: **www.dcsf.gov.uk/research/data/uploadfiles/RBX16-03. pdf** (accessed 11 November 2019).

Smith, A, Lovatt, M and Wise, D (2005) *Accelerated Learning: A user's guide*. Stafford: Crown House Publishing.

Strand, S (2015) *English as an Additional Language (EAL) and Educational Achievement in England: An analysis of the National Pupil Database*. Oxford: Oxford University Press.

Tabors, P (1997) *One Child, Two Languages: A guide for preschool educators of children learning English as a second language*. Baltimore, MD: Paul Brookes.

Tower Hamlets EMA Team (2009) Progression in language structures: some suggestions for class teachers in planning for children's academic language development. Available at: **file:///C:/Users/Ami/Downloads/ Progression%20in%20Language%20Structures%20Tower%20Hamlets%20sentence%20starters. pdf** (accessed 11 November 2019).

Vygotsky, L (1962) *Thought and Language*. Cambridge, MA: MIT Press.

12

Supporting children in learning about difference

Richard Woolley

 This chapter will

- explore some of the differences between children and their families;
- consider strategies to help learn about difference;
- support you in valuing difference and helping children to feel included;
- acknowledge the importance of difference and reflecting differences in the classroom.

 Links to the Teachers' Standards

Part Two: Personal and Professional Conduct, specifically:

Teachers uphold public trust in the profession and maintain high standards of ethics and behaviour, within and outside school, by:

- treating pupils with dignity, building relationships rooted in mutual respect;
- having regard for the need to safeguard pupils' well-being, in accordance with statutory provisions;
- showing tolerance of and respect for the rights of others;
- not undermining fundamental British values, including democracy, the rule of law, individual liberty and mutual respect, and tolerance of those with different faiths and beliefs.

Teachers must have an understanding of, and always act within, the statutory frameworks which set out their professional duties and responsibilities.

Introduction

Difference is not unusual. Sometimes we shy away from speaking about difference, worried that it will cause division or highlight the dissimilarities between us. Sometimes we focus on finding similarities and common-alities, things that unite us in order to try to establish a sense of cohesion, a sense of homogeneity within our classrooms or schools. However, difference is not unusual. In fact, the one thing that we all have in common is that we are different. Every single one of us, and every single person we have ever met and will ever meet, is different from us: a unique, special individual and a total *one-off*. Surely that is something to celebrate and not to avoid?

In our classrooms, difference will be evident in many shapes and forms. The children in our care are all of different ages, heights and physical builds; they come from different homes and each has their own particular hobbies, interests, hopes and fears. Each has different learning abilities and aptitudes. Some differences will be apparent because they are clearly visible to us, but others, including those relating to identity, disability and personal viewpoints and values, may not be visible. Sometimes information about children's homes and families will not be known to us. It is important that we consider these unseen differences as well as those overt and in the public domain.

 Reflection activity

Consider the range of differences between children with whom you have worked. What kinds of differences immediately come to mind? Might there have been other differences that you did not think to consider or which did not show themselves in that setting?

 Case study

Jamie is in Year 5 and lives with dad much of the time, staying with grandma when dad is away working. Dad has to travel extensively for work a couple of times each month. Mum moved out of their home when Jamie was 3 years old. Jamie is in touch with mum, but this varies in frequency as mum now lives in New Zealand with her new partner. Mum and her partner have two children, but Jamie has not yet met these new sisters in person, although they have seen each other during video messaging calls. Jamie is very aware that life is different from other children in the class at school who mainly live with mum or with mum and dad. Within Jamie's friendship group there aren't friends who have parents or carers who work away from home for significant amounts of time. Jamie also is not aware of any friends whose mothers live a significant distance away.

Reflection and discussion activity

Reflection

Consider Jamie's situation. How might the apparent differences between life at home and those of friends and peers impact upon Jamie's experience in school?

How might Jamie feel if the resources used in school always focus on families with a mum and dad who live at home with their child(ren)?

Jamie doesn't often speak about mum at school and has never spoken about mum's partner Sarah or their two children. How might Jamie feel about having members within the family that it feels awkward to him to mention at school?

Trainee: think about how you might create an environment in which Jamie feels comfortable either to know that having a different family pattern from others is perfectly OK, and might even feel able to speak about if he wished.

When you imagined Jamie's situation, did you give Jamie a gender identity and, if so, what was this and why? Did you initially make any assumptions about Jamie's mum's partner?

Mentor: consider how this situation might be different if Jamie were not a pupil in your class but was a colleague or a trainee working in your school. How would you help to ensure that all members of the school community felt welcomed and valued?

Discussion

Mentor and trainee: discuss what resources are available in your school, showing diverse families and representing the world in which children are growing up. Additional resources are flagged up later in this chapter.

Reflecting the world around us

It is interesting to consider how our school environments reflect the world around us. Even if we feel that we live in a fairly homogeneous community (one where everyone seems the same or similar) in terms of social class, 'race', ethnicity, culture and sexual orientation, this does not mean that there are not unseen differences. In addition, it is likely that many of the children in our care will move beyond our community later in their lives and experience very different worlds. They will meet people from different communities, traditions and with different ideas from themselves. We need to remember that in whatever community children live, they are already part of wider worlds through interconnection provided by mass media. You only have to watch an episode of a popular soap opera to see that very diverse families, human relationships, and often tricky and complex situations are easily visible to children even in the potential comfort of their own homes.

To suggest that children are not aware of diverse ways of being family suggests that they have no friends, little wider family, do not mix with anyone in their street or local community, and have no access to television or other media products. In fact, that would be a very naive suggestion. Those who talk about schools that 'teach' children about families with same-sex parents, for example, imply that children are not aware of such families already. That seems highly unlikely in the modern age. Furthermore, talking with children about different families does not mean discussing sexual acts or practices with those children. Just as speaking with pupils about a family with a mummy and a daddy and two children does not require an explanation of how those children came into being, sharing a story about a family with two dads and their children also does not require an explanation. There is a danger that when straight (i.e. heterosexual) relationships are being discussed, there is a focus on the relationship, and when gay relationships are being spoken about immediately people think about sexual acts. There is no logic or reason to this, except for people's prejudices and it is important to make sure that we do not fall into such a trap.

 Reflection and discussion activity

Reflection

Think about the resources you have seen used in English or literacy lessons in school. Have any of them shown family relationships? If so, what kinds of families were represented? Did they all have two parents of different sex, or have you seen a range of resources showing children living with one or two parents, of the same and different genders, with other family members, in public care or other ways of being family?

Trainee: consider the impact that a limited range of resources might have on children from a wide variety of family backgrounds.

Mentor: consider how you can encourage your trainee to make the resources they use inclusive, to reflect the world in which children are learning and growing.

Discussion

Mentor and trainee: consider a strategy you might implement in the coming days to introduce an additional element of diversity and inclusion in a lesson that you are planning.

 Find out more from ... history

In 1988, the introduction of the Local Government Act (legislation.gov.uk, 1986) prohibited the promotion of homosexuality as a pretend family relationship. Technically, the Act did not apply to schools, but at the time this was not clear and many teachers working in schools felt this legislation limited what they were able to speak about with their pupils. The idea that same-sex relationships constitute a pretend family is itself interesting, and the thinking and attitudes of very many people have moved on in the intervening years. The Act was not repealed until 2003 (2000 in Scotland), although during its lifetime no one was ever prosecuted.

What it did do was to cause much caution and self-censorship. Recent reviews of policies in schools has revealed that a significant number have not revised their documentation following the repeal of the Act.

Contrast that with the Equality Act of 2010 (legislation.gov.uk), and the inclusion of the protected characteristics from that Act within the National Curriculum for England (DfE, 2014) and you get a sense of how approaches to difference and diversity have changed over past decades.

The Equality Act (2010) identifies nine protected characteristics, building upon a raft of equalities legislation that developed during the later twentieth and early twenty-first centuries, namely:

- age

- disability

- gender reassignment

- marriage and civil partnership

- pregnancy and maternity

- race

- religion or belief

- sex

- sexual orientation.

These protected characteristics form a basis for a broad understanding of inclusion within both our schools and wider society. Sometimes the term 'inclusion' is used as a synonym for provision for learners with special educational needs or disabilities. I think this is limiting and a wider interpretation provides the opportunity to draw in equality for all. The protected characteristics are not in themselves all-encompassing, neglecting to address issues including social class, family income and other areas causing social disadvantage. However, they are a starting point and cause us to think about inclusion as a term that involves us all and not just a subset of society. We all need to be included, however we identify and whatever our differences and personal traits.

Case study

I heard the story of a child who had been taught by their mum how to draw a house whenever the topic of "homes" came up at school. The child learned to draw a square house with a pitched roof, four windows and a door (Tierney, 2007). The parent felt that there would be a stigma attached to the fact that they lived in a trailer as part of a traveller community

(Woolley, 2010, p41)

Reflection and discussion activity

Reflection

Consider the situation outlined in the case study.

Trainee: reflect on how a child may feel if they are unable to speak about home, friends or family in school for fear of being marginalised or ostracised.

Mentor: reflect on any tensions within your local community, where differences between people cause discomfort or segregation. How might you help your trainee to be aware of these in order to help them avoid aggravating situations?

Discussion

Mentor and trainee: consider how the school environment can be enhanced to acknowledge, and even celebrate, diversity so that children see that difference is valued, even if they choose not to share their own differences.

Relating to others who are different

From September 2020, Relationships Education is mandatory in primary schools in England (DfE, 2019). This new curriculum brings the possibility of developing the profile of supporting learning about relationships and relatedness. It is not to be confused with Sex Education, which schools may choose to include in their curriculum, and from which parents and carers can choose to withdraw their child.

This is an interesting development in the range of statutory requirements given to schools. In essence, everything that a school does is about relationships and forms a part of relationships education. Each interaction between people – for example, the way the head teacher treats their staff, the way members of staff interact with each other, with parents and carers and with the children, and the ways in which children interact with one another and the kinds of behaviours that are tolerated or permitted, all of these help children to learn about how they fit into the world, their sense of value and self-worth, the value of others and what is acceptable or unacceptable in their community. In essence, this is Relationships Education.

The new curriculum indicates that:

> Today's children and young people are growing up in an increasingly complex world and living their lives seamlessly on and offline. This presents many positive and exciting opportunities, but also challenges and risks. In this environment, children and young people need to know how to be safe and healthy, and how to manage their academic, personal and social lives in a positive way.

(DfE, 2019, p4)

By the end of their time in primary school, it is expected that children will have learned about aspects of five key areas of study (DfE, 2019, pp20–2), namely:

- Families and people who care for me.

- Caring friendships.

- Respectful relationships.

- Online relationships.

- Being safe.

One way of exploring the diversity of family life in the UK is the use of children's picture books. The *Family Diversities Reading Resource* (Morris and Woolley, 2017) is a collection of over 150 high-quality stories and illustrations showing a broad spectrum of ways of being family. Originally developed by a group of students, a specialist librarian and an academic, this resource provides signposts to books ideally suited for inclusion in a school library. The resource is freely available online to all educational and not-for-profit groups, and can be downloaded from a link included later in this chapter. Drawing from the range of books, the differences experienced by children are clearly outlined. Key examples (adapted from Morris and Woolley, 2017) include the following.

Broken Bird (Broad, 2006)

Broken Bird doesn't realise that he is different from other birds when he hatches, but soon he senses that he is different from his brothers as he has only one wing. When the others fly away, he is left to make the best of his situation, walking around to explore his location. He meets different creatures and sees different places meeting Scary Bird along the way, named by her sisters because her one wing is expected to scare others away. The two birds discover friendship and love. They build a nest together and even learn to fly. This is a heart-warming and endearing tale of difference and love with the two birds finding that they complement each other perfectly. This book focuses on differences relating to physical attributes, disabilities and aptitudes.

Come Home Soon (Thomas, 2013)

This book explains that saying goodbye to a parent is not an easy process, and why it may be necessary for them to be away from home. It provides insight into a family where a member works in the armed forces. It acknowledges that feelings of anger or loneliness may occur, and provides opportunity to pause for thought and discuss such issues with children. The book is very inclusive, making it ideal to use whether mum or dad is working away from home. The sense of being under the same sky, even when separated is a lovely touch, and there is also a sense of optimism in looking forward to the parent's return home. This is a very reassuring book, and additional support on how to use it is included in a final section. This book focuses on differences relating to home backgrounds and changing family patterns.

If I Had a Hundred Mummies (Carter, 2006)

This book considers the trials and tribulations that would be faced if a child had just that – a hundred mums. There would be endless bedtime stories, masses of kisses and people to care, the need for a huge house and a whole range of clutter and junk. However, there might also be plenty of holidays, lots of sweets and plenty of ice-creams. The punch line is that one hundred mothers is not an exciting prospect, but having two is just fine. This is an unexpected end to the book. It provides an affirming message to children with two mums. Of course, there are many reasons why a child might have two mothers: mum and dad may be separated and there is a new partner; mum may have a female partner; some children refer to auntie or grandma as mum; and a child may have a birth mother and an adoptive mother. This book focuses on a range of ways of being family, using humour and exaggeration to amplify key issues in a warm and tender way.

Mum and Dad Glue (Gray, 2009)

This rhyming book reads with pace and an engaging lilt that addresses the difficult issue of parents divorcing in a thoughtful and sensitive manner. The main character is a young boy who seeks a pot of glue to mend his parents' relationship. He considers lots of options and ends up in a glue shop where the wise shopkeeper offers advice and support. The boy realises that while his parents' relationship may be broken, their love for him is not. This book represents the split in the parents' relationship through its illustrations which will provide a great deal of stimulus for discussion. As a metaphor, this book provides plenty of opportunity for reflection and developing perspectives on separation and divorce. This book explores separation in a sensitive and extremely thought-provoking manner, with a powerful impact.

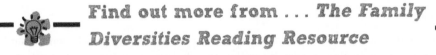

Find out more from ... *The Family Diversities Reading Resource*

The *Family Diversities Reading Resource* is freely available online to settings, schools and not-for-profit organisations (**https://eprints.worc.ac.uk/5921/**). It is an annotated bibliography of over 150 children's picture books for learners across the primary phase of education showing diverse forms of family life. A subject-focused index indicates groupings of books relating to different ways of being family, including one- and two-parent families and children living with a range of adults and in different types of home.

Strategies to support children's learning

Children's picture books provide one means of raising issues 'one step removed' from the experience of children. There is a wide range of other approaches that can be used to explore difference, raise issues and consider sensitive topics and structure lessons. Specific approaches can include the following (extended from Woolley, 2010, pp10–11).

- Engaging in a campaign – for example, writing to the local member of parliament, inviting them to visit the school, or supporting a think tank or campaign group on environmental or human rights issues.

- Involving visits and visitors – for example, a campaigner, member of the uniformed services or a local councillor.

- Role play, including considering the feelings of others who are facing challenging circumstances or local community issues.

- Forging international links, but in a mindful way that does not cause those in less privileged contexts to presume that resources or other benefits will be forthcoming.

- Visualisation, including imagining different worlds, communities or relationships.

- Role play, considering perspectives from others, but not 'standing in their shoes' as this is impossible. One can never actually know what it is like to be another person or know their situation.

- Debates and Philosophy for Children, a strategy to support questioning and reasoning and well worth further reading beyond this chapter.

- Buddying, putting in place and nurturing positive relationships to encourage mutual learning and support.

- Circle Time, a very common activity in primary school classrooms that facilitates turn-taking, active listening and developing empathy.

Each is worth exploring in its own right, and a wealth of reading and lesson plans are easily searchable online to support the development of your own approaches.

Key issues in the new statutory guidance for Relationships Education

The statutory guidance for Relationships Education (DfE, 2019) stipulates that each school will develop its own policy, outlining how the subject will be developed and delivered. This policy should:

- define Relationships Education;

- set out subject content;

- outline how it will be taught and by whom;

- describe how it will be monitored and evaluated;

- indicate why parents do not have a right to withdraw their child from the subject (although they retain the right to withdraw their child from Sex Education delivered outside the curriculum for science);

- identify a date for reviewing the policy.

The guidance makes clear that teaching about relationships should be inclusive, reflecting the communities in which the children are growing up, being respectful of their backgrounds and family beliefs, and also being sensitive about the range of families from which the children come.

Teaching about families requires sensitive and well-judged teaching based on knowledge of pupils and their circumstances. Families of many forms provide a nurturing environment for children. (Families can include for example, single parent families, LGBT parents, families headed by grandparents, adoptive parents, foster parents/carers amongst other structures.) Care needs to be taken to ensure that there is no stigmatisation of children based on their home circumstances and needs, to reflect sensitively that some children may have a different structure of support around them; e.g. looked after children or young carers.

(DfE, 2019, p19)

For some, this idea is controversial and there have been examples where teaching about same-sex parents, for example, has caused tensions within communities. It is important to make clear that the focus is not on sex or sexual acts, but rather on families and relationships. As noted earlier in this chapter, many, if not all children are aware that there are many different kinds of families represented in their schools, local communities and even in the television programmes that they watch. It is important to acknowledge this diversity and not to confuse speaking about relationships with talk about sex.

⚡ Find out more from ... internet clips

The following internet clip illustrates children's responses to the notions of equal (or same-sex) marriage:

www.huffingtonpost.com/2013/11/04/kids-react-gay-marriage_n_4212543.html

It is worth considering children's views when exploring curriculum content. Sometimes they are far more able to consider ideas than we give them credit for. Erricker (2003) suggests that the notion of protecting childhood innocence is flawed. Indeed, it may be more about giving adults a reason not to talk about issues that they themselves find difficult, sensitive or controversial. Creating safe and supportive environments in school where children are able to ask questions and develop their own ideas is one means of helping them to grow as confident and thoughtful individuals. As teachers, we have school policies – for example, on inclusion, anti-bullying, relationships education, and equality and diversity to support our approaches to valuing difference. We also work in an education system where the Equality Act (2010) is enshrined in the values outlined within the National Curriculum (DfE, 2014).

These build on aspects of the UN Convention on the Rights of the Child (United Nations General Assembly, 1989) which highlights the importance of children finding their own voice and developing their own views. It is important that we enable children to learn about and reflect upon the diverse range of relationships they will encounter as they learn and grow in order to help them have the self-confidence to feel comfortable with difference.

Taking it further . . . research

My own research looks at the sensitive and controversial issues that student teachers anticipate coming across in their first teaching post (Woolley, 2010, 2011; King-Hill and Woolley, 2018). The following quotations come from students in their final year of teacher training courses, both undergraduate and postgraduate, in England.

Consider how you react to each viewpoint and note any questions these student teachers raise for you.

I wouldn't have a problem teaching [about homophobia] but I feel that it is an issue that many parents may have strong feelings about towards the teaching of it and I think this is where the main difficulties lie.

> (Female undergraduate student, teaching children age 3-7 years, East Midlands, cited in King-Hill and Woolley, 2018, p133)

How do you begin to explain to a child what is happening in the world? People are committing horrendous crimes in the name of Islam. But how can this be explained to a child without causing religious hatred or unnecessary fear?

> (Female final-year undergraduate (third year), teaching children age 5-11 years, West Midlands)

Children refusing to play with others due to religion/ethnicity has already been witnessed by myself during placement. I assume it will happen again and I understand how to deal with it, although I feel it is an issue because the children are learning this behaviour from home.

> (Female PGCE student, teaching children age 5-9 years, London & South East)

At primary age I have found that children may display non-heteronormative behaviours and mannerisms however they tend to be too young to identify as LGBT, making it difficult to address homophobia as children may not realise that specific bullying is homophobic if they do not know they are gay etc or if another child is.

> (Female PGCE student, teaching children age 5-11 years, North East, cited in Mason and Woolley, 2019, p198)

I think that there are so many instances where gender stereotypes are present in the schools and it is not noticed and considered normal. It is also something that children encounter a lot at home and if this is something that children are struggling with then this is really going to affect their progress in their education. As a teacher, it is a subject that is really hard to get children to think about what it means to be a particular gender as they are so ingrained in our society and there is not a lot of awareness within schools themselves. I don't expect that there would be a great deal of support in a school for teachers should a situation arise.

> (Female PGCE student, teaching children age 5-11 years, North East, cited in Mason and Woolley, 2019, p196)

This is frequent at a low level (you can't do that because you're a girl) and almost excepted [sic] so will be hard to know when to confront it.

> (Male PGCE student, teaching children age 5-11 years, London & South East, cited in Mason and Woolley, 2019, p197)

Reflection and discussion activity

Reflection

The comments above from student teachers cover a range of differences encountered in everyday life, including gender stereotypes, religions, and belief and sexual orientation.

Trainee: consider whether your own concerns about the issues you will face in your first teaching post resonate with these from final year student teachers. How do your own perceptions and concerns about difference compare or contrast?

Mentor: consider how you can support your trainee in preparing to face difference and diversity in their first teaching post. What strategies do you use to promote inclusion, celebrate difference and ensure that the protected characteristics enshrined in the Equality Act (2010), the National Curriculum (2014) and the Statutory Guidance for Relationships Education (2019) are embedded in your setting?

Trainee and mentor: what hopes and apprehensions do you feel, anticipate and feel able to share in order to explore how to take forward effective practice?

Chapter summary

This chapter has explored some of the differences that exist between children and their homes and families. Importantly, it has focused on the normality of difference rather than viewing it as 'other' or the exception. If we can accept that approach to difference and diversity, confident in our own identities, there is less likelihood that difference will make us feel threatened, and prejudice and bigotry are less likely to flourish. Preparing children to live in a world pervaded by difference will help them not only to get on with their peers in the present day, but to be prepared for 'different others' as yet unknown to them.

References

Broad, M (2006) *Broken Bird: A true tale of love*. London: Puffin Books.

Carter, V (2006) *If I Had a Hundred Mummies*. London: Onlywomen Press.

Department for Education (DfE) (2014) *National Curriculum in England: Framework for Key Stages 1–4*. London: Department for Education. Available at: **www.gov.uk/government/publications/national-curriculum-in-england-framework-for-keystages-1-to-4/** (accessed 11 October 2019).

Department for Education (DfE) (2019) *Relationships Education, Relationships and Sex Education (RSE) and Health Education: Guidance for governing bodies, proprietors, head teachers, principals, senior leadership teams, teachers.* London: Department for Education.

Equality Act 2010. Available at: **www.legislation.gov.uk/ukpga/2010/15/contents** (accessed 19 October 2019).

Erricker, C (2003) Against the protection of childhood innocence. *International Journal of Children's Spirituality*, 8(1): 3–7.

Gray, K (2009) *Mum and Dad Glue.* London: Hodder Children's Books.

King-Hill, S and Woolley, R (2018) Sexual behaviours and development, in Woolley, R (ed.) *Understanding Inclusion: Core concepts, policy and practice.* London: Routledge.

Local Government Act 1986. Available at: **www.legislation.gov.uk/ukpga/1986/10** (accessed 19 October 2019).

Mason, S and Woolley, R (2019) *Relationships and Sex Education 3–11* (2nd edn). London: Bloomsbury.

Morris, J and Woolley, R (2017) *Family Diversities Reading Resource.* Lincoln: Bishop Grosseteste University and University of Worcester.

Tierney, A (2007) Travellers and Gypsies. Presentation at a conference to launch the local authority inclusion strategy Turning the Tables: Perception and Realities. North Lincolnshire Council, 2 March.

Thomas, P (2013) *Come Home Soon.* London: Wayland Books.

United Nations General Assembly (1989) *The UN Convention on the Rights of the Child.* New York: United Nations.

Woolley, R (2010) *Tackling Controversial Issues in the Primary School: Facing life's challenges with your learners.* London: Routledge.

Woolley, R (2011) Controversial issues: identifying the concerns and priorities of student teachers. *Policy Futures in Education*, 9(2): 280–91.

13
Professional responsibilities
Sue Lambert

 This chapter will

- help you to consider what safeguarding is (including the anti-radicalisation agenda);
- help you to be prepared if a child discloses something to you or you are concerned about what a child is saying or doing;
- encourage you to reflect on what is meant by 'fundamental British values' (FBV), to be aware of your own values and beliefs, and how this could impact on practice.

 Link to Teachers' Standards

1   **Set high expectations which inspire, motivate and challenge pupils**, specifically:
   - establish a safe and stimulating environment for pupils, rooted in mutual respect.

8   **Fulfil wider professional responsibilities** (all elements of this Standard).

Part Two. Personal and Professional Conduct

Introduction

The importance of the wider professional role is key to you becoming a well-rounded and effective teacher, who acts within the statutory frameworks. These set out your professional duties and responsibilities (DfE, 2011). Within Part Two: Personal and Professional Conduct of the current Teachers' Standards (DfE, 2011), teachers are required to demonstrate consistently high standards of personal and professional conduct. However, it is more than this. As a teacher, you are in a position of trust and you need to create a safe environment for children. They may feel comfortable telling you things they are struggling to understand or that are upsetting or confusing for them. They will also look to you as a role model, so you need to be aware of the impact you can have through your words, actions and role modelling.

It is also important for you to be involved in the school as part of the wider community too. As Ewens (2015) notes, when you start in a new school you need to find out as much as you can about the social and cultural setting from which the children are drawn. You need to know about *the preconceptions and expectations that children bring with them to school, which reflect the beliefs and values of their parents and carers* (p213). You also need to listen to school staff, look carefully at the school environment and read the school policies so that you are confident in your role as part of the school community, and know the school expectations for you in the wider professional role.

In this chapter, through reflection, case studies and ideas for discussion with mentors, you will consider approaches and strategies that develop your professional role. You need knowledge and understanding about freedom to choose, tolerance and avoiding prejudicial or discriminatory behaviour, however unintentional. You will also explore your role and responsibilities in relation to child protection. You need to be confident about your responsibilities and when you may need advice and help in matters of child protection or confidentiality. This chapter will also help you to think about strategies you need to have in place to support children who may share safeguarding issues with you.

Values, beliefs and FBV

We all have our own values and beliefs which are the result of our own experiences – personal, educational, social, and wider environmental and cultural influences. As a teacher, you need to think about what your own values and beliefs are so that you do not, however unintentionally, undermine the values of others or show intolerance or a lack of respect. Equally, you need to avoid imposing your values or beliefs on children, which is challenging. As Butroyd (2015) notes: *as teachers we are not always aware of the values that we transmit. Pupils interpret values and are not simply passive receptors. We need to be aware of values and consider their impact.* (p31)

Hayes (2015) also notes that you need to think about how you develop the positive classroom behaviours you want *while resisting the temptation . . . that your way is the only way.* (p175)

There needs to be a balance because children do not need you to be their friend, although they do want you to be friendly. They will look to you to model expectations on how you interact with them and how you expect them to interact with each other. It can be difficult to get this right when you first start teaching, especially if you are not in the class teacher role all the time until later in your training.

Reflection and discussion activity

Reflection

Trainee and mentor: separately, think about what your answer to the following question would be.

If you had ten words to describe what you value and believe a teacher should be and/or do, what would those words be? List them.

Discussion

Share your lists and look for similarities and differences. Discuss what this highlights about our own values and beliefs, and why we need to be aware of these when working with children.

Your values and beliefs about teaching may grow and change as you gain more experience, observe others teaching and in their wider role, and learn what works well and less well in the classroom. It is always important to be able to reflect on how children may see you in terms of modelling appropriate values and beliefs.

As a teacher, you will be expected to demonstrate consistently high standards of personal and professional conduct. The following statements are from Part Two of the Teachers' Standards and define the behaviour and attitudes expected.

- *Teachers uphold public trust in the profession and maintain high standards of ethics and behaviour, within and outside school, by:*

  o *treating pupils with dignity, building relationships rooted in mutual respect, and at all times observing proper boundaries appropriate to a teacher's professional position*

  o *having regard for the need to safeguard pupils' well-being, in accordance with statutory provisions*

  o *showing tolerance of and respect for the rights of others*

  o *not undermining fundamental British values, including democracy, the rule of law, individual liberty and mutual respect, and tolerance of those with different faiths and beliefs*

  o *ensuring that personal beliefs are not expressed in ways which exploit pupils' vulnerability or might lead them to break the law*

(DfE, 2011, p14)

The new Core Content Framework for ITT (2019) also specifically notes:

providers should continue to ensure that trainees have a clear understanding of the expectations regarding personal and professional conduct of a teacher and the ethics of the teaching profession.

This includes how Fundamental British Values can be upheld in schools and the importance of showing tolerance and respect for the rights of others.

(DfE, 2019a, p7)

 Reflection and discussion activity

Reflection

Trainee: think about a teacher you had when you were in school or a teacher you have observed teaching. Can you list aspects of how they behaved, or what they did or said that reflected the professional role of the teacher outlined in the section above?

Mentor: reflect on your understanding of the wider professional role of the teacher. What do you do, say and display in the classroom to reflect the expectations noted above? Think about things you can share with the trainee to help them model professionalism in the classroom.

Discussion

Trainee and mentor: look at and discuss the things you have both identified. Are they the same or different? Discuss how some of the things discussed can be modelled by the trainee in the classroom.

Fundamental British values

The terminology 'fundamental British values' (FBV) has caused some confusion and much discussion in the media and for schools. Some say that the term 'British' is divisive and not inclusive, while others have commented that the values expressed within the definition are positive values for all and promote inclusive citizenship. However, it is part of your role to promote these values in school as part of the whole-school duty to promote FBV, and Ofsted include this in their inspection reports. The promotion of FBV is largely done through the Spiritual, Moral, Social and Cultural (SMSC) curriculum and citizenship education underpins this, particularly in Key Stages 3 and 4.

 Reflection and discussion activity

Reflection

Trainee: look at the fourth point of the Teachers' Standards (2011) above to see how fundamental British values are defined. Can you think about examples that would explain this to someone else? If it helps, think about how you might explain this to someone who knew nothing about Britain.

Discussion

Mentor and trainee: discuss the examples that the trainee has suggested. Are they similar or different from to how you would define FBV?

 Reflection and discussion activity

Scenario: In the classroom you overhear a child comment negatively about what another child is wearing: 'You can't have nice things like me because your dad doesn't work.' Other children laugh and the child who has been mocked is upset and goes to sit on their own away from all their classmates.

Reflection

Trainee: think about what strategies you could use to address this sort of comment in terms of building respect, tolerance and understanding in your class. Do you know who you would tell, what you would record? Do you know about the school policies that address this? If not, find out about anti-bullying policies and procedures so you are confident about what to do and raise this in your discussion with your mentor.

Mentor: think about things you have used successfully in the classroom or playground that have helped in similar situations. What did you record and who did you share this with?

Discussion

Trainee and mentor: discuss the relevant policies and procedures that relate to this sort of incident, and strategies you could use in the classroom to address this. There are some suggestions at the end of this section that may be helpful.

Ideas for developing respect, tolerance and understanding

Some of the things suggested below may be helpful classroom practice for exploring values and beliefs. Schools may also have specific materials and visiting speakers who also help to address issues raised, so make sure you talk to your mentor about this. The resources and activities suggested in the following sections may also be useful. There are also ideas in Chapter 15 that may be helpful.

- Circle Time: encourage children to say something positive about the child next to them in the circle, or start a circle discussion with 'I feel sad when . . .', then 'I feel happy when . . .'. Make sure that children know that the circle is a safe place to explore feelings and that it is important to respect each other and that all responses are valued and not to be ridiculed.

- Create a circle of friends or use a buddy system to support the child and build friendship groups.

- Role play: putting yourself in someone else's shoes. Create scenarios and ask children how they felt in the role of someone being bullied or teased to raise awareness about feelings and empathy. Discuss strategies that they can use, who they could go to for help and teach them how to use their voice in an assertive manner.

- Create golden rules for the class – for example, rights to learn, be listened to and respected – and discuss why these are important and what they might look like in practice. This will help children to have ownership of their environment.

- Put the character back together again. Cut up a character and get the children to put it back together. This can promote discussion about whether the character is still the same after being broken and can again lead to discussion of feelings, respect and how bullying or not being valued can change a person.

- Social, moral, spiritual and cultural (SMSC) taught sessions and resources and use of stories (see the Find out more from websites section below).

- Making use of the restorative approaches discussed in Chapter 9 can also be helpful.

Find out more from ... websites

Booklists about difference, acceptance and bullying can be found by searching the Book Trust website: **www.booktrust.org.uk/books-and-reading/bookfinder/** (accessed 22 November 2019).

Promoting fundamental British values as part of SMSC in schools. DfE advice for maintained schools: **www.gov.uk/government/uploads/system/uploads/attachment_data/file/380595/SMSC_Guidance_Maintained_Schools.pdf** (accessed 7 November 2019).

Safeguarding

In this section you will learn more about child protection. It links closely to the previous section about values, beliefs and FBV. It is important for you to think about how you support children to develop knowledge, skills and understanding so that they have strategies to deal with difficult situations, can minimise risk-taking behaviours and allow them to make informed choices. You need to be prepared so that you know what to do, who you need to tell and what to record should a child disclose something to you, or if you have concerns about something a child does or says.

Safeguarding and promoting the welfare of children is defined as:

- *protecting children from maltreatment;*

- *preventing impairment of children's health and development;*

- *ensuring that children grow up in circumstances consistent with the provision of safe and effective care;*

- *taking action to enable children to have the best outcomes.*

(DfE, 2019b, p6)

Child protection refers to the activity undertaken to protect specific children who are suffering, or are likely to suffer, significant harm.

It is important for you to be familiar with the safeguarding policies of the schools in which you work. It can be very upsetting to hear what has happened to children, but you need to be confident in the policies and procedures, and schools will talk to you when you first go in about safeguarding. Make sure you know what to do and ask questions if you need to. Schools also have to consider confidentiality as do you, so always be professional and do not try to ask for information about children that might breach this. Table 13.1 outlines the types of abuse you need to be aware of.

Table 13.1 *Definitions of abuse from Working Together to Safeguard Children*

Neglect	Emotional abuse
The persistent failure to meet a child's basic physical and/or psychological needs, likely to result in the serious impairment of the child's health or development. It may occur during pregnancy as a result of maternal substance abuse. Once a child is born, neglect may involve a parent or carer failing to: • provide adequate food, clothing and shelter (including exclusion from home or abandonment); • protect a child from physical and emotional harm or danger; • ensure adequate supervision (including the use of inadequate care-givers); • ensure access to appropriate medical care or treatment. It may also include unresponsiveness to, or neglect of a child's basic emotional needs.	The persistent emotional maltreatment of a child such as to cause severe and persistent adverse effects on their emotional development. It may involve: • conveying to them that they are worthless, unloved, inadequate, or valued only insofar as they meet the needs of another person; • not giving them opportunities to express their views, deliberately silencing them or 'making fun' of what they say, or how they communicate. • developmentally inappropriate expectations being imposed; interactions that are beyond the child's developmental capability; • overprotection and limitation of exploration and learning; • preventing the child participating in normal social interaction; • seeing/hearing the ill-treatment of another; • serious bullying causing them frequently to feel frightened or in danger; • exploitation or corruption of them. Some level of emotional abuse is involved in all types of maltreatment of a child, though it may occur alone.

(Continued)

Table 13.1 (Continued)

Sexual abuse	Physical abuse
• forcing or enticing a child to take part in sexual activities, not necessarily involving a high level of violence, whether or not the child is aware of what is happening; • physical contact: including assault by penetration - e.g. rape or oral sex; or non-penetrative acts - e.g. masturbation, kissing, rubbing and touching outside of clothing; • Non-contact activities - e.g. involving children in looking at/in the production of sexual images/activities, encouraging children to behave in sexually inappropriate ways, grooming a child in preparation for abuse.	A form of abuse which may involve: • hitting, shaking, throwing, poisoning, burning, scalding, drowning, suffocating, or otherwise causing physical harm to a child; • physical harm may also be caused when a parent or carer feigns the symptoms of, or deliberately induces illness in a child; • injuries in babies and non-mobile children.
Child sexual exploitation	
is a form of child sexual abuse. It occurs where: • an individual or group takes advantage of an imbalance of power to coerce, manipulate or deceive a child or young person under the age of 18 into sexual activity (a) in exchange for something the victim needs or wants, and/or (b) for the financial advantage or increased status of the perpetrator or facilitator; • victim may have been sexually exploited even if the sexual activity appears consensual; • child sexual exploitation does not always involve physical contact; it can also occur through the use of technology.	

Source: (DfE, 2019a, pp102–3)

Some possible indicators of abuse

Remember that professional judgement is most important and no list can be comprehensive enough to show all indicators of abuse.

There are some behaviours that can suggest that a child is being abused, but equally children can show some signs that may not mean they are being abused. It is sometimes changes in behaviour, appearance and/or health that can ring alarm bells, but not always. The important thing is to take each case individually. Never ignore your concerns. The child:

• may be late, or stays away from school, or arrives early and stays late. Seems to want to avoid going home;

• may be quiet, withdrawn and uncommunicative;

- talks about someone 'doing things' to them;

- has bruising on the face, arms, legs, buttocks etc. and may try to explain these, but what they say is not consistent with the injuries;

- may show signs of obvious neglect (see Table 13.1);

- may be thin or appears not to be thriving;

- may have other signs of injury which are difficult to explain, such as burns, grazes, teeth marks, scratches.

 Reflection and discussion activity

Discussion

Mentor and trainee: talk about the safeguarding policy for the school. After you have done this, see if the trainee can answer the questions below. If you (trainee) do not know the answers to some of the questions, talk to your mentor to make sure you are really clear about what to do.

Who is the Designated Safeguarding Lead (DSL) in school and have you had an opportunity to speak to them?

Do you know who to speak to and what to record?

Do you know about the role of the Local Authority Designated Officer (LADO)?

Have you seen key documents and read any guidance that all staff are expected to read (such as the expectation to read Part 1 of DfE, 2019c, *Keeping Children Safe in Education.*

For any child to disclose something to you, they need to feel safe and know that they are going to be listened to and not judged. There are some guidance ideas at the end of this section, but try to think about your approach by reading the scenarios first and having discussions with your mentor.

Read the scenario below and think about what you would do.

 Reflection and discussion activity

Scenario: You have noticed that a child who is usually happy and enjoys playing with other children is very quiet, not eating their lunch and is often upset, and that this has been going on for a few days. At breaktime

(Continued)

(Continued)

they stay in the classroom until all the other children have left and ask to speak to you. They ask you if you can keep a secret.

Reflection

Trainee: think about what your response to the child would be.

Mentor: share the sort of responses that you give to a child if they say something like this to you.

Discussion

Mentor and trainee: can you think of a 'script' that the trainee can use so that they say the right thing in this situation?

 Reflection and discussion activity

Scenario: You hear two children talking about Jake and saying that they have heard loud arguing coming from his house and that their parents have seen Jake out on his own in the garden late at night. Jake seems to be quite tired and withdrawn in class but has not said anything about home.

Reflection

Trainee: think about what you need to do in this situation. Are there any things you are not sure about? Note these and share them in the discussion with your mentor.

Mentor: think about what the important things are for the trainee to consider in this situation and how you would handle it. Share this in the discussion.

Discussion

Mentor and trainee: discuss things the trainee is unsure about and what must be done in this situation, and what could be done that might be helpful. Use the following prompts if they are helpful.

- What makes this a tricky situation to deal with?

- What needs to be recorded and how should it be recorded – factual, dated, etc.?

- What could be helpful next steps for the child and family?

- Who will follow this up?

It is really important that you never promise confidentiality. If the child decides not to tell you, then you should not push them to do so. You need to make sure you record that they had asked if they could tell you something but did not do so, after you had said that you might not be able to keep it confidential. It is helpful for you to give them other opportunities to talk to you, but do not ask them to tell you or lead them.

The following should summarise some of the points raised from reflection, discussion and the scenarios. If a child discloses a safeguarding issue you need to:

- *Be an effective listener.* Think about your facial expression and how you can show the child you are really listening to them and appreciate that they felt able to speak to you. Remain calm. Think about what you can say to them when they have finished talking. For example, 'I'm glad that you felt you could talk to me and I have listened really carefully. This is what I am going to do now . . .'.

- *Be non-judgemental.* It is really hard not to show how you feel, but if you look shocked or angry the child might think you are judging them and stop talking to you.

- *Never stop a child who is recalling events.* Try to listen rather than question, but if you do need to ask, make sure it is an open question – e.g. 'Is there anything else you want to tell me?'. Do not do anything that may jeopardise the record of what a child tells you, such as asking leading questions or attempting to investigate further yourself.

- *Be honest.* Do not promise confidentiality or something you cannot achieve. The child needs to know that you will need to do what is best for them to keep them safe.

- *Make a record of the discussion.* Include time, place, persons present and what was said. Use the language that the child used. Do this as soon as you can after a child has spoken to you. Talk to the designated safeguarding lead who will be able to help you with this.

 Find out more from ... websites

A useful clip about how to be a good listener: **https://learning.nspcc.org.uk/research-resources/2019/let-children-know-you-re-listening/** (accessed 25 November 2019).

The NSPCC website has lots of information and advice about supporting children who may be at risk of, or are being abused. It also links to Childline and resources and ideas to help children: **www.nspcc.org.uk** (accessed 25 November 2019).

Cyberbullying

Some elements of cyberbullying are child abuse and should be treated as such, with the same procedures followed, as already discussed. Cyberbullying can include:

- sending rude and abusive messages or humiliating someone;

- sending untrue information with the intent to ridicule, spread rumours or gossip;

- deliberately sending offensive and/or extreme language because they enjoy causing distress;

- impersonating someone and posting untrue, embarrassing or vicious content and exclusion of someone from a group deliberately;

- There is also cyber stalking which may lead to legal action depending on what is being done.

(Points adapted from the BullyingUK website: **www.bullying.co.uk/cyberbullying/** (accessed 25 November 2019).

For children, cyberbullying can be very distressing and you need to think about what you do in school to help prevent this, and what to do if you are made aware that this is happening to a child. Make sure you know what the school anti-bullying policy says and what children are taught about cyberbullying.

 Reflection and discussion activity

Scenario: Although mobile phones are not allowed in class, you hear a group of children talking about messages and pictures they have seen of another child in the class that an older child has sent threatening to 'get them' when they leave school, and saying that no one will help them because they have no friends. You have noticed that the child being threatened has been upset and not wanting to leave at the end of the day.

Reflection

Trainee: what would you do in this situation. Think about what the school policy says situation?

Discussion

Mentor and trainee: discuss what the trainee has said they would do. Were there things they were not sure about? What can you both do to address this sort of situation?

Child protection and exploitation online

There are a number of areas that need to be considered, including online grooming of children and radicalisation, which is discussed in the following section in more detail. Children and young adults can be very naive about who they talk to online. This is particularly true of vulnerable children who may feel that they do not have many friends, or they do not fit in, but this is not necessarily the case. There are several websites that can be helpful for supporting children and there are links to these in the Find out more from websites section above. These include helping children and young people think about friendships and relationships, raising awareness of risky behaviours, and knowing what to do and who to contact or speak to if they are concerned for themselves or someone else. The strategies in the values and beliefs section are also useful for exploring this and the school may also have specific resources and displays that help children to know what to do, or who to contact, so talk to your mentor about this and become familiar with the materials that the school uses.

 Reflection and discussion activity

Scenario: Jane is worried because a friend has told her that she has a new boyfriend. Her friend has never met him, but they have been in touch through Facebook and text messages for a few weeks, and she thinks they will soon want to meet. He has asked her to keep it a secret. In class recently there have been sessions about online safety and Jane asks you questions about how you know if someone is really a friend online. She does not mention her friend directly, but you are worried about the nature of her questions and that someone may be at risk of online grooming.

Reflection

Trainee: do you know what to do if you have concerns about a child being exploited online? Think about what you might do in this situation. Make a note of things to discuss with your mentor and anything you are not sure about.

Mentor: have you had a situation like this arise? If you have, what did you do? If you have not, what would you do?

Mentor and trainee: discuss what you would do. Did you have the same approach? If not, what were the differences? If it helps, use the following prompts:

- What resources are used in school to support in educating children about exploitation?

- Are there posters and displays in school to support children and taught sessions in computing and SMSC?

- Which policies do you need to be aware of?

- What are the procedures for this in school and did you follow these in your reflection?

- Who do you speak to about concerns?

- What do you record and where?

 Find out more from ... websites

Child Exploitation and Online Protection (CEOPs) website has sections for different age groups exploring games, information and advice. There is also a section for teachers and parents and carers: **www.thinkuknow. co.uk/** (accessed 25 November 2019).

NSPCC materials to help children be 'Share aware' with links to games and apps: **www.nspcc.org.uk/fighting-for-childhood/about-us/partners/nspcc-o2-online-safety-partnership/** (accessed 25 November 2019).

This site has information and advice about bullying and how to address it, and also about dealing with bullying in school: **www.bullying.co.uk/bullying-at-school/** (accessed 25 November 2019).

Anti-radicalisation agenda

This links closely to all the previous sections, as it is a safeguarding issue and needs to be treated as such if you have concerns that a child is at risk of extremism or radicalisation. The whole school has a key role in this. You will know from the news media of cases where children and young people have been radicalised or influenced to behave in certain ways by extremist materials and/or people, both online and in person. Some schools are in Prevent priority areas, so you need to check and make sure you know if the schools you train in are in these areas.

Schools need a broad and balanced curriculum that promotes FBV and robust safeguarding policies and procedures. As part of the Prevent agenda, they also need trained staff who can identify at-risk children and know the referral procedures. They also need to protect children from extremist or terrorist materials online at school. Schools have a duty to challenge extremist views in the same way as they would challenge other prejudicial or discriminatory language or actions.

The values and beliefs section is also important because it is through creating a classroom environment that promotes respect, tolerance and understanding of others that you can help to prevent children and young people becoming as susceptible to extremism and radicalisation.

The Prevent agenda for schools is based on the following non-statutory guidance:

> *Protecting children from the risk of radicalisation should be seen as part of schools and childcare providers' wider safeguarding duties, and is similar nature to protecting children from other harms (e.g. drugs, gangs, neglect, sexual exploitation), whether these come from within their family or are the product of outside influences.*

(DfE, 2015, p4)

 Reflection and discussion activity

Scenario: You have been doing a session about immigration and encouraged the children to pin where they are from on a map of the world. You have also talked about historical migration from the times of the early invaders and settlers to more recent times, including people moving from the UK to other parts of the world. In the playground you overhear a group of children discussing what you have been doing in class and a child is overheard saying, 'My Dad says you should go back to where you came from because you don't want to fit in and your kind cause trouble'.

Reflection

Trainee: what would you do straight away? What would you do to follow this up with your mentor, with the child, with the class?

Mentor: think of what you would do to support the trainee if a situation like this arose.

Trainee and mentor: discuss what the trainee has thought about in terms of following up the incident, and also what would be recorded and reported. Who else might you involve to deal with the wider issues this raises?

Find out more from ... websites

Some resources which might be helpful are the Prevent for Schools (P4S) materials, which are available for KS1 to KS4. These look at a range of issues and approaches.

- Respect for yourself and your friends, the abolition of slavery, materials to support understanding and tolerance of different faiths and cultures and the importance of the school in the wider community: **www.preventforschools.org/** (accessed 25 November 2019).

- A site for teachers and children with information about being internet smart: **www.gov.uk/govern ment/uploads/system/uploads/attachment_data/file/251455/advice_on_child_internet_safety.pdf** (accessed 25 November 2019).

- A guide for social networking for trainee teachers and NQTs: **www.childnet.com/ufiles/Social-networking.pdf** (accessed 25 November 2019).

- Videos and resources for primary and secondary age to help raise awareness of cyber bullying and strategies to prevent it and deal with it: **www.childnet.com/teachers-and-professionals/for-working-with-young-people/hot-topics/cyberbullying** (accessed 25 November 2019).

- CEOPs resources and materials for teachers for different age groups to raise awareness of cyber bullying, promote discussion and develop strategies to help children deal with cyber bullying, report it and avoid it: **www.thinkuknow.co.uk/** (accessed 25 November 2019).

- Link to a range of resources and sites that have materials to help address bullying issues and promote respect and tolerance: **www.anti-bullyingalliance.org.uk/tools-information** (accessed 25 November 2019).

- Bristol Guides are a handbook for education professionals and are updated annually. They contain information about statutory guidance for teachers and roles and responsibilities: **www.bristol.ac.uk/education/expertiseandresources/bristolguide/** (accessed 25 November 2019).

- DfE article about social media and how it can be a mechanism for radicalisation: **www.gov.uk/government/uploads/system/uploads/attachment_data/file/440450/How_social_media_is_used_to_encourage_travel_to_Syria_and_Iraq.pdf** (accessed 25 November 2019).

Chapter summary

This chapter has addressed a number of aspects of your professional role and may have raised questions as well as giving opportunities to think about the wider professional role, and your own values and beliefs. Think about what you need to do next to develop your confidence in your professional role.

The most important message for you to remember is that any safeguarding issue always needs to be addressed, and there will be a whole-school approach. As a teacher, you are part of the wider school

(Continued)

(Continued)

community, and knowing the children you teach, the staff you work with, the parents and carers and the community in which the school is based, are important to you being able to develop this professional role effectively. Your classroom needs to be a safe environment where children and young people feel able to ask questions, explore situations and be supported in developing strategies to keep themselves safe and develop tolerance, respect and resilience.

References

Butroyd, R (2015) Relationships with children and young people. In Denby, N (ed.) (2015) *Training to Teach: A guide for trainee teachers* (3rd edn). London: SAGE, pp19–32.

Department for Education (DfE) (2011) *Teachers' Standards*. Available at: **http://media.education.gov.uk/ assets/files/pdf/t/information%20sheet%201%20final.pdf** (accessed 7 November 2019).

Department for Education (DfE) (2015) *The Prevent Duty Departmental Advice for Schools and Childcare Providers*. Available at: **www.gov.uk/government/uploads/system/uploads/attachment_data/file/439598/ prevent-duty-departmental-advice-v6.pdf** (accessed 7 November 2019).

Department for Education (DfE) (2019a) *Initial Teacher Training (ITT) Core Content Framework*. Available at: **www. gov.uk/government/publications/initial-teacher-training-itt-core-content-framework** (accessed 14 November 2019).

Department for Education (DfE) (2019b) *Working Together to Safeguard Children*. Available at: **www.gov.uk/ government/publications/working-together-to-safeguard-children--2** (accessed 7 November 2019).

Department for Education (DfE) (2019c) *Keeping Children Safe in Education*. Available at: **www.gov.uk/govern ment/publications/keeping-children-safe-in-education--2** (accessed 7 November 2019).

Ewens, T (2015) The school community: being part of a wider professional environment. In Hansen, A (ed.) *Primary Professional Studies* (3rd edn). London: SAGE, pp204–20.

Hayes, D (2015) Establishing your own teacher identity. In Hansen, A (ed.) *Primary Professional Studies* (3rd edn). London: SAGE, pp170–86.

Ofsted (2018) *Safeguarding Policy*. Available at: **www.gov.uk/government/publications/ofsted-safe guarding-policy/ofsted-safeguarding-policy** (accessed 7 November 2019).

14

Working with other adults

Emma Clarke

 This chapter will

- develop your understanding of how to work with other adults in schools;
- consider how best to deploy other adults and specifically Teaching Assistants (TAs);
- be aware of some recent research and guidance on deploying TAs;
- reflect on some of your own values and beliefs which will impact on the way you work with TAs.

 Links to the Teachers' Standards

8 **Fulfil wider professional responsibilities**, specifically:
  - deploy support staff effectively

Introduction

Deploying other adults, specifically support staff, effectively is a requirement within Standard 8 of the Teachers' Standards (DfE, 2011) and relates to fulfilling your wider responsibilities as a teacher. Working with other adults, TAs in particular, is a fact of life for most teachers now with the Education Endowment Foundation research (Sharples *et al.*, 2015) stating that there are now more TAs than teachers in primary schools. Your chances of working with a TA are therefore very high, and it is essential that you get this important relationship right. However, TAs are not the only group of adults working in schools: you may also encounter parent helpers, office staff, governors, administrators, faith leaders, and many more. Although this chapter focuses specifically on working with TAs, many of the strategies, skills and key points discussed will also relate to other adults.

 Reflection and discussion activity

Reflection

Trainee: think of all of the different adults you may encounter in school.

Mentor: share with the trainee some of the roles that other adults in you school undertake.

Discussion

Mentor and trainee: discuss together some of the advantages of other adults working in schools.

Different expectations and roles of TAs

A key issue which often arises when working with TAs is that their role is very varied, and different schools use TAs in different ways. Historically, TAs were viewed by some as a *mum's army* of *paint pot washers* (Bach *et al.*, 2006). This somewhat negative and belittling view has thankfully long since gone and TAs are now viewed by some as 'paraprofessionals', taking on many of the roles of qualified teachers. However, in research (Bland and Sleightholme, 2012), pupils did not comment on the pedagogical role of TAs, but on the fact that they were required to *fetch coffee and biscuits for the teacher*. This is clearly not an effective use of support staff.

The roles that TAs play in schools have changed significantly over the years. TA numbers first experienced a significant increase with the introduction of the 1981 Education Act which encouraged pupils with special educational needs to move from special into mainstream schools. TA numbers continued to rise with the advent of the National Curriculum in the late 1980s, when increasing TA numbers were seen as a way of easing the increasing bureaucratic demands on teachers. In 2003, with the publication of *Raising Standards and Tackling Workload: A National Agreement* (DfES, 2003), the role of Higher Level TA (HLTA) was created, and later when the requirement for teachers to be freed up for planning, preparation and assessment (PPA) time was brought in, the role that TAs undertook expanded. Many HLTAs were used by schools to cover PPA times when teachers were not in classrooms. This raised some concerns for both HLTAs and teachers.

It is the expectation that TAs play an increasingly pedagogical role in schools that has been the most controversial, and has caused apprehension for teachers and TAs alike. Some changes were welcomed, with suggestions that being a TA was now a *profession* rather than being a *second class citizen* (Galton and MacBeath, 2008). The evolving TA role was also described as increasingly *interesting and professional*, and was shifting away from the perception that a TA is someone who only *staples something to a board for eight hours a day* (Cockroft and Atkinson, 2015). Nevertheless, the blurring of roles between the teacher and the TA was seen by some as producing a decline in teacher's professional status (Blatchford *et al.*, 2007) and *role creep* was viewed as a threat to teachers. This *role creep* was seen as a concern for both teachers and TAs, where TAs felt to some extent coerced into responsibilities they were not trained or qualified for (Anderson and Finney, 2008), while some teachers viewed TAs' encroaching role as a threat to their autonomy and professionalism.

TAs' roles have now changed beyond recognition since the days where the job was viewed by some as *a bit of money for housewives* (Smith *et al.*, 2004), and research (Blatchford *et al.*, 2007) has shown that TAs' *direct pedagogical role* is now greater than time spent helping either the teacher or the school. However, this has resulted in many schools having a lack of a shared clear and cohesive understanding of TA expectations. This can make working with TAs in the classroom difficult as it can leave you in a position where you are unsure of what you can and cannot reasonably ask them to do. Schools will have job descriptions for TAs, but teachers often do not get to see these.

 Reflection and discussion activity

Reflection

Trainee: think about the range of tasks that a TA or other adult may be asked to undertake. Rehearse having a discussion with a TA or other adult about some of these specific tasks you would like them to do.

Discussion

Mentor: briefly explain how TAs are deployed in your school and the range of responsibilities they have.

Mentor and trainee: consider how the wide variety of ways in which TAs are deployed may be beneficial or problematic for teachers.

It might be beneficial when you sit down to meet with any other adults you work with in the classroom and particularly your TA to ask them what types of work they usually do in the classroom, what they would like to do, and possibly what they would not like to do. It is also important to know about any specific skills or strengths that TAs working with you possess, and if they are willing to share them. For example, if you have a TA who is highly skilled in art or music, this could enhance the teaching you provide; if your TA is bilingual, they could support your languages provision, and so on.

Different schools and teachers use TAs differently, with some TAs having largely pedagogical roles while others are deployed to support teachers, and it is important you find out how your class teacher or school deploys certain TAs. For example, some TAs may work one-to-one with a pupil with specific difficulties, others may carry out administration tasks, some (often HLTAs) may cover whole classes, while others may teach specific interventions. TAs are employed under different contracts at differing grades and some, specifically HLTAs, may have greater responsibilities than others and, therefore, you may deploy them in different ways and expect different things from them.

This chapter will look specifically at TAs who are allocated either to you as a class teacher or to your class more generally and are working under your direction.

How to develop professional working relationships with other adults in the classroom: research

Mackenzie (2011) found in her research that teacher–TA relationships were exemplified by *tensions, misunderstandings and even antagonism*. Almost 20 years before that, Thomas (1992) noted that *good teamwork is notoriously difficult to achieve*, and he raised concerns over issues of cooperation between professionals who may hold radically different ideas on what should be done in the classroom as well as *on what education is all about*.

This all clearly contradicts the *close partnership* between teachers and TAs which was cited as providing *a marked improvement in the quality of teaching* (HMI, 2002). Yet research (Blatchford *et al.*, 2007) showed that teachers believed that TAs had a positive impact on pupils' *motivation, social skills and behaviour*. Teachers reported that working with TAs also had advantages in improving pupils' learning outcomes, providing increased support for learning and teaching, and improved classroom management (Blatchford *et al.*, 2004). This was echoed in later research by Galton and MacBeath (2008) who found that teachers particularly valued TAs' contributions when working with small groups or specified pupils. Recent research by the Education Endowment Foundation (Sharples *et al.*, 2015) confirmed the benefits of teachers working with TAs, which included freeing up the teachers so that they were able to spend more time *on the core functions of teaching*. Advantages were also seen in the reduction of teacher workload and, as echoed in other research, an improvement in *teachers' perceptions of stress and job satisfaction*. Importantly, teachers stated that having a TA present also increased their confidence and ability *to cope* (Galton and MacBeath, 2008).

 Reflection and discussion activity

Reflection

Trainee: have you seen or heard about any of the advantages or pitfalls of working with other adults in the classroom? Were there any that have not been mentioned above? How might you manage some of the issues mentioned?

Mentor: share your experiences of working with adults in the classroom, both positive and negative. How did you manage the negative and foster the positive aspects of the relationship?

Discussion

Mentor and trainee: research stated that TAs improved the teacher's ability *to cope*. What do you think is meant by this? How might TAs do this?

As a result of TAs' changing and evolving role, it is often rather difficult to clarify expectations. Research showed that where there was no clear definition of the TA role, the gap was often filled by an unsatisfactory reliance on the teacher and TA 'getting on' with each other. It could be seen that that this is not a professional way to conduct the teacher–TA relationship. It is important to ensure that you can have both a professional and friendly relationship with your TA. This will support you in getting the best out of the working relationship for you, the TA, and most importantly the pupils in your class. It will be key to understand some of the main issues emerging from research. These include the following.

- *Time*: this is probably one of the most important issues to consider in developing a professional relationship with your TA or TAs.

Webster *et al.* (2011) found that three-quarters of teachers questioned had no formal time to plan and talk over sessions with TAs, which resulted in *brief and ad hoc* discussions. This supported earlier research (Marr *et al.*, 2001), which found similar issues, but also reported that where joint planning and feedback took place, only one in five TAs were paid for the additional time. Gerschel's (2005) research showed that the *lack of prior notice* and necessity to *interpret teaching in the lesson* was a source of frequent complaints from TAs. Similarly, Blatchford *et al.*, (2012), reported that two-thirds of teachers and three-quarters of TAs rated preparation and feedback time as *less effective*, reiterating reliance on TAs' *goodwill*. These themes also recurred in Sharples *et al.*'s (2015) research, with TAs stating they often *went into lessons blind*, and that communication, as previously stated, often relied on TAs generosity meeting during unpaid hours.

It can be seen, then, that it is imperative that you liaise carefully with any TAs and other adults you work with, and ensure (unless it has already been done on a whole-school level) that you have time to discuss with your TAs the content of your lesson, and what you expect them to do, as well as ideally providing some forum for feedback at the end of the session. In some schools, this can take place in assembly time; others, where time is short, rely on 'communication books'. However, if you depend on writing rather than talking, ensure that at some point in the day or week you make time to chat with your TA. Be mindful, though, that playtimes and lunchtimes are not always convenient, and many TAs do not get paid for time before or after school. Several of the practical ideas later in this chapter rely on the assumption that you will have spent time discussing these with your TA, rather than simply surprising them in the middle of a session.

- *Training*: this is a key aspect to be aware of.

Much research (including, but not only, Tucker, 2009; Symes and Humphrey, 2011; Sharples *et al.*, 2015) has shown a *mismatch* between the level of training that TAs receive and their increasingly demanding role. The DfEE (1997) cautioned that many *TAs had little or no training for the work they do* and Ofsted (2008) conceded that *weaknesses remained* in training and deployment. The same point was highlighted later (Webster *et al.*, 2011; Sharples *et al.*, 2015) with concerns continuing to be raised about the level of training that TAs had. It is important, therefore, that you take some time to discuss with your TA(s) whether they have had any specific training and in what. If your TA has not received any recent training, bear in mind that they may need support and guidance if you have asked them to carry out specific focused intervention tasks, for example.

Case study

Kahina, an experienced teacher, and Jo, her TA, invested time in meeting together before the start of the year. They used this time to discuss the strengths and skills that each could bring to the classroom. Kahina discovered that Jo was a talented artist and they discussed how these skills could be shared with the pupils. They also considered how to keep each other informed about planning and progress for specific pupils, and decided a shared book would be useful. Kahina added the weekly plans when they were completed, and Jo added notes about specific pupils and more general feedback on progress. They also agreed to have an informal chat about the week when they were on playground duty together. This ensured that there was a range of strategies to keep communication open between them and they were clear about the specific strengths each other had.

 Reflection and discussion activity

Reflection

Trainee: how does the school you are in or other schools you have worked in manage some of these challenges? What have you seen that works well?

Discussion

Mentor: discuss what your school does or is planning to do to manage some of these challenges.

Trainee: what do you feel is 'best practice' here? How will you cope with these issues?

How to deploy other adults effectively: what research has shown

There has been a steady increase in the guidance on how schools should work with other adults and specifically TAs, but some of the proposed strategies rely on whole-school negotiation and cannot always be implemented by individual teachers. However, some of the key ideas from research which you can implement will now be discussed.

- *Working with low-attaining pupils or pupils with SEND*: historically, TAs usually worked with these pupils, either in the classroom or in withdrawal groups which worked outside the classroom.

Evidence from research (Webster *et al.*, 2012; Webster, 2014) has highlighted the continuing beliefs of some schools and parents that TAs were 'hardwired' to support pupils with SEND. Yet, findings (Blatchford *et al.*,

2012) demonstrated that when TAs worked with lower attaining or SEN pupils, they actually had a negative impact on their achievement.

However, there are ways to deploy TAs with pupils who need the most support that positively impacts on their progress, which is through structured interventions for short periods. Sharples *et al.* (2015) highlighted that *positive effects are only observed when TAs work in structured settings with high-quality support and training*. These elements are, therefore, essential to keep in mind when planning interventions and deploying TAs to work with specific groups.

- *Supporting not replacing the teacher*: it is important that you do not expect the TA to take on your teaching role.

Think carefully about where your skills and expertise are most needed, and how your TA can support you in freeing up time to work with those pupils in order to ensure that all pupils are making progress. When planning, make sure that you do not use your TA to support the same group of pupils for an extended period. Try to ensure that if you have asked your TA to work with a group outside the classroom on a specific planned intervention this is not for a prolonged period. Both the pupils and the TA should be included in whole-class activities; constantly working outside the classroom is not beneficial for either the pupils or for the TA.

 Case study

Lucy, an experienced TA, found that the teachers she now worked with asked her to undertake short-term interventions with a range of pupils usually outside the classroom. Lucy felt marginalised and was concerned that she was not seen as part of the class. She felt that being asked to work outside the classroom resulted in her not building relationships with the teacher or the pupils. As a result, she felt this hindered any specifically tailored work, as she did not know the pupils well and she found it difficult to understand what the teacher wanted because she did not know how the pupils achieved in class or the usual routines and expectations.

Developing pupils' independence

Research (Webster, 2014) showed that pupils who worked with TAs for extended periods, particularly those on a one-to-one basis, had significantly less contact with the teacher and their peers, with the TA being their main source of interaction.

This model of the TA closely working with the same pupil or same small group of pupils also raises the issues of 'stereo teaching', where the TA simply repeats what the teacher says, and the 'velcro' model, where the TA works so closely with a pupil or pupils that they unintentionally reduce their interaction with others. These both promote reliance on the TA and reduce the pupil's, or pupils', independence, which is something that you as a teacher need to foster. Research (Russell *et al.*, 2013; Webster and Blatchford, 2013; Sharples *et al.*, 2015) has shown that TAs' interactions with pupils are different from teacher interactions. Task completion as opposed to a clear understanding of the objective is often prioritised by TAs, and closed, rather than open, questions are asked. A difference in the amount of support versus 'spoon feeding' provided was also seen, with TAs often not giving pupils long enough to answer questions. This effectively *closes down* (Russell *et al.*, 2013) discussion and, coupled with the *vague explanations*, some TAs were observed to give constrained rather than enhanced learning. Nevertheless, with careful deployment, these issues can be minimised. Sharples *et al.* (2015) suggested encouraging your TA to focus on the following:

- *Providing the right amount of support at the right time*: this will help to develop pupils' independence and enquiry, rather than simply waiting for the TA to tell them the answer.

- Encouraging *pupils to be comfortable taking risks with their learning*: this links with the previous point. Encourage your TA to sit and wait, and to support the pupil in developing their own thoughts, ideas and understanding, rather than focusing on simply getting the task finished.

- *Giving the least amount first to help support pupils' ownership of the task*: again, this links closely with the above points. Support your TA in enhancing pupils' independence: this can be done by ensuring that your TA does not work with the same group or individual pupils all the time.

- *Use of open-ended questions*: the grid in Figure 14.1 was suggested to help TAs (and also teachers) develop open-ended, challenging questions.

		Complexity →					
		Is . . .	Did . . .	Can . . .	Would . . .	Will . . .	Might . . .
Complexity ↓	Who						
	What						
	Where						
	When						
	Why						
	How						

Figure 14.1 Use of open-ended questions, from Sharples et al. (2015) Making Best Use of Teaching Assistants: Guidance report. London: Education Endowment Foundation

Reflection and discussion activity

Reflection

Trainee: consider how questioning supports pupils' learning. Use the format in Figure 14.1 to ask some increasingly complex questions in the classroom.

Mentor: model for the trainee some questions using the grid in Figure 14.1. Taking a topic you or they are currently teaching, coach the trainee in using the grid to devise questioning, moving on to formulating increasingly more complex questions.

Discussion

Trainee: discuss how the issues from research will affect how you deploy TAs within your own classroom.

How to deploy other adults effectively: practical ideas

The preceding sections have highlighted some of the advantages and issues that may arise when working with other adults, specifically TAs. This section will provide you with some ideas on how to deploy TAs effectively in your lessons. Research (Webster *et al.*, 2012) showed that TAs spent half their time in lessons being 'passive' and listening to the teacher. When this 'passive' time is unplanned, it is clearly not an effective use of anybody's time and is not good practice. It is essential that you think about how to minimise this 'passive' time and ensure that pupils, and you, as the teacher, are benefiting from having a TA in the classroom.

You could try using some of the following strategies to involve other adults during the main teaching or teacher exposition:

The other adult could scribe pupils' suggestions on the board

This strategy ensures that the other adult is actively involved in the session while you are teaching the whole class and has many advantages, including:

- improving the pace of your teaching – you do not have to pause to write;

- support for your management of behaviour – you do not lose eye contact with pupils;

- direct teaching does not stop – ideas generated are not paused mid-flow while you write them down;

- if the other adult is a TA, this strategy puts them 'up front' – they can be an additional pair of eyes, assessing who understands, who may need support, who is focused, and so on.

However, this approach needs practice and negotiation between you and your other adult/TA to ensure that you both understand what will be written, where and how. You will also need to check that the other adult is comfortable doing this, and that their handwriting, grammar and spelling are at least as good as yours.

During discussions, a TA could have specific questions to ask specific groups – for example, high-attaining (HA) or low-attaining (LA) pupils

This questioning could either support or extend learning, depending on the individual pupils. It is important to bear in mind, however, that as previously discussed, working with the same pupils for extended periods is not good practice. However, this approach can be very useful for:

- encouraging reticent pupils to contribute;
- extending high-attaining pupils and taking their learning in a different direction;
- enabling the teacher to spend time with these specific groups while the TA supports the rest of the class, checking that pupils are on task, encouraging participation, etc.

During discussion time, a TA could act as a 'roving reporter'

Here, the TA could move around and listen to pupils acting on the teacher's direction while the teacher works with a specific group, pair or pupil. The TA could listen for:

- the 'best discussion';
- the 'best question asked';
- the 'best answer given';
- the 'best use of correct vocabulary'.

The TA could then feed back to the class on who (and why) had given the 'best answer', 'most thought-provoking discussion', and so on. This strategy might support the TA as it gives them a clear purpose as opposed to 'keeping an eye on pupils'. It may also encourage pupils' discussions and debates if they know that an adult is listening carefully to them.

A TA could act as a scribe

The TA could work with specific pupils (behaviour difficulties, attention difficulties, etc.) and scribe their key points/vocabulary/ideas on 'sticky-notes' which either the pupils or TA can share with the class. This is a useful way to gather ideas from pupils who, for whatever reason, find it difficult to record their suggestions.

A TA could work with a specific group of pupils during the teacher's exposition to extend learning, set challenges or consolidate prior learning

This is effective when the TA can follow up detailed comments in the teacher's marking to support pupils with specific aspects of their work. Again, it is important that this is not used with the same group of pupils or at the start of every lesson, but it can be a helpful way of ensuring that key aspects are addressed, and the necessary support is given, so that pupils' learning can move on in the main part of the lesson.

A TA could work with high-attaining pupils to draw up list of success criteria

Using the lesson objective(s) provided by the teacher, the TA could work with pupils specified by you to devise a list of success criteria. This activity would work well to stretch high-attaining pupils. Again, this would need careful discussion with you and your TA so they feel confident supporting their discussions.

Reflection and discussion activity

Reflection

Trainee: think about the ways of using TAs that have just been discussed. What are the strengths and limitations of these approaches?

Mentor: think about which strategies you use more or less. Why might that be? Are there additional approaches that might be helpful or tips for the trainee?

Discussion

Devise a list of strategies, building on those suggested above that you would like to trial in the classroom with a TA. Begin to work together to evaluate their success.

Things to remember

- Consider when you plan for your TA the range of pupils you are asking them to work with.

- Ensure that your TA is not routinely working with the lower attaining pupils, unless it is on a short, focused intervention with clear links made to classroom learning.

- Think about how your TA's skills and experience can support your teaching. For example, while you are working with a focus group, can they take on the role of keeping the rest of the class on task, encouraging and supporting, answering questions and so on?

- Careful thought and detailed consideration of how your TA can add value to, and support what you do early on in your relationship will result in a classroom where everyone is informed and clear about what they are doing.

- Cockroft and Atkinson's (2015) research found that *approachability* in teachers *contributed to how effective they (TAs) could be*. With this in mind, it is essential that you find time to talk to your TA and work together to be the most effective team possible.

 Chapter summary

Throughout this chapter, effective ways of using what can be highly skilled and experienced individuals have been discussed. Research evidence has been considered when discussing some of the advantages and issues when working with other adults. It can be seen that TAs and other adults are a real asset to both you and your class, and can enhance provision when deployed effectively.

Find out more from . . .

Making Best Use of Teaching Assistants: Guidance report: **https://educationendowmentfoundation.org.uk/ tools/guidance-reports/making-best-use-of-teaching-assistants/** (accessed 17 October 2019).

'Maximising TAs' website has lots of up-to-date resources and research, and is very accessible and helpful. Their blog is particularly interesting: **http://maximisingtas.co.uk** (accessed 17 October 2019).

The DISS research report:

Blatchford, P, Russell, A and Webster, R (2012) *Reassessing the Impact of Teaching Assistants*. Abingdon: Routledge.

 Taking it further . . . research

Clarke, E (2019) Paint pot washers or pedagogues? Is gender an issue for teaching assistants?, *Educational Review*, DOI: 10.1080/00131911.2018.1559800. Available at: **https://www.tandfonline.com/doi/full/10.1080/0 0131911.2018.1559800** (accessed 23 March 2020).

Clarke, E and Visser, J (2016) Teaching assistants managing behavior – who knows how they do it? A review of literature. *Support for Learning*, 31(4): 266-80. Available at: **https://onlinelibrary.wiley.com/doi/ full/10.1111/1467-9604.12137** (accessed 23 March 2020).

Cockroft, C and Atkinson, C (2015) Using the wider pedagogical role model to establish learning support assistants' views about facilitators and barriers to effective practice. *Support for Learning*, 30(2): 88-104.

Stoll, L and Seashore Louis, K (2007) *Professional Learning Communities: Divergence, Depth and Dilemmas.* Maidenhead: McGraw-Hill Education.

Watson, D, Bayliss, P and Pratchett, G (2013) Pond life that 'know their place': exploring teaching and learning support assistants' experiences through positioning theory. *International Journal of Qualitative Studies in Education*, 26.

Wilson, E and Bedford, D (2008) 'New partnerships for learning': teachers and teaching assistants working together in schools – the way forward. *Journal of Education for Teaching*, 34 (2): 137-50. Available at: **https:// doi.org/10.1080/02607470801979574**

References

Anderson, V and Finney, M (2008) *I'm a TA not a PA!* In Richards, G and Armstrong, F (eds), *Key Issues for Teaching Assistants: Working in diverse classrooms*. London: Routledge.

Bach, S, Kessler, I and Heron, P (2006) Changing job boundaries and workforce reform: the case of teaching assistants. *Industrial Relations Journal*, 37(1): 2–21.

Bland, K and Sleightholme, S (2012) Researching the pupil voice: what makes a good teaching assistant? *Support for Learning*, 27(4): 172–6.

Blatchford, P, Russell, A and Webster, R (2012) *Reassessing the Impact of Teaching Assistants*. Abingdon: Routledge.

Blatchford, P, Russell, A, Bassett, P, Brown, P and Martin, C (2004) The role and effects of teaching assistants in English primary schools (Years 4 to 6) 2000–2003. Results from the class size and pupil–adult ratios (CSPAR) KS2 Project. *British Educational Research Journal*, 33(1): 5–26. Available at: **https://onlinelibrary.wiley.com/doi/abs/10.1080/01411920601104292** (accessed 23 March 2020).

Cockroft, C and Atkinson, C (2015) Using the wider pedagogical role model to establish learning support assistants' views about facilitators and barriers to effective practice. *Support for Learning*, 30(2): 88–104.

Department for Education (DfE) (2011) *Teachers' Standards*. London: DfE. Crown copyright.

Department for Education and Employment (DfEE) (1997) *Excellence for all Children: Meeting special educational needs*. London: DfEE.

Department for Education and Skills (DfES) (2003) *Raising Standards and Tackling Workload: A national agreement*. London: DfES.

Galton, M and MacBeath, J (2008) *Teachers Under Pressure*. London: SAGE.

Gerschel, L (2005) The special educational needs coordinator's role in managing teaching assistants: the Greenwich perspective. *Support for Learning*, 20(2): 69–76.

Her Majesty's Inspectorate (HMI) (2002) *Teaching Assistants in Primary Schools an Evaluation of the Quality and Impact of their Work* (PDF format). London: HMI.

Mackenzie, S (2011) "Yes, but . . .": rhetoric, reality and resistance in teaching assistants' experiences of inclusive education. *Support for Learning*, 26, 64–71. Available at: **https://onlinelibrary.wiley.com/doi/full/10.1111/j.1467-9604.2011.01479.x** (accessed 23 March 2020).

Marr, A, Turner, J, Swann, W and Hancock, R (2001) *Classroom Assistants in the Primary School: Employment and deployment*. London: The Open University.

Ofsted (2008) *The Deployment, Training and Development of the Wider School Workforce*. London: Ofsted.

Russell, A, Webster, R and Blatchford, P (2013) *Maximising the Impact of Teaching Assistants*. Abingdon: Routledge.

Sharples, J, Webster, R and Blatchford, P (2015) *Making Best Use of Teaching Assistants: Guidance report*. London: Education Endowment Foundation.

Smith, P, Whitby, K, and Sharp, C (2004) *The Employment and Deployment of Teaching Assistants*. Slough: NFER.

Symes, W and Humphrey, N (2011) The deployment, training and teacher relationships of teaching assistants supporting pupils with autistic spectrum disorders (ASD) in mainstream secondary schools. *British Journal of Special Education*, 38(2): 57–64.

Thomas, G (1992) *Effective Classroom Teamwork: Support or intrusion?* London: Routledge.

Tucker, S (2009) Perceptions and reflections on the role of the teaching assistant in the classroom environment. *Pastoral Care in Education*, 27(4): 291–300.

Webster, R (2014) Code of Practice: how research evidence on the role and impact of teaching assistants can inform professional practice. *Educational Psychology in Practice*, 30(3): 232–7.

Webster, R and Blatchford, P (2013) *The Making a Statement project final report. A study of the teaching and support experienced by pupils with a statement of special educational needs in mainstream primary schools*. London: Institute of Education.

Webster, R, Blatchford, P and Russell, A (2012) Challenging and changing how schools use teaching assistants: findings from the Effective Deployment of Teaching Assistants project. *School Leadership & Management*, 33(1): 78–96.

Webster, R, Blatchford, P, Bassett, P, Brown, P and Russell, A (2011) The wider pedagogical role of teaching assistants. *School Leadership & Management*, 31(1): 3–20.

15

Well-being and resilience for all

Sue Lambert

 This chapter will

- help you understand how resilience and well-being might be defined;

- support you in understanding why well-being and resilience are important for all;

- support you to reflect on your own well-being;

- give you some understanding of the value of self-awareness to support well-being;

- provide possible strategies to promote well-being and self-awareness for all;

- encourage you to reflect on your role supporting children's well-being and resilience.

 Links to Teachers' Standards

1 **Set high expectations which inspire, motivate and challenge pupils,** specifically:

- establish a safe and stimulating environment for pupils, rooted in mutual respect.

5 **Adapt teaching to respond to the strengths and needs of all pupils,** specifically:

- have a secure understanding of how a range of factors can inhibit pupils' ability to learn, and how best to overcome these.

Part 2: Professional and Personal Conduct, specifically:

- treating pupils with dignity, building relationships rooted in mutual respect, and at all times observing proper boundaries appropriate to a teacher's professional position;

- having regard for the need to safeguard pupils' well-being, in accordance with statutory provisions.

What do we mean when we talk about being resilient?

Resilience comes from *resilire*, the Latin verb to jump back or rebound, but resilience is more than being able to bounce back from something that is traumatic or stressful. It is not something that is easy to define. Masten *et al.* (2001) see resilience as getting good outcomes in spite of serious threats to ability to adapt to the environment and situations or development. Newman and Blackburn (2002, p1) identify resilient children as *better equipped to resist stress and adversity, cope with change and uncertainty, and to recover faster and more completely from traumatic events or episodes.* Rutter (2006, p2) sees resilience as *an interactive concept that is concerned with the combination of serious risk experiences and a relatively positive psychological outcome despite those experiences.*

There is still much debate about what resilience is, whether it can be developed and what factors have a bearing on this. The debate is moving away from assuming that some of us are naturally more resilient than others, to recognising the impact of external factors, both positive and negative, including minimising risk factors to help maintain or develop resilience (Hart *et al.*, 2016). Some now argue that resilience is something that evolves as an interactive process between an individual, family and the features of their environment, including, for your consideration, the school environment (Gilligan, 2001; Schofield, 2001).

This is true throughout life, if you are not resilient or do not develop resilience in terms of capacity to cope and deal with traumatic events. As trainee teachers, being resilient and self-aware about what affects your well-being will be important, because the nature of training and teaching will be demanding and at times challenging.

Find out more from ... YouTube

Inside resilient children: Ann Masten discusses her work and research and what supports children in being resilient: **www.youtube.com/watch?v=GBMet8oIvXQ** (accessed 11 November 2019).

What is well-being and self-awareness?

The government defines well-being as having a positive physical and mental state (DoH, 2010). Marmot (2010) discusses the importance of mental health and states that material circumstance, social environment, psychosocial factors, behaviours and biological factors are all important for both physical and mental health, which means that the broader context of people's lives needs to be recognised. The annual report for YoungMinds (2016) also noted how mental and physical health are interlinked and that

> *Our mental health is a continuum that changes during our lifetime and is influenced by what we are born with (genetic factors), our environment (how we are nurtured and socio-economic factors) and events (such as bereavement, bullying). Our physical health is affected by our mental health and our mental health is also affected by our physical health.*

(YoungMinds, 2016)

Musgrave (2017) says that a child's ability to withstand adversity is impacted by their capability to develop *deep pockets of resilience* (p78) and this is true for you, too. Mental health is linked with resilience; however, it is important to recognise that while they are related, mental health and well-being are distinct (DfE, 2019a) and many people with mental health issues are often resilient. Schools and teachers have a key role in supporting health and pastoral care. Good schools understand the importance of how physical and mental health and an environment where children feeling safe impacts on well-being and hence attainment (DoH, 2010). However, teachers are not the experts in mental and physical health care, and it is important to work with experts from other agencies as a team to support children with diagnosed mental and physical health needs.

Self-awareness is an essential element of maintaining well-being and resilience. You need to ask yourself what your body is telling you and to take time to think about this, as well as recognising your emotions at particular times and the impact this may have on your well-being. Daniel Goleman (2005) explains that emotional understanding of yourself, your goals, intentions, responses and behaviour, and managing these elements well, is an essential aspect of emotional intelligence, as is understanding others' emotions. You need to make sure that you are self-aware to recognise what affects your well-being, which will help you to understand how to support children to be self-aware, and in supporting them to help them maintain their well-being too.

There is evidence that an 'active approach' is a hugely important factor in deciding effectiveness, creativity and happiness (Petty, 2014). Conversely, there is also a strong link that a 'passive approach' creates negativity, unhappiness, time-management issues and possibly depression (Petty, 2014). You have a choice to be active or passive.

 Reflection and discussion activity

Reflection

Trainee: are you an active or passive learner, or does this depend on the situation?

Think about the quotations in the table below. Think about when/if you have said or thought something similar. Which approach do you think is better for your well-being?

Table 15.1 Active and passive learners

Active	Passive
• Process: 'What might be a good next step?' • Improvement: 'What might make it even better?' • Positive: 'I can see that . . . went well.' • Learning: 'What is this telling you is needed to learn/develop next?'	• Process: 'I know this won't go well.' • Perfection: 'I can't get it all right.' • Negative: 'All of these things were wrong in the lesson.' • Blaming: 'That wasn't my fault because they should have already known that from last year and then my plan would have worked.'

Source: Adapted from Petty (2014).

(Continued)

(Continued)

Discussion

Trainee and mentor: think about how you can work together to develop an active approach - e.g. following observations and when discussing planning and teaching. Would some of the active suggestions above be helpful?

It is hard sometimes to focus on a positive and active approach. Talk to most teachers and they will tell you that they can always find things they can do better but find it much harder to see the positives. You often have blind spots too, which can have a negative effect on your well-being – for example: setting unrealistic goals; finding it hard to accept you are wrong, or not being able to see any positives in constructive criticism. There is also a temptation to just work harder or for longer rather than stepping back and thinking about how to work smarter and be kind to yourself, which, as a teacher with a demanding workload, you need to be able to do.

Workload will not go away, but the importance of managing this to maintain teacher well-being has been recognised more widely over the last few years. There have been a number of government publications linked to workload, recognising that this is an issue that has an impact on teacher retention within the profession. The Independent Teacher Review Groups have published guidance about marking, planning and data management (DfE, 2016a, b, c). In 2019, a workload toolkit was published to help schools with this aspect (DfE, 2019b) and the new Ofsted framework (2019) specifically asks *the extent to which leaders take into account the workload and well-being of their staff, while also developing and strengthening the quality of the workforce.* (p64)

Reflection and discussion activity

Trainee: read the *Reducing Teacher Workload* pamphlet or poster, available at: **www.gov.uk/government/publications/teacher-workload-poster-and-pamphlet**, and discuss with your mentor how the workload for planning and marking is managed. Think about strategies that will help you to make this manageable.

Taking it further . . . research about emotional resilience in trainee teachers

Braine, M and Turner, S (2019) *Embedding Wellbeing Knowledge and Practice into Teacher Education: Building emotional resilience.* University of Cumbria. Available at: **http://194.81.189.19/ojs/index.php/TEAN/index** (accessed 23 October 2019).

Managing your well-being is not about keeping calm and carrying on in the same way. Everyone is different – know yourself and what works for you.

There are some suggestions below which you might find more or less helpful. Think about what your response to the suggestion tells you about yourself.

- Give yourself some time every day for yourself: reading, writing, meditating, doodling, doing crosswords, sewing, etc.

- Picture yourself somewhere where you felt really relaxed or think about something that you have to look forward to.

- Write things down (much better than venting on social media where it could be seen by someone you may not want to see it or be misinterpreted). This can be just a release or can be used to help you reflect, especially if it is done some time after the event – e.g. a taught session that you thought had not gone well or having dealt with a specific challenge.

- Put yourself in someone else's shoes: see it from the mentor's point of view, a specific child's point of view, etc.

- Note some highlights of the day so your focus is positive not negative.

- Regulate breathing to help you feel calm: 3 in, hold for 4 and breathe out for 5, or sing along to a song.

- Be active: go for a walk, to the gym, dance around the kitchen. Exercise has been proven to be a big influence on well-being.

- Phone a friend or talk to someone. If you have a friend who is not involved in teaching, you can sometimes vent to them and it might make you feel better. They may not know a lot about what you are saying, but just letting it out can be really helpful.

- Take a break from what you are doing, but also from technology.

- List the things that are causing you to feel anxious or stressed. Divide it into things within your control at the moment and things outside of your control at the moment. Do something about the things that you can control and set others aside. We tend to focus on the things outside of our control.

Some things that might be stressful for you may be a way of reducing stress for others. For example, making lists and ticking things off can make you feel under pressure if it seems overwhelming, or otherwise can help you feel organised and able to prioritise.

Managing your time and workload should help you, but feeling stressed can be perfectly normal. There are some times when being stressed motivates and helps you focus on something important, such as planning an effective lesson, doing something you compete in or being observed when teaching. However, at other times, it can feel overwhelming, which makes it difficult to concentrate on anything. Stress affects everyone in different ways; it triggers physical responses as well as emotional ones. However, stress that does not go away can be very detrimental and lead to other health issues. It is important to have a sense of belonging, but the problem is that we tend to isolate ourselves when we feel anxious, stressed and under pressure. Social isolation is harmful, so knowing yourself and making a conscious effort not to socially isolate yourself is important.

Reflection

Trainee: how could being more aware of the causes and effects that stress has on a person both physically and mentally make you more self-aware and able to maintain your own well-being?

Reflect on what you have read so far and make a note of the top ten things you can do to support your well-being and manage your workload. Keep it somewhere that you can see it to remind yourself about what is important for you and why.

Find out more from . . . TED talk

Kelly McGonigal, health psychologist, looks at research about stress and its impact, and suggests practical strategies for managing health and happiness: **www.ted.com/talks/kelly_mcgonigal_how_to_make_stress_your_friend?language=en** (accessed 24 October 2019).

Understanding how to support children's well-being and resilience

The DfE (2019, p5) states that current evidence on the influences on children's well-being are varied and this variation increases as children grow into young adults. There is evidence that indicates that their peer and family relationships, alongside their wider school and neighbourhood environment, have the strongest links to children and young people's well-being (DfE, 2019a). This is reflected by the bio–psycho–social model that psychologists use when considering psychological disorders based on the work of Engel (1977).

The idea of several aspects coming together is also reflected in the quotation below from Pearce (2011).

Psychological strength, or resilience, is directly implicated in a child's capacity to cope with adversity . . . . Resilience strengthens a child and enables them to try new experiences, accept challenges, and cope with frustration and failure. Resilience sustains a child through hardship and supports the realization of personal dreams and aspirations.

(pp17–18)

Thinking about this quotation and the DfE (2019) report demonstrates the importance of supporting children to be resilient and develop resilience. However, as noted before, for some children – e.g. those with diagnosed attachment issues and diagnosed mental and physical needs – your role will be in support of experts in the field. Having said this, there are things you can do in the classroom to make it a resilient environment. One of the most important things is recognising that all emotions are acceptable, and it is what you do with them that matters. You also need to be aware that it is non-verbal communication that can have the most impact on how children perceive feelings and attitudes which has an impact on their self-esteem and motivation and consequently their resilience. In Chapter 2, you were introduced to Mehrabiran's (1972) work who found that only 7 per cent of messages about feelings and attitudes were in the words that were spoken, with 38 per cent in the way the words were said and 5 per cent were about the feelings and attitudes being in the facial expressions. As a teacher, you need to be very aware of how children perceive what you say and how it is said.

 Case study

The teacher notices that Aroon is sitting by himself and not communicating with the other children in his group. She sighs and while walking away says, 'Come on, Aroon, you are such a good listener but I know you have some great ideas that the others would love to hear.' Aroon does not join in. After a few minutes the teacher returns to the group and stops to speak to Aroon. She faces him and says, 'Aroon, can you look at me, please' and repeats what she said before. Aroon smiles and starts to join in with his group.

Trainee: what made the difference? How might the teacher have been standing; what might she have been doing with her facial expression and words that made a difference? Why is it important to think about this and what it might mean for your practice? Think about other chapters that might be helpful - e.g. behaviour, particularly restorative and solution-focused approaches, teacher presence and the chapter about inclusion.

You need to be an active listener so that you are aware of things that impact on children's well-being. As a teacher, you will have many interactions with children, so really listening to what they say is very important so that your actions and reactions are supportive of them as individuals and learners. This is about really paying attention to other people's emotions, body movement/language, what is said and how it is said. It is about trying to understand and be empathetic. Many of the things that make you struggle in terms of well-being are the same for children. As already mentioned, emotional literacy is very important. If children do not have the language of feelings/emotions, they struggle to address things, so anxiety and/or frustration build up. Adults need to do the detective work to help children understand and develop their emotional language and literacy, and model ways to express emotions, feelings, acceptable behaviours, how to problem solve and how to learn from mistakes.

The importance of being a positive role model and giving children opportunities to learn through trial and error are really important. Role model the value of making mistakes as part of a learning process, using positive language such as 'that was very tricky and you did really well, so tell me what could we do differently next time to make it even better?' Managing mistakes and navigating disappointment/perceived failure is important, and knowing that reacting emotionally is normal.

—— 🧩 —— **Case study** ————————————————————

Jess is often quiet in class and gets upset when she can't do something quickly or is not pleased with the results of her work. She is involved in an art lesson drawing a vase of flowers and suddenly gets angry and screws up her paper and throws her pencil down, before leaving the table and going into a huddle in the corner of the room. The teacher goes over with her work and unscrews it before speaking to her. She kneels down and speaks to her quietly and the teacher starts to draw her own version of the vase of flowers as Jess watches. After a little while, they both get up and go back to the table.

Trainee: why might the teacher have done this? What do you think she could have said that encouraged Jess to return to her table? What would you do in a situation like this? Make a note of some of the responses that you might have used to support a child in seeing that trial and error are important and that it is all right to make mistakes.

Trainee and mentor: mentor, share with the trainee some of the ways you would support a child in a similar scenario.

——

There are things you can do to empower children, and many of the things that were discussed earlier about the importance of having self-awareness and how to develop this can be just as helpful for children. It may be helpful to discuss things as a class during Circle Time and turn-taking games and when other opportunities arise. There are some examples below of other things that you could do.

- Be in the hot seat as a character who is a model of calm (could be a real person or fictional character). Encourage children to ask questions about what you do to keep calm or how you manage situations that make you feel anxious.

- Use scenarios with the children so they can role play situations that allow them to explore different feelings and ways of communicating. You can do this in pairs or small groups, or have children playing the role as actors being directed by others in terms of the words and actions they use – e.g. you are playing and someone takes your ball to play with their friends, calls you a nasty name and won't let you play. What could you do? What could you say? How do you feel? How do you think the other people feel? This gives opportunities to develop the language of emotional literacy.

- Explain and model how you are feeling. Children with low self-esteem may believe that you are unhappy with them if you do not explain how you are feeling, or if your expression and gestures suggest you are not happy or interested – for example, 'I am sorry if I am not as smiley as usual today but my roof at home is leaking and I am a bit worried about it. I am sure I will feel much better once we start our exciting work for today.'

- Use emotion cards. A range can be found and downloaded, or you could ask children in pairs to show each other how they look, move or stand when they feel a particular emotion.

- Use stories to discuss the emotions of the characters – e.g. why was . . . sad; why do you think . . . made him cry? (See 'Find out more from' section below for a useful website.)

- Suggest ways to find out how children are feeling before a lesson/when they come in to school in the morning, after their break or lunch – e.g. choose a face or colour (red, yellow or green) to put beside their names on a display, or position their name card on a feelings thermometer. This can also help children who do not have the language to show you at different times of the day how they are feeling or show another adult they trust in the classroom.

- Although not promoted by government, some schools still use some of the SEAL (Social and Emotional Aspects of Learning) materials, which provide some useful activities to support social and emotional development.

Find out more from ... websites

The SEAL materials can be found on the following website: **https://webarchive.nationalarchives.gov.uk/20110809155339/http://nsonline.org.uk/inclusion/behaviourattendanceandseal/seal** (accessed 12 November 2019).

Storybooks that can be used to promote discussion about resilience: **https://afineparent.com/gift-guides/childrens-books-about-resilience.html** (accessed 12 November 2019).

Book Trust has a wide range of recommendations for books about resilience, well-being and dealing with emotions, available at: **www.booktrust.org.uk/books-and-reading/** (accessed 12 November 2019).

There are a number of risk factors that can have an impact on resilience and affect well-being, but there are also factors that can help you protect well-being or that mean you are more likely to be resilient or develop resilience. Resilience and well-being for children is about reducing or minimising risks. Risk is not causal but cumulative (MacKenzie *et al.*, 2011). As noted in Maslow's hierarchy of need, if basic psychological needs and the need to feel safe are not met, then higher level needs may be inaccessible. As Taylor *et al.* (2016) note, if basic structures are in place, then children will feel a greater sense of security and peace of mind.

> *Although some of these (basics) may seem beyond the reach of 'school duty' and are linked to family life and social circumstances they can still be addressed through taking an interest or exploring sensitively with students and could make significant changes to your student's wellbeing and enhance their ability to learn.*

(pp6–7)

Goodman *et al.*'s (2015, p7) review for the Early Intervention Foundation, *Social and Emotional Skills in Childhood and their Long-term Effects on Adult Life*, identified a number of areas for developing social and emotional skills, many of which are reflected in Taylor *et al.* (2016), The Resilient Classroom, and Hart *et al.*'s (2007) Resilience Framework. The table below notes areas that can help to support resilience and well-being, and what good influences can do to help children. Many of the characteristics are absent when a child is solitary, shy or withdrawn.

Table 15.2 What helps develop well-being and resilience for a child and what can good influences do?

Areas that develop well-being and resilience	Characteristics	Role of good influences
Self-perceptions and self-awareness	Values oneself, has confidence to believe in abilities to achieve.	Good influences help children's understanding of who they are and their own personal strengths.
Sense of belonging	Able to make and maintain good relationships. Values belonging to groups who accept them for who they are (important to find something they are good at).	Belonging has a positive effect. Good influences can help them make sense of where they have come from and their place in the world. They help them to try out different things so they find something they are talented at.
Motivation, ownership and empowerment	Strives towards goals; distinguishes whether goals are set by other people or by themselves; sees value of the goal; has aspiration and ambition. Creates a positive approach to learning. Having aspirations helps them become more resilient.	Good influences can help children develop talents, interests and life skills. They can help with allowing them to develop new skills that are an essential part of them increasing their learning and thinking about where they want to go in life; they have ambition.
Self-control and self-regulation	Manages and expresses emotions. Has ability to overcome short-term impulsive behaviour in order to prioritise future goals, so sees a bigger picture.	Good influences help them to be self-aware and take responsibility for themselves and their behaviour towards others, while at the same time believing in them.
Social skills	Ability to interact with others, forge and maintain relationships, and avoid socially unacceptable responses. Ability to communicate, empathise, be kind, share and cooperate.	Good influences encourage children to see other children's and adult's perspective, and to be sensitive to how to others feel. This helps them to understand how they feel and how their behaviour can affect other people's feelings. They model effective ways to communicate and ask children 'how' questions rather than 'why' questions to help them build social skills.
Resilience and coping	Adapt positively and with purpose in the face of stress and otherwise difficult circumstances. Show strength in adversity.	Good influences encourage children to cope by helping them develop a 'have a go' approach and to see mistakes as an opportunity to learn. They support them to solve problems, be confident in their own views and beliefs, encourage their interests and make them feel good about themselves.

Source: Adapted from Goodman et al. (2016) and Taylor et al. (2016).

Reflection and discussion activity

Trainee and mentor: think about each of the points above and what you have read in this chapter. Use the following questions to structure a discussion together.

- What do you do as part of your classroom practice to promote each area?

- How do you give children a sense of belonging and confidence?

- How do you empower them and give them ownership of learning?

- What do you do or say so that they know you are supporting them to succeed academically, socially and emotionally?

- How do you help them to express their emotions and develop good relationships with other children and adults?

- How do you support them to overcome challenges, whether academic, social or emotional?

Make notes of things you need to think about when planning, teaching and interacting with children to promote these areas.

 Find out more from ... websites

Building Resilience in Children: 20 Practical, Powerful Strategies (supported by science):

www.heysigmund.com/building-resilience-children/ (accessed 20 October 2019).

Resilience Framework (Children & Young People): boingboing.org.uk (2012), adapted from Angie Hart and Derek Blincow with Helen Thomas (2007):

www.boingboing.org.uk/wp-content/uploads/2010/10/Resilience-Framework-children-and-young-people-2015.pdf (accessed 20 October 2019).

 Taking it further ... research about resilience

Ann Masten discusses how resilience can be developed, calling it 'ordinary magic':

Masten, AS (2001) Ordinary magic: resilience processes in development. *American Psychologist*, 56(3): 227-38: **http://dx.doi.org/10.1037/0003-066X.56.3.227** (accessed 2 October 2019).

—◆— **Chapter summary** ————

In this chapter you have had a chance to reflect on your own understanding of resilience and well-being and the importance of self-awareness. It has shown the importance of understanding what affects your well-being and resilience, and what approaches to managing your well-being, workload and resilience might be helpful for you. You will be aware that there are many factors that impact on well-being and resilience. It has enabled you to consider the importance of your role in supporting children by being a positive role model, and what strategies and approaches you might use in the classroom to help them develop skills and understanding so that they too have positive well-being and can be resilient. This needs to be an integral part of your practice as a teacher in supporting children to thrive in school.

As noted by Pearce (2011), *the promotion of resilience is a universal concern of all adults with a caring concern for children* (pp17-18).

—— **References** ——

Department for Education (DfE) (2016a) *Reducing Teacher Workload: Data Management Review Group Report*: **www.gov.uk/government/publications/reducing-teacher-workload-data-management-review-group-report** (accessed 16 October 2019).

Department for Education (DfE) (2016b) *Reducing Teacher Workload: Marking Policy Review Group Report*: **www.gov.uk/government/publications/reducing-teacher-workload-marking-policy-review-group-report** (accessed 16 October 2019).

Department for Education (DfE) (2016c) *Reducing Teacher Workload: Planning and Resources Review Group Report*: **www.gov.uk/government/publications/reducing-teacher-workload-planning-and-resources-group-report** (accessed 16 October 2019).

Department for Education (DfE) (2019a) *State of the Nation 2019: Children and Young People's Wellbeing: Research Report*. **www.gov.uk/government/publications/state-of-the-nation-2019-children-and-young-peoples-wellbeing** (accessed 14 September 2019).

Department for Education (DfE) (2019b) *Reducing Teacher Workload* Available at: **https://www.gov.uk/guidance/school-workload-reduction-toolkit** (accessed 23 March 2020).

Department of Health (DoH) (2010) *Healthy Lives, Healthy People: Our strategy for public health in England*. London: The Stationery Office. Available at: **www.gov.uk/government/uploads/system/uploads/attachment_data/file/216096/dh_127424.pdf** (accessed 11 October 2019).

Engel, GL (1977) The need for a new medical model: a challenge for biomedicine. *Science*, 196 (4286): 129–36 (8 April).

Gilligan, R (2001) *Promoting Resilience: A resource guide on working with children in the care system*. London: BAAF.

Goleman, D (2005) *Emotional Intelligence: Why it can matter more than IQ*. London: Bloomsbury.

Goodman, A, Joshi, H, Nasim, B and Tyler, C (2015) Review for the Early Intervention Foundation. *Social and Emotional Skills in Childhood and their Long-term Effects on Adult Life*. Institute of Education: **www.eif.org.uk/files/pdf/social-and-emotional-skills-in-childhood-and-their-long-term-effects-on-adult-life.pdf** (accessed 9 October 2019).

Hart, A, Blincow, D and Thomas, H (2007) *Resilience Framework (Children & Young People)*, adapted from boingboing.org.uk (2012): **www.boingboing.org.uk/wp-content/uploads/2010/10/Resilience-Framework-children-and-young-people-2015.pdf** (accessed 12 October 2019).

Hart, A, Gagnon, E, Eryigit-Madzwamusel, S, Cameron, J, Aranda, K, Rathbone, A and Heaver, B (2016) *Uniting Resilience Research and Practice With an Inequalities Approach*. SAGE Open October–December 2016: 1–13.

MacKenzie, MJ, Kotch, JB and Lee, Li-Ching (2011) Toward a cumulative ecological risk model for the etiology of child maltreatment. Children and Youth Services Review, 33(9): 1638–47, September.

Marmot, M (2010) *Fair Society, Healthy Lives: Strategic review of health inequalities in England post 2010*: **www.instituteofhealthequity.org/** (accessed 11 October 2019).

Masten, A (2001) Ordinary magic: resilience processes in development. *American Psychologist*, March.

Mehrabian, A (1972) *Nonverbal Communication*. Chicago: Aldine-Atherton.

Musgrave, J (2017) *Supporting Children's Health and Well-being*. London: Sage.

Newman, T and Blackburn, S (2002) *Transitions in the Lives of Children and Young People: Resilience Factors (Barnardo's Policy, Research and Influencing Unit)*. Edinburgh: Scottish Executive Education Department.

Ofsted (2019) *The Education Inspection Framework*. Manchester: Crown Publishing. **https://assets.publishing.service.gov.uk/government/uploads/system/uploads/attachment_data/file/801429/Education_inspection_framework.pdf** (accessed 14 October 2019).

Pearce, C (2011) *Promoting Resilience in Children: A short introduction*. London: Jessica Kingsley.

Petty, G (2014) *Teaching Today: A practical guide*. Oxford: Oxford University Press.

Rutter, M (2006) Implications of resilience concepts for scientific understanding. *New York Academy of Sciences*, 1094: 1–12. **https://doi.org/10.1196/annals.1376.002** (accessed 21 October 2019).

Schofield, G (2001) Resilience and family placement: a lifespan perspective. *Adoption and Fostering*, 25(3): 6–19.

Taylor, S, Hart, A and Hove Park School (2016) *The Resilient Classroom: A resource pack for tutor groups and pastoral school staff*. **https://youngminds.org.uk/media/1463/the_resilient_classroom-2016.pdf** (accessed 14 October 2019).

YoungMinds (2016) *YoungMinds Annual Report 2015–16*: **https://youngminds.org.uk/media/1233/youngminds-annual-report-15-16-final.pdf** (accessed 14 October 2019).

YoungMinds (n.d.) What is academic resilience? **https://youngminds.org.uk/media/1465/what-is-academic-resilience.pdf** (accessed 16 October 2019).

16

Guidance for ITT mentors

Coaching and mentoring (including communities of practice for trainees)

Adam Hounslow-Eyre

 This chapter will

- introduce you to the differences between mentoring and coaching;
- discuss how and when to use mentoring and coaching approaches so they are most effective;
- consider the complexities of mentoring and coaching in the context of communities of practice at different 'levels' and what tensions there might be, if any.

 Links to the Teachers' Standards

8   Fulfil wider professional responsibilities

Part 2: Personal and Professional Conduct

Introductory analogy

As an initial starting point, mentoring might be characterised as a more directive, 'hands-on' relationship between a protégé and a more experienced other. The discussions of the two partners in this mentoring relationship will be centred around considering the novice's achievement compared to professional, often national, standards. Coaching might be characterised as a more 'arm's-length' relationship between two professional colleagues. The discussions of the two partners in this coaching relationship will be centred around the participant's achievement compared to agreed or self-generated criteria. Both mentoring and coaching are based on the formation of a relationship of trust between trainee and mentor, or between colleagues (respectively).

An analogy might be to the process of teaching someone to ride a bicycle. In this analogy the initial stages of learning represent a mentoring relationship; the experienced bike rider might be literally 'hands-on' with the novice, holding the back of the bicycle seat and the handlebars while offering advice and encouragement. The advice offered will reflect the 'standards' required to successfully ride a bicycle: 'Start with one pedal raised, one foot on the floor, one foot on the pedal, push hard.' The later stages of learning to ride a bicycle would be analogous to a coaching relationship. Both individuals can now ride a bicycle; the more proficient rider might now stand at a distance from the less experienced rider and offer encouragement and ask questions. The questions asked will reflect the criteria for more efficient bicycle riding: 'What do you need to remember when you change riding surface? How sharply do you need to turn the handlebar for this corner?' Even from this initial analogy, it is possible to discern that the differences between mentoring and coaching might not be discrete and fixed.

 ── **Reflection and discussion activity** ──

Reflection

Trainee and mentor: write a brief definition of mentoring and/or* a brief definition of coaching. Bullet point three significant differences between mentoring and coaching.

Discussion

Trainee and mentor: now share your definitions and three bullet pointed significant differences.* Start to discuss how your definitions and differences* compare; are they similar or widely divergent? How might this impact upon your mentoring and/or* coaching experiences? How might you begin to overcome any differences?

(* This activity can be focused on one or other term, or be completed as two different activities separated by a number of weeks or months. In either case, omit bullet pointing differences and move on to sharing your definitions.)

Mentoring

Mentoring of trainees is currently a ubiquitous approach to professional development across a wide range of settings in education, healthcare and industry. The widespread use of mentoring is perhaps surprising given its paradoxical origin. The term 'mentor' is derived from the character of Mentor in Homer's *Odyssey*. In that epic poem, Mentor is an elderly family friend left by Odysseus to look after both his son, Telemachus, and his palace while Odysseus leaves to fight the Trojan wars. However, Mentor's role within the *Odyssey* as a trusted 'family retainer' is questionable. He is an experienced elder, the teacher and overseer of Telemachus, but also rather ineffectual in his wider role. When Odysseus returns from his 20-year odyssey, he finds his palace overrun by young nobles attempting to persuade Odysseus's wife Penelope to remarry, and so deny Telemachus his birthright.

This characterisation of the original Mentor as ineffectual is reinforced by contemporary research that suggests that while mentoring is a ubiquitous term and approach, it is poorly defined and implemented. A recent systematic review by Ghosh (2013) identifies twelve different definitions of mentoring from within education alone.

Table 16.1 Definitions of mentoring

Author(s)	Definition/description of mentoring in education
Anderson and Shannon (1988)	Mentoring is a nurturing process in which a more skilled or more experienced person, serving as a role model, teaches, sponsors, encourages, counsels and befriends a less skilled or less experienced person for the purpose of promoting the latter's professional and/or personal development.
Jacques (1992)	Mentoring is more than dealing effectively with practical, craft skills; it is a process of transmitting practice and also principles to another adult.
Adey (1997)	Mentoring is an interrelationship of an experienced teacher and a beginning teacher wherein the expectations of the latter are that their 'critical friend' will help to provide the challenges essential to their early development as teachers in the classroom and the wider school.
Boreen and Niday (2001)	Mentoring is more than an opportunity to give advice; it is a two-way exchange of listening and questioning.
Fairbanks *et al.*, (2000)	Mentoring consists of complex social interactions that mentor teachers and protégé teachers construct and negotiate for a variety of professional purposes and in response to the contextual factors they encounter.
Feiman-Nemser (2001)	Mentoring is an educational practice that rests on an explicit vision of good teaching and understanding of teacher learning, leading to growth over and beyond the conventional approaches that emphasise situational adjustment, technical advice and emotional support.
Awayaa *et al.* (2003)	Mentoring is a particular kind of personal developing relationship between the mentor teacher and the protégé teacher that avoids the hierarchical stricture associated with supervision models and in which there is some degree of choice between the parties to it.
Smith and Ingersoll (2004)	Mentoring is the personal guidance provided, usually by the seasoned veterans to the beginning teachers in schools.
Lopez-Real and Kwan (2005)	Mentoring can be seen as comprising an important duality; it is both a relationship and a process of collaborative work.

(Continued)

Table 16.1 (Continued)

Author(s)	Definition/description of mentoring in education
Lindgren (2005)	Mentorship can be seen as a process where the novice (mentee), as the learner, is optimally engaged and has a constructive self-awareness and there is potential for the development of mentors themselves as the questions, values and acts of the mentees provide unrealised and new possibilities.
Lee and Feng (2007)	Mentoring is the socialisation of the mentee through the leadership and support of the more experienced professional.
Hobson *et al.* (2009)	Mentoring is defined as the one-to-one support of a novice or less experienced practitioner (mentee) by a more experienced practitioner (mentor), designed primarily to assist the development of the mentee's expertise and to facilitate their induction into the culture of the profession (in this case, teaching) and into the specific local context (here, the school).

Source: Adapted from Ghosh (2013).

 Reflection and discussion activity

Reflection

Trainee and mentor: review Ghosh's definitions of mentoring above. Which definition of mentoring resonates with you, or 'jumps out' at you? Exactly what aspect of the definition is it that appeals to you?

Discussion

Trainee and mentor: now share your chosen definition and the exact aspect that appeals to you. Do your selections coincide or contrast with each other? What might this signify as your mentoring relationship is forged and develops?

Common features of mentoring

It is clear from Ghosh's systematic review that the definition of mentoring in education is often poorly defined and open to multiple interpretations. However, across all the definitions it is possible to see some commonalities emerging. Unsurprisingly, perhaps, it is defined as involving the interaction of a novice and a more experienced or skilled practitioner. However, this interaction is variously described as 'befriending', 'acting as a critical friend', 'supporting' and a 'process' or 'nurturing process' sometimes with an element of challenge. Beyond this description of a relationship between a lesser and more experienced practitioner there is also a common emphasis on mentoring being a process of 'socialisation' or an introduction to 'practice and principles' and an emphasis on mentoring skills such as listening and questioning.

Reflection and discussion activity

Discussion

Trainee and mentor: what are the relative benefits and risks of a mentoring relationship becoming a 'friendship'?

- Is it easier to receive developmental feedback in a relaxed, friendly relationship, so maximising the trainee's uptake and future performance?

- Is it more difficult to hold a friend to account, making the mentoring relationship ineffectual and too 'cosy'?

Discuss this together.

The remainder of this section will focus on the emerging commonalities of forming the mentoring relationship and the 'skills' of mentoring, often cited as listening and questioning (Whitmore, 2017); the third commonality of socialisation will be addressed at the end of this chapter in relation to communities of practice.

Aspects of successful mentoring: forming the relationship

From the preceding it is clear that entering into a mentoring relationship is not likely to be a simple 'event' that is consistent throughout the mentoring period; rather, the mentor and trainee will enter into a dynamic process. This dynamic relationship will, of necessity, be influenced by a range of factors. These factors might be personal or professional; personal factors could include the respective ages and genders of the mentor and trainee. While professional factors could include the participants' underlying 'philosophy of education'– for instance, being child-centred to a greater or lesser degree – these factors do not inherently prevent the forming of a strong mentoring relationship, and indeed an explicit focus on such personal and professional aspects might form an interesting starting point to develop a mentoring relationship.

Reflection and discussion activity

Trainee and mentor: consider potential ice-breaking activities as a way to build rapport with one another. At its most simple, a 'getting to know you' initial meeting will be extremely useful in founding a mentoring relationship. However, such an initial meeting might be 'strained' due to the mentor and trainee being strangers to each other. A pre-arranged ice-breaking activity similar to those listed below might offer a starting point.

- Share your 'professional vision' or 'educational beliefs' either through five written bullet points or five images.

(Continued)

(Continued)

- 'CV' swap, completed on a common pro-forma with categories to discover the wider experiences of the mentor and trainee – e.g. 'hidden talent', 'all pets ever owned', 'guilty television pleasure'.

- 'My Learning Journey' Pecha Kucha: The Pecha Kucha (or 20 x 20) presentation format is an approach where you show 20 images, each for 20 seconds, usually using electronic presentation software. The images advance automatically and you talk along to the images.

 Find out more . . . from research

Pecha Kucha is an innovative and highly effective way of transmitting information in a concise format. It can have many applications within educational settings beyond its possible use in mentoring. Examples of a range of Pecha Kucha presentations can be explored at: **www.pechakucha.com/** (accessed 21 January 2020).

Having initiated the relationship, a next step might be to establish (or reflect upon, if specified in documentation) the roles and responsibilities of the mentor and trainee. Adhering to daily or weekly routines will be conducive to driving forward a profitable collaborative relationship; it might be important for both sides to consistently meet these expectations in the initial stages of the mentoring relationship to help build trust. As the relationship matures, it might be possible for these roles and responsibilities to be reviewed or be met more flexibly – for instance, moving the weekly meeting from one day to the next due to other school commitments.

 Reflection and discussion activity

Scenario: A weekly meeting has been agreed at the end of the day on Thursday to review progress towards planning for the next week.

Trainee: your week has not gone as planned. It is Thursday morning and you do not have the materials you agreed to bring to the weekly meeting. What do you do?

- Wait until the meeting to disclose you do not have the agreed materials.

- Try to 'pull together' some materials during the day.

- Disclose the lack of materials to your mentor via email (late Wednesday night or Thursday morning).

- Disclose the lack of materials to your mentor face-to-face first thing Thursday morning.

Mentor: your week has not gone as planned. It is Thursday morning and there is no possibility of holding the weekly meeting at the end of the day, as you are required to attend a Senior Leadership Team (SLT) meeting at short notice. What do you do?

- Ask to be excused from the SLT meeting to meet your trainee.

- Ask to join the SLT meeting late, after meeting your trainee.

- Cancel your weekly meeting with the trainee via email.

- Cancel your weekly meeting with the trainee face-to-face.

Sustaining the dynamic mentoring relationship will be predicated on both the mentor's and trainee's ability to collaborate to resolve problems as they emerge, and the degree to which the mentor feels the trainee should resolve emerging challenges independently. The ability to solve problems will in turn be influenced by whether the emerging relationship is quite 'formal' or more 'personal'. Both approaches are successful, but can become significant if there is a mismatch in expectation between the mentor and trainee. As discussed above, some definitions of mentoring see it as incumbent upon the mentor to 'befriend' the trainee (in a more personal relationship). Others stress the 'induction into the profession' (in a potentially more formal relationship). Any mismatch in expectations, which the suggestions in the activity above attempt to mitigate, can lead to a trainee perceiving the mentor's practice as 'toxic'. The origin of the term 'toxic mentor' or 'disabling mentor types' is often attributed to Darling's work in healthcare in the 1980s. Darling (1986) identifies four types of 'toxic mentoring', described in Table 16.2.

Table 16.2 Types of 'toxic mentoring'

Type	Characteristics
Avoiders	The elusive mentor who is never available to the learner to set and review their practice and goals, or to provide support, challenge and role modelling.
Blockers	The mentor who blocks the learner's development by preventing them from accessing learning by either over-supervising or withholding knowledge or information.
Destroyers	The mentor uses challenges and tactics such as humiliation that set out to destroy the learner's self-confidence.
Dumpers	This type of mentor believes in 'sink or swim', and will often deliberately leave the learner in situations where they are out of their depth.

Source: Darling (1986).

It is essential to highlight that at least some of these behaviours (the Avoider or Dumper) could be driven by wider institutional pressures, and that a 'sink or swim' moment might be an appropriate response to a situation. It is the persistent application of these types of mentoring that makes them 'toxic'. A focus on the forming of a mentoring relationship in whatever guise it ultimately takes on is important. Chambers *et al.*

(2002) discovered three broad concerns among trainees that prompted in-course withdrawal from Secondary PGCE courses: mentor/student relationships, the workload expected of students and the image of the profession as perceived by students in school.

Reflection and discussion activity

Chambers *et al.* (2002) found that Secondary PGCE withdrawal rates rose from a fairly constant 5-6 per cent per year to 11 per cent per year from 1996 to 1997. Current withdrawal rates seem to hover around 15 per cent per year. What could have impacted on these changes? How does this impact on mentoring and coaching practices in schools?

Find out more . . . from research

Read more about teacher retention in this research article by the National Foundation for Educational Research (nfer) at: **www.nfer.ac.uk/publications/LFSAO1/** (accessed 21 January 2020).

Extend your reading with this online article: **https://schoolsweek.co.uk/what-do-the-statistics-say-about-teacher-shortages/** (accessed 21 January 2020). The article discusses emerging evidence for longer term (4-5 years from entry into teaching) trends in teacher retention via different training routes.

To maintain and develop an effective relationship between mentor and trainee, in either its personal or formal approach, an outcomes-focused attitude of collaborative problem solving is powerful. The focus on the outcomes contained in the Teachers' Standards and any course-specific documentation can form a central, 'neutral' focus around which discussions can reflect on what developments might be required to attain these outcomes. Such collaborative discussions can clearly set an attainable target for the trainee and a clear observation focus for the mentor. Subsequent discussion is then of what evidence was provided (seen) to justify the mentor and trainee agreeing an outcome has been met. Lee *et al.* (2006) characterise this overall outlook as 'Solve, Resolve, Evolve'. This formulation draws out the initial collaborative problem solving, followed by a commitment to change practice and a review of the impact this change has in a memorable phrase. (This phrase will also be informative for the subsequent discussion of coaching, where the element of 'solving' is resisted by the coach and taken on by the coachee.)

Reflection and discussion activity

Is it possible to apply the 'Solve, Resolve, Evolve' approach to the Thursday meeting scenario outlined above?

Trainee and mentor: reflect on your 'solution' to the scenario. What 'resolution(s)' would emerge from it to inform the evolving mentoring relationship?

Aspects of successful mentoring: listening and questioning

Open and clear channels of communication between mentors and trainees are obviously paramount in the dynamic and expanding mentoring relationship. A successful period of mentoring will require both mentor and trainee to develop strong listening and questioning skills.

Active listening, fully concentrating on what is being said, 'listening' with all the senses (observing body language and facial expressions) and giving full attention to the speaker is required from both mentor and trainee. However, listening can fall short of being truly active. An interesting analysis of potential barriers to good, active listening is offered by Jones *et al.* (2006) and is shown in Table 16.3.

Table 16.3 Barriers to good and active listening

Barriers to good and active listening	
'Open ears–closed mind' listening	Jumping to conclusions about what the speaker will say, therefore closing the mind because 'we will learn nothing new'.
On-off listening	This is where we are using the time to think about what we are going to say next; when this happens we are not listening to what is being said.
'Glazed look' listening	We are looking at the speaker, but not listening because our minds are on other things.
'Red flag' listening	We block out or interrupt the speaker because keywords have engendered an emotional response.
'Obviously' listening	Repeating facts, constantly missing new facts; this is the over-use of affirmative feedback. Repeating back phrases, nodding, saying 'hmm' too frequently.
Avoiding the issue	Not listening to or asking for clarification because the subject appears too difficult or complex.
'Matter over mind' listening	We have already decided on the outcome, therefore refuse to have our own ideas and points of view challenged.
Focusing on the subject instead of the speaker	Details and facts about an incident become more important than what people are saying about themselves. There is a danger here of missing key facts and the speaker's expressions.
Not listening	Allowing external distraction (corridor noise, telephone, etc.) to take over our attention.

Source: Adapted from Jones et al. (2006).

These poor active listening practices can be driven by time pressures and workload, or by 'resistance' on the part of the trainee to accept constructive, critical feedback, or on the part of the mentor to recognise innovative practice that challenges their assumptions. An understanding of the dangers of these barriers to active listening will support the mentoring relationship to be open and effective.

Reflection and discussion activity

Trainee: you have planned and delivered an 'innovative lesson'. Your mentor expressed some reservations about the lesson at the weekly planning meeting, but agreed to you trying the approach. The lesson did not go as well as planned; indeed, many of the potential issues the mentor raised occurred. During feedback on the lesson, how do you maintain active listening?

Mentor: the trainee has planned and delivered an 'innovative lesson' you had reservations about and clearly expressed at the weekly planning meeting. The lesson has exceeded even the trainee's expectations, with pupils vocally expressing their desire for 'all lessons to be taught like this'. During feedback on the lesson, how do you maintain active listening?

A mentor's ability to employ a range of question types alongside an appropriate approach to questioning will significantly impact on the mentoring relationship. Questioning will of necessity form a part of giving feedback to a trainee, with feedback often occurring at 'pivotal' (and thus stressful) moments in a trainee's development. While there is a well-understood distinction between closed questions (eliciting a 'yes' or 'no' response) and open questions (prompting more expansive answers), it is the variety of open questions asked and the wider approach in the 'question chain' adopted that will have the greatest impact on successful questioning alongside active listening.

In terms of a sequence of questions, or a 'question chain', the most common approaches taken are usually compared to the analogy of a funnel or pyramid. In the funnel approach, the question chain proceeds from very general questioning to increasingly focused (and potentially pointed) questioning; in the pyramid approach, the chain is reversed, proceeding from a very focused initial question (perhaps pointedly addressing a critical incident that has occurred). While the approach to the question chain is significant, so is the range of questioning utilised. Table 16.4 outlines a number of possible question types, addressing their purpose and offering possible exemplar questions.

Table 16.4 Possible question types

Question type	Purpose	Starting ideas
Diagnostic	To find the root of a problem, separate symptoms from cause and prompting reflection on experience.	• 'Why do you think they responded that way?' • 'What happened immediately before this event?' • 'How do you feel about that?'
Information seeking	To gather facts and to avoid making assumptions and ensure you have a real understanding of the situation.	• 'How did you respond to that?' • 'What did you do about this?' • 'What options have you considered?'
Probing	To get a person to talk more.	• 'Can you say a little more about …' • 'Would you expand on that idea …' • 'Perhaps you'd like to tell me …'

Question type	Purpose	Starting ideas
Challenging with cushion	To explore alternate points of view. To soften any sense of confrontation using a challenging question (if deemed necessary).	• 'What are your reasons for saying that?' • 'What has led you to that conclusion?' • 'Do you think other people would see it that way?' • 'I'm curious . . . ' • 'I'm wondering . . . ' • 'Would you like to tell me . . . ?'
Action	To prompt deeper reflection and action planning.	• 'What could be done to improve the situation?' • 'How might you go about achieving that?' • 'What, specifically, do you plan to do?'
Priority and sequence	To further unpick what is to be done and in what order, clarify thinking and break the task into manageable chunks.	• 'What will you do first?' • 'What is the next step?' • 'Is there a logical order in which to proceed?'
Prediction	To manage risk, to address any problematic outcomes the proposed course of action might have.	• 'What are your intended outcomes if you take this course of action?' • 'What are the likely consequences of this?' • 'Are there other possible repercussions?'
Hypothetical	To aid rehearsal or 'envisioning' of a proposed course of action.	• 'What would you do if . . . ?' • 'How would you handle . . . ?' • 'If you do . . . , what do you think will happen?'
Extension	To develop critical thinking skills.	• 'What are the implications of . . . ?' • 'What insights have you gained as a result of . . . ?' • 'What have you learned from this incident?'
Generalisation	To prompt further reflection and embed changes into future repertoire of responses.	• 'Are there some general principles here you could apply in other situations?' • 'What could you do differently next time?' • 'How is this situation like others you have dealt with?'
Summarising	To ensure or check for understanding.	• 'So, what you're saying is . . . ' • 'What I'm hearing is. . . ' • 'From your point of view . . . '

Source: Adapted from University of Melbourne Mentoring Tools (n.d.).

Beyond the funnel or pyramid approach to a question chain, there is also the analogy of a sand timer, from general to specific questioning before returning to general questioning again.

Reflection and discussion activity

Mentor: using the open-question types outlined in the table above, construct a question chain using a sand-timer approach. Start by listing the order of question type, and then include one question from the examples above (or of your own) for each type.

Can you think of a recent situation when you could have used this type of question chain?

Aspects of successful mentoring: the process of mentoring

Having established the importance of forming a mentoring relationship and the key mentoring skills of listening and questioning, it is important to consider the process of mentoring more deeply. It has been implicit in the preceding discussion and activities that mentoring is also a process that moves the trainee on in their professional development. The trainee and mentor become increasingly confident that professional and national standards are being attained. The process of development through mentoring is captured by a wide variety of theoretical models. A clear and effective model is offered by Whitmore (2017), described using the acronym GROW, illustrated in Figure 16.1.

Figure 16.1 The GROW model (Whitmore, 2017)

In an education context, the initial goal(s) (the G of the GROW model) that the trainee wishes to realise can be drawn from standards documents or from areas for development identified in previous professional assessment. A mentor, utilising active listening and skilful questioning, can collaborate with the trainee to raise their awareness of how closely they are attaining standards, gaining a clear understanding of where they are – the reality of their situation (the R of the GROW model). It is possible for there to be some misconception on the behalf of the trainee as to how well they are meeting professional standards (be this an over-estimation or underestimation of their attainment). In Lindgren's (2005, as cited in Gosh, 2013) terms, it is important to develop the trainee's 'constructive self-awareness'.

 Reflection and discussion activity

It is common for professional standards to be broken down into progressive steps to assist with the assessment of trainees. If such a matrix or rubric exists, after a short period of relationship building, both the trainee and mentor could indicate (perhaps by using a highlighter pen) their assessment of the trainee's attainment against the standards.

Share the two highlighted rubrics: focus on the areas of agreement first before moving on to consider any mismatch. Initial goals for the trainee can be identified and drawn from this discussion of mismatching assessments.

The role of the mentor in helping a trainee to identify options (the O of the GROW model) to address identified goals can be significant. The mentor has a more extensive understanding of what improvement will involve and what precise aspects of development are required. The 'will' aspect (the W of the GROW model) has two facets which a mentor can support. There is the sense of 'will' as in narrowing the range of options discussed to a single focus (or perhaps to two or three focus aspects) – what the trainee will actually do. There is, perhaps, a second sense of 'will' implicit in the model, which is having 'the will' to action the changes and attain the goal(s) discussed and targeted. This second sense of will links to the mentoring relationship formed. In some definitions of mentoring, the mentor should actively encourage the trainee to have confidence in their ability to attain their goal(s).

The outcome of the GROW process can be captured in points for development or targets for assessment over an agreed period of time. This capturing of outcomes, in education mentoring, is often achieved by the setting of SMART development targets that will be the focus of observation and assessment for the following week(s). The acronym SMART stands for Specific, Measurable, Agreed, Realistic and Timeframed (Whitmore, 2017). The use of a SMART approach to target setting can be particularly useful to gain 'the will' of the trainee to successfully develop their professional practice and achieve their goal(s). By agreeing next steps for development with the trainee while explicitly discussing and applying realism, a time frame and a specific measurable focus for future assessment can be motivating for both mentor and trainee.

 Reflection and discussion activity

Scenario: Following a mentor meeting structured around the GROW model, the trainee and mentor have agreed a development focus on increased use of open questions in maths lessons.

Trainee and mentor: can you turn that goal into a development target using SMART?

S - (specific) - to use more open questions to children in maths lessons.

M - (measurable)

A - (agreed) - for this exercise you may wish to assume agreement.

R - (realistic)

T - (time frame)

Share your SMART target - where do your two versions match or differ?

Interestingly, the creator of the GROW model, John Whitmore, while advocating SMART approaches to target and goal setting, also recommends that targets are PURE and CLEAR.

PURE:

Positively stated

Understood

Relevant

Ethical

CLEAR:

Challenging

Legal

Environmentally sound

Appropriate

Recorded

(Whitmore, 2017)

A desire to provide SMART, PURE and CLEAR targets for development to trainees at all times is a suitable aspiration for any mentor. In summary then, Clutterbuck (2004) offers an acronym for the rich complexity of being a mentor as:

Manage the relationship

Encourage

Nurture

Teach

Offer mutual respect

Respond to the learner's needs

Having discussed mentoring in some depth, it is now possible to turn to a discussion of coaching.

Coaching

In the analogy used at the beginning of this chapter – of teaching someone to ride a bicycle – coaching was characterised as a more 'arm's-length', less directive, approach to professional development. The focus within a coaching relationship is to hone and maximise performance often against criteria that colleagues have agreed as an important focus. In a school context, a pair or group of colleagues might come together to address a perceived area of development at an individual, class, departmental, Key Stage or whole-school level. While the coaching focus might be related to professional or national standards, it may have a more specific, local significance.

As suggested before, a coaching approach has much in common with mentoring: both require a dynamic and developing relationship of trust (though in coaching this may be more collegiate in nature), and utilise active listening and questioning. The preceding, extensive consideration of mentoring reflects this commonality between mentoring and coaching, and raises an important observation here: mentoring and coaching approaches can be seen to form a continuum of practice, rather than two different, 'water-tight' categories. In terms of mentoring, when working with a high-performing trainee, it may be appropriate to adopt a coaching approach in some aspects of their professional development. Within coaching, it may be appropriate, at specific times, to deploy a 'moment' or element of mentoring. This overlap is exacerbated by a spectrum within coaching itself, which may be practised at one end of the spectrum in 'solution-focused', more directive forms (as discussed above in a school context) or, at the other end of the spectrum, in entirely 'non-directive' forms, often utilised in leadership development such as National Professional Qualification for Headteachers.

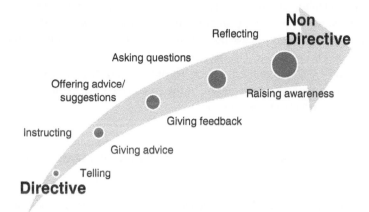

Figure 16.2 Spectrum of approaches to coaching (Downey, 2003)

Thus, the mentoring approach detailed so far in this chapter could be regarded as 'directive coaching' with reference to Downey's analysis. Utilising Clutterbuck's acronym for mentoring, perhaps the most significant difference is the lack of teaching in non-directive forms of coaching.

Coaching is often initially compared with sports coaching, and this perspective may be seen in the preceding discussion where coaching has been characterised as a collegiate approach to hone performance. Coaching's heritage is, however, more closely connected to the humanistic tradition. The humanistic outlook in non-directive coaching is that the individual being coached has the resources within themselves to address and solve the area for development under consideration. In Kline's (2014) memorable formulation, *Usually the brain that contains the problem also contains the solution.*

From its foundation in the work of Rogers, through its wider impact in psychology, counselling, education and business organisation, the person-centred or humanistic approach is focused on facilitating an individual in becoming a *fully functioning person* (Rogers, 1961). The aim is to allow the individual themselves to explore and find solutions to the issue under consideration. At the non-directive end of the coaching spectrum, this will require the use of a skill not present in a mentoring relationship. The coach will 'play back' the coachee's thoughts and words to facilitate them to make connections and commitments to change future practice. The skill of playing back has two important aspects that require drawing out: resisting the urge to heal and the necessity of using 'clean language'.

In a non-directive coaching relationship, it is essential that the coach does not teach, does not 'slump' into directive practices. Downey (in West and Milan, 2014) argues that a coach must resist solving, fixing or healing a coachee's problem or focus area. Downey, perhaps controversially, goes further and argues that it is essential that the coach does not make things better for the coachee or offer their 'wisdom' to the coachee. From the perspective of mentoring, this might be regarded as a toxic practice, as 'blocking' or 'dumping'. However, from a humanistic, non-directive coaching perspective, it is facilitating the brain of the coachee to find the solution that is within it.

To truly ensure the highest degree of non-directive coaching, it is also essential to use 'clean language'. The concept of clean language develops out of Grove's work with trauma victims (Sullivan and Rees, 2009) which paid explicit attention to the metaphors and phrasing patients used, utilising and repeating (playing back) these terms to the patients in any subsequent questioning. In non-directive coaching practices, the focus is similarly on playing back words and phrases that coachees have used in any discussion and questioning; thus, the language of the exchange is kept 'clean' as it is not 'polluted' by rephrasing. This deliberate focus by the coach on not rephrasing the terminology used can be highly significant, as any rephrasing may be perceived by the coachee to betray a bias (of praise or sanction) in the coach's perspective. If the coach is to resist being wise or healing the coachee's issue, then the use of clean language will be paramount.

 Reflection and discussion activity

Scenario: A coaching relationship has been formed around the focus of increasing teacher use of open questioning. During an observed lesson, the coachee initially employed some open question; upon receiving limited responses from the pupils, the coachee's questioning becomes persistently closed. During feedback the coachee says, 'It was just dreadful, I thought it would be like that. They're just not capable of it, they're just not ready for it. There's so much to get through, if they're not secure with this, how are they going to make progress?'.

Reflection

Coach: using clean language, how would you begin to play back the coachee's thinking to them? Write a possible first question to ask the coachee (refer to the 'question types' table above).

The skills for coaching encompass those for mentoring, requiring active listening and questioning. However, coaching is commonly recognised as having a further skill – that of silence. As suggested earlier in the chapter, the silence that coaches employ can be viewed as a toxic practice (from the perspective of mentoring).

However, silence is an essential aspect of coaching as it can allow 'the brain that has the problem' the time to formulate its own solution(s). Interestingly, it is sometimes suggested that the teaching profession can be a challenging environment in which to undertake coaching, as the members of the teaching profession are expert at offering support and advice on next steps in development. The teaching profession is in some senses a hostile environment for coaching, as it 'cuts against the grain' of everyday teaching practice.

It is apparent, then, that at this non-directive end of the coaching spectrum, practice is significantly removed from that of being a mentor. An essential aspect of mentoring, it will be remembered, might be regarded as 'serving as a role model' with 'an explicit vision of good teaching' which non-directive coaching would regard as 'polluting' and a barrier to a coachee's self-development. This disparity between the two roles helps to explain why it is commonly felt that a coach does not need to be an expert in or be knowledgeable about the profession or setting of a coachee. The two approaches are also sometimes viewed as aligning with different timescales, with mentoring persisting over a longer time period than a coaching relationship. However, given the complexity and spectrum of opportunity in both mentoring and coaching previously discussed, it is unsurprising that such a straightforward alignment is contestable. This chapter will conclude with a consideration of the concept of a 'communities of practice' making connections to both the socialising function of mentoring and coaching, and the timescales employed.

Communities of practice

The concept of a community of practice (CoP) emerged initially from the work of Lave and Wenger, and was later extended by Wenger (1998) with his definition as *groups of people who share a concern or a passion for something they do and learn how to do it better as they interact regularly*. Wenger argues that a CoP can be characterised by three essential features. First, it has a 'domain', a shared area of interest – e.g. education or the teaching of English. A CoP further entails a community – in other words, an active group who engage in shared activities. Lastly, it requires the participants to be practitioners, to develop a repertoire of practical resources to apply to their practice.

It is clear, then, how mentoring and coaching may be seen to embody the essential aspects of a CoP. Both mentoring and coaching involve pairs or groups of individuals engaging together around a common focus, developing a range of strategies to develop more effective practice. With specific reference to teaching, it is possible to observe a CoP operating at various levels; at the level of a classroom, a Key Stage, a department, a school, a chain of schools, a geographical region, a nation and perhaps an international profession. There are increasing opportunities through digital technology for teaching a CoP at a global level. It could be argued that the spread of international research into 'what works' in education is a positive outcome of just such a development of an international CoP in teaching.

 Reflection and discussion activity

Trainee and/or coachee, mentor and/or coach: What or who are the essential constituents of your CoP? How extensive (broad and deep) is your CoP? How could you expand your CoP if necessary?

However, such optimistic assessments of contemporary practice can be challenged by a characterisation of global educational developments towards increasingly fragmented and competitive markets in education between nations and between different school types within national boundaries. In a context of competition between nations and between schools within a country, the scope for developing communities of practice might be marginalised. This less optimistic outlook has points of contact with both mentoring and coaching, and the timescales attached to each practice.

The less optimistic assessment of CoP suggests that there is an increasing shift towards more short-term coaching practices in professional development. This approach can have very positive outcomes, optimising performance within a specific context. Thus, a school chain may identify a common area of concern and develop a repertoire of approaches that can be used across the chain to improve teacher performance and learner outcomes. This can be characterised as 'growing your own' targeted solutions and your teaching professionals. In the less positive outlook, such coaching is unfavourably contrasted with a more long-term, mentoring process in which there is a commitment to the trainee in a lifelong learning journey. This can be characterised as inducting reflective practitioners into the profession. Such a less optimistic view is captured by Pring when he says:

> *So, the teacher (or 'the workforce') is a 'deliverer of improved outcomes' or a trainer of those who have to hit targets – not the thinker of what those outcomes might be. As Peter Abbs . . . describes the situation we are in: '*
> *. . . teachers become the technicians of subjects, not the critical guardians of a long culture; nor the midwives of the creative potentialities of living children.*

(2011, p3)

The tension that Pring, citing Abbs (1994), is trying to capture can be applied to professional development and is seemingly committed to a CoP at a national or international level, requiring a practice of long-term mentoring over short-term coaching.

 Chapter summary

As this chapter has sought to explore, the tensions and ambiguities between mentoring and coaching are complex. Navigating this complexity will be more sure-footed within a community of fellow professionals critically aware of the scope of choices between, and within, mentoring and coaching approaches to support professional development.

References

Abbs, P (1994) *The Educational Imperative: A defence of Socratic and aesthetic learning.* London: Falmer Press.

Chambers, GN, Coles, J and Roper, T (2002) Why students withdraw from PGCE courses. *The Language Learning Journal*, 25(1): 52–8 (6 September).

Clutterbuck, D (2004) *Everyone Needs a Mentor*. London: Chartered Institute of Personnel and Development.

Darling, LA (1986) What to do about toxic mentors. *Nurse Educator*, 11(2) (1 January).

Department for Education (DfE) (2011) *Teachers' Standards in England from September 2012*.

Downey, M (2003) *Effective Coaching: Lessons from the coach's coach*. New York: Cengage Learning.

Ghosh, R (2013) Mentors providing challenge and support: integrating concepts from teacher mentoring in education and organizational mentoring in business. *Human Resource Development Review*, 12(2): 144–76 (1 June).

Jones, J, Jenkin, M and Lord, S (2006) *Developing Effective Teacher Performance*. London: Paul Chapman.

Kline, N (2014) *Time to Think: Listening to ignite the human mind*. London: Cassell Illustrated.

Lee, S-H, Theoharis, R, Fitzpatrick, M, Kim, K.-H, Liss, JM, Nix-Williams, T, Griswold, DE, Walther-Thomas, C (2006) Create effective mentoring relationships: strategies for mentor and mentee success. *Intervention in School and Clinic*, 41(4): 233–40 (1 January).

Pring, R (2011) *Bring Back Teaching*. Available from: **www.abdn.ac.uk/education/documents/journals_documents/Volume_24_Issue_1_Democracy_and_Education/EITN_Journal_ARTICLE_Final_EitN_Dem_Pring.pdf** (accessed 21 January 2020).

Rogers, CR (1961) *On Becoming a Person: A therapist's view of psychotherapy*. New York: Houghton Mifflin Harcourt.

Sullivan, WJ, and Rees, J (2009) *Clean Language: Revealing metaphors and opening minds*. Bancyfelin: Crown House.

University of Melbourne (n.d.) *Mentoring Tools*. Retrieved from: https://ahebgusite.wordpress.com/ (accessed 21 January 2020).

Wenger, E (1998) *Communities of Practice: Learning, meaning, and identity*. Cambridge: Cambridge University Press.

West, L and Milan, M (2014) *The Reflecting glass: Professional coaching for leadership development*. Basingstoke: Palgrave Macmillan.

Whitmore, J (2017) *Coaching for Performance*. London: Nicholas Brealey.

Index